AF701697

Parklawn Health Library
5600 Fishers Lane Rm. 13-12
Rockville, Maryland 20857

ADVANCES IN HEALTH ECONOMICS AND HEALTH SERVICES RESEARCH

Volume 12 • 1991

RISK-BASED CONTRIBUTIONS TO PRIVATE HEALTH INSURANCE

ADVANCES IN HEALTH ECONOMICS AND HEALTH SERVICES RESEARCH

A Research Annual

RISK-BASED CONTRIBUTIONS TO PRIVATE HEALTH INSURANCE

Volume Editor: MARK C. HORNBROOK
Center for Health Research
Kaiser Permanente
Portland, Oregon

Series Editors: RICHARD M. SCHEFFLER
Graduate Schools of Public Health and Public Policy
University of California, Berkeley

LOUIS F. ROSSITER
Department of Health Administration and The Williamson Institute
Medical College of Virginia

VOLUME 12 • 1991

JAI PRESS INC.

Greenwich, Connecticut *London, England*

Copyright © 1991 JAI PRESS INC.
55 Old Post Road, No. 2
Greenwich, Connecticut 06836

JAI PRESS LTD.
118 Pentonville Road
London N1 9JN
England

All rights reserved. No part of this publication may be reproduced, stored on a retrieval system, or transmitted in any form or by any means, electronic, mechanical, photocopying, filming, recording or otherwise without prior permission in writing from the publisher.

ISBN: 1-55938-241-4

Manufactured in the United States of America

W
74
R311
v. 12
1991

CONTENTS

PART II. DEFINING AND MEASURING RISK

PART III. RISK-ASSESSMENT MODELS

LIST OF CONTRIBUTORS

Richard V. Anderson	Kaiser Foundation Health Plan Oakland, California
Marjorie D. Bennett	Center for Health Research Kaiser Permanente Portland, Oregon
Bruce D. Bowen	Kaiser Foundation Health Plan Oakland, California
Michael J. Goodman	Center for Health Research Kaiser Permanente Portland, Oregon
Nancy P. Gordon	Kaiser Foundation Health Plan Oakland, California
Merwyn R. Greenlick	Center for Health Research Kaiser Permanente Portland, Oregon
Stephen T. Hayes	Kaiser Foundation Health Plan Oakland, California
Mark C. Hornbrook	Center for Health Research Kaiser Permanente Portland, Oregon
Karl R. Iorio	Kaiser Foundation Health Plan Oakland, California
George A. Kaplan	California Department of Health Services Berkeley, California
John P. Mullooly	Center for Health Research Kaiser Permanente Portland, Oregon

Douglas W. Roblin Kaiser Foundation Health Plan
Oakland, California

Elizabeth L. Slavin Kaiser Foundation Health Plan
Oakland, California

PREFACE

The nation is experiencing continued and rapid changes in the financing of health care. The combined impact of rising costs and numbers of individuals without adequate health insurance is receiving attention at the national and state levels. Almost every major "stakeholder" in health care has put forward a proposal for restructuring the health care system.

A key element in virtually all of these proposals is risk selection. Adverse selection leads to a breakdown of the health insurance market. Insurers in a competitive environment take measures to avoid high-risk (sick) patients and seek to attract low-risk (healthy) patients. Proper risk adjustments are necessary so that the market can operate efficiently and create what some policy makers have called a "level playing field."

This volume of *Advances in Health Economics and Health Services Research*, edited by Mark C. Hornbrook, presents a set of state-of-the-art papers on risk adjustment. The volume has three goals: (1) describe the methodological techniques and apply them to multi-option health benefit plans; (2) define risk measures and demonstrate their use; and (3) present a set of risk-assessment models. The papers are data-based and many deal with real-world problems faced by Kaiser Permanente and other HMOs, in particular, and by private and public health insurers, in general.

We are pleased to present these contributions in this year's volume. It represents a logical extension of previous volumes in this series, namely, Biased Selection in Health Care Markets (Volume 6), and Risk-Based Payments Under Public Programs (Volume 10). We believe that Volume 12 will be heavily used by the field and has the potential of becoming a standard reference in risk selection and private health insurance markets.

Richard M. Scheffler
Louis F. Rossiter

FOREWORD

Mark C. Hornbrook

This volume of *Advances in Health Economics and Health Services Research* contains ten papers produced by a special research and development effort undertaken by Kaiser Permanente (KP) to address policy and operational problems deriving from employers' perceptions about their employees' choice of health plans. Specifically, many employers have expressed concerns that HMOs disproportionately attract healthy, "low-risk" persons compared to indemnity plans. This problem is especially salient in health benefit programs where all HMOs are more recent offerings compared to the long-established indemnity plans. This selection effect associated with initial HMO market penetration is viewed as creating an unfair competitive advantage for HMOs and as raising premiums to unaffordable levels for persons who are enrolled in indemnity plans with higher risk members. Employers believe that if nothing is done to stop this effect, their total health care costs will continue to increase and adversely selected health plans will fail.

To maintain viable choice for their employees, employers have resorted to manipulating their premium contribution formulas to counteract perceived selection bias—contributions to favorably selected plans are reduced and those to adversely selected plans are increased. In many cases, contributions are altered without objective measures of relative risks among the health plans and in seemingly arbitrary amounts apparently without considering the underlying cause of any selection effects or responses by health plans and employees to new "surcharges." Employers are re-examining their contribution formulas and health benefit programs and searching for ways to reduce the portion that health care represents in their total wage bills. The general thrust of employers' health benefit strategies is to impose different rates and benefits for different classes of employee, moving primarily in the direction of experience rating and employee cost-sharing (Kramon, 1991).

As insurers and employers have sought to minimize health insurance costs, the most vulnerable members of society have been left either in high-cost, low-coverage options or with no coverage at all. For example, exclusion of pre-existing conditions from coverage under health plans offered to small businesses has trapped many chronically ill persons in their jobs and health plans. This change in traditional social insurance principles has important implications; specifically, the number of Americans with health insurance fell in absolute terms during the mid-1980s (HIAA, 1990). This resulted from a combination of factors, but mostly from a change in health insurers' goals from risk pooling to risk avoidance.

The policy issue of who should pay what rate with respect to such employee characteristics as marital status, number of dependents, retiree status, and health status, interacts with the goal of ensuring effective competition among health plans. Current rating systems that do not discriminate between three-person and six-person families impose a redistribution from smaller to larger families. One response by employers is to drop contributions for dependent coverage, which may lead to lack of insurance for workers' families.

From a health plan perspective, charging premiums that reflect expected utilization by an enrolled group may protect the financial status of health plans in the short run but can lead to long-run instability that undermines the competitive positions of health plans. When plan choice is correlated with health status, a self-energizing disequilibrium can arise. If high utilizers are not uniformly distributed across health plans, for example, imposing a surcharge on these persons will affect health plans differently according to differences in their enrollment proportions (Enthoven, 1988).

In 1988, Kaiser Permanente established the Inter-regional Risk Adjustment Task Force to investigate alternative methods for measuring the risk of the various health plans in an employer's program and to develop options for adjusting employer contributions to compensate equitably and efficiently for selection effects. While one function of the Task Force was to help KP develop internal policy options and competitive strategies to offer to its employer groups, an equally important goal was to disseminate improved risk-assessment models to health plans, employers, and health benefits consultants. The Task Force members reasoned that if employers had valid risk-assessment models, their health benefit decisions would be based on better information and would not introduce yet another source of bias and distortion into the health insurance market.

With the apparent failure of the HMO Act to stimulate the growth of community rating as a competitive and social strategy (that is, pooling risk inside health plans), the time has come for new policy initiatives. While national health insurance is one option designed to address access and selection bias issues, establishment of an accurate risk-adjustment mechanism to redistribute risk within public and private multi-option health benefits programs would serve two purposes: first, it would help reverse the perverse effects of the movement to experience rating, and second, it would stabilize private health insurance markets. If the viability of the private health insurance market cannot be sustained—that is, insurers are not willing to underwrite all workers and to participate in public risk-based contracting programs—one scenario is that the government will intervene to pick up all the risk, insurers will become carriers and fiscal intermediaries, and HMOs will revert to fee-for-service providers.

AIMS OF THIS VOLUME

This issue of *Advances* is aimed at a broad audience interested in private health insurance. This includes researchers, actuaries, employers, unions, consumers, health plans, and benefits consultants. While some of the papers are highly "academic," in the sense of being very complex and technical, other papers attempt to present the issues and methods to a wider audience. Our goal is to stimulate greater discussion and experimentation with risk-assessment and risk-adjustment techniques, with the ultimate goal of improving the state of the art in risk modeling through research and experimentation.

This volume of *Advances* presents the major research and policy analysis papers produced by the Kaiser Permanente Risk Adjustment Task Force. We are especially pleased that the editors of *Advances,* Richard Scheffler and Louis Rossiter, have agreed to disseminate these papers to the scientific and professional health care audience. In this manner, they have greatly accelerated the dissemination process. Moreover, appearing as a coordinated set, the contribution of the papers is greater than if they had appeared separately.

The issue is divided into three parts. The first part contains five papers addressing the policy issues involved in designing risk-adjustment schemes to remove health status selection effects in health plan enrollments. The second part contains two papers addressing the empirical and technical issues in developing risk-assessment models. The third part presents three empirical risk-classification schemes. The contributions of each paper are outlined in the following sections.

RISK-ADJUSTMENT POLICY OPTIONS

In the first paper, Anderson poses the question "Can Risk Assessment Tools be Feasibly Used in the Health Benefits Marketplace?" This paper presents a case study of one employer's approach to adjusting health plan contributions made on behalf of employees. While the case study is obviously not generalizable to all employer/health plan relationships, this scenario serves two important purposes. First, it highlights the differing and often conflicting objectives of employers and health plans; and second, by presenting specific details of premiums, contributions, and enrollments, the case study serves the heuristic purpose of describing a selection phenomenon and provides a background for the more abstract and theoretical papers appearing later in this volume.

So-called "switcher" studies are often used to assess selection bias. The health status of the most recent cohort of new members from an employer group is assessed, usually by demographic or prior use indicators. These studies often find that health maintenance organizations (HMOs) attract healthier and lower-utilizing members (that is, experience favorable selection) than conventional health insurance plans. The paper by Gordon and Kaplan, titled "Some Evidence Refuting the HMO 'Favorable Selection' Hypothesis: The Case of Kaiser Permanente," tests the hypothesis that favorable selection was occurring for Kaiser Permanente of Northern California, the largest prepaid group practice model HMO in California. This study is not a true risk-assessment analysis because the relationship of health status to future health care cost is not estimated. The paper does serve to indicate that it is possible, by using a different analytic approach, to come to a different conclusion about selection bias for one of the health plans described in Anderson's paper.

Voluntary choice of health plan under multi-option health benefit programs may lead to differences in the health status of enrollees in the various plans; such differences can destabilize the market. The paper by Hornbrook and Goodman, entitled "Adjusting Health Benefits Contributions to Reflect Risk," contends that models assessing relative risk—defined as expected per capita annual expense deriving from differences in enrollee health status and propensity to consume health services—could be used to improve the efficiency of health insurance markets by spreading risk over larger population groups. This would enable health plans to compete on the basis of quality of service rather than risk skimming. Without risk adjustment, employees, Medicare beneficiaries, and Medicaid recipients who happen to select high-cost risk pools carry an unfair share of their medical care expenses. Risk adjustments can be applied either to health plan revenues, thereby allowing health plans to specialize in selected case types, or to employer contributions, thereby providing incentives for consumers to switch to high-risk health plans and equalize risk across plans. Risk adjustment is not a panacea for all sources of inefficiency. Indeed, it is not appropriate for many employers and many circumstances. Large groups with dual- or multi-option health benefit programs are best suited for risk adjustment.

Once it is determined that employer contributions are to be adjusted to reflect health risk, the paper by Bowen and Slavin, entitled "Adjusting Contributions to Address Selction Bias: Three Models for Employers," illustrates three computational methods. These methods are: the ratio method, which adjusts the contribution based solely on the ratios of the risks that each health plan faces; the absolute difference method, which calculates iso-risk rates for the health plans and maintains those absolute differences in the budget-neutral contributions by the employer; and "everyone in fee-for-service" method, which prices the base plan (fee-for-service) as though it had all of the risk. Each method is evaluated in terms of the information needed for the calculation, the results of the method, and the method's ability to meet the employer's policy objectives. The greater the dispersion of risk coefficients from the overall average, the more the methods will differ in their impact on employer contributions.

The paper by Iorio, entitled "Risk Adjustment of Employer Contributions: How Well Will It Work?," compares the risk weights derived from competing HMO and indemnity sources. The relative structure of each weighting scheme is examined for age, gender, and family size cross-subsidies. The incentives presented by these different weights for health plan choice and their interactions with risk-adjustment efforts are analyzed. This paper illustrates that a valid risk-assessment model is necessary for any risk-adjustment scheme.

DEFINING AND MEASURING RISK

Voluntary choice of health plan under multi-option benefit programs often leads to differences in risk (that is, case mix) among the plans that may be unrelated to health plan or provider performance. In their paper, titled "Health Plan Case Mix: Definition, Measurement, and Use," Hornbrook and Goodman define "risk" as the expected value of the distribution of per capita costs of efficiently provided preventive, diagnostic, and therapeutic health care services delivered to a defined group of enrollees for a specific future period. Classification of this risk variation is critical to measuring and understanding health plan performance. This paper identifies eight types of prospective risk-assessment models and outlines issues related to specification, estimation, and validation of these models. Alternative applications of risk-assessment models are outlined, including third-party reimbursement systems, internal budgeting, and marketing. Priorities for research to increase the accuracy and stability of risk taxonomies are summarized.

Some employers have argued that risk assessment should focus on persons who are switching health plans. Assuming that every enrollee had to switch to enroll in a health plan at some point, and that the switchers in any one year are a random sample of all switchers, then the risk characteristics of the switchers are indicative of the overall health plan membership. In their paper, titled "Persistence of Health Care Expense in an Insured Working Population," Goodman et al. argue that these assumptions are testable hypotheses—Are switchers the same as stayers? If not, how many years must elapse before switchers attain the overall mean? This study seeks to assess the degree of persistence of use in nonaged, employed populations. This is shown by age- and gender-adjusting expected expense, and then using Markov chain techniques to characterize longitudinal patterns of use. The findings indicate that some persistence of use exists among the lowest utilizers and much less persistence in the remaining groups. Also, the research shows that extreme deviations from expected values tend to disappear over time. The findings of the Markov Chain analysis imply that modeling of future expense risk should include at least two prior years of data.

RISK-ASSESSMENT MODELS

The first priority of the KP Risk Adjustment Task Force was to estimate simple demographic risk-assessment models to obtain empirical iso-risk weights that could be used immediately by employers in analyzing the relative risks within their multi-option health benefits programs. The paper by Hayes, titled "Demographic Risk Factors Derived from HMO Data," develops a series of demographic risk-assessment models from data on a very large HMO population. These models rely on variables that are relatively permanent characteristics of individuals and are easy to collect. Models are estimated for subscriber units and for individuals. In many firms, only basic demographic characteristics of the employee (subscriber) are known, so that no data are available on the spouse and dependents. Aggregated risk-assessment models are required in this circumstance.

Hornbrook, Goodman, and Bennett in their paper entitled "Assessing Health Plan Case Mix in Employed Populations: Ambulatory Morbidity and Prescribed Drug Models," test several diagnostic and prescribed drug models for measuring the expense risk of health plan memberships. Health status and propensity to use medical care are assessed by the number of treated morbidity episodes and prescribed drugs for a sample of nonaged employed members of a large HMO for the years 1980-1987. A pooled time-series cross-section sample of 51,633 observations is randomly split into two data sets for deriving and validating prediction models. Serious chronic diseases are found to have the strongest associations with future health care expense. Morbidity and drug-use models predict next year's overall health care expense for a defined population more accurately than simple demographic factors. Nevertheless, age and gender still contribute prediction power independent of disease and drug use. Interactive regression modeling does not create models that perform better than a priori specifications. These models are effective in detecting selectivity effects in health plan enrollment.

The final paper in this volume, titled "Assessing Health Plan Case Mix in Employed Populations: Self-reported Health Status Models," examines self-reported health status for assessing selection bias in enrollment patterns of employees under multi-option health benefits programs. Validity, bias, and stability of per capita medical care expense predictions are examined for self-reported health status relative to demographic factors, a linear prior-use model, and a combined health status/prior-use model. Data for two samples of HMO beneficiaries for 1980 and 1985 are used to estimate and validate these models. Self-reported health status more accurately predicts expense than do demographic factors, although both approaches are very unstable. Self-reported prior use captures more of the high cost tail of an expense distribution than demographic factors alone and may help correct for selection bias. Much work is needed to develop more powerful predictors based on social survey techniques. The compelling rationale of the self-report approach is that it can be applied consistently across different health plans. Approaches that use health plan clinical or administrative data are subject to selection bias induced by different treatments and data capture. Thus, while morbidity data are more accurate and reliable predictors than self-reported health status, the latter approach carries its own methodological validity that warrants high priority for research and demonstration projects in risk assessment and risk adjustment.

CAVEAT

While these papers were sponsored by Kaiser Permanente and are the products of KP employees, they do not represent official policy of Kaiser Foundation Health Plan or Kaiser Foundation Hospitals and should not be inferred as such.

ACKNOWLEDGMENTS

All of the papers in this volume evolved from the work of the Technical Subcommittee of the Kaiser Permanente Inter-regional Risk Adjustment Task Force. The meetings of this committee represented a seminar in risk-adjustment methods. The members of the committee should be acknowledged for their perseverance and commitment to sorting out the complexities of the principles of social risk sharing: Jerry Fleming (chair, 1988-1989), Bruce Bowen (chair, 1989-1991), Richard Anderson, Mark Blumberg, Ann Evans, Bruce Fireman, Michael Goodman, Merwyn Greenlick, Stephen Hayes, Mark Hornbrook, Jack Hudes, Karl Iorio, Bill Kramer, and Douglas Roblin. The members of the primary task force included Irwin Goldstein (chair), Jim Lane, Robert Crane, Alan Silvestone, Dick Anderson, Alain Enthoven, Bruce Bowen, and Jerry Fleming.

In July 1990, a workshop was sponsored by the Center for Health Research to review the Task Force's conceptual and empirical work on risk-assessment models and to evaluate policy options for adjusting risk. The participants in this workshop included the following five outside consultants who labored mightily to review a very large volume of material and provided new insights regarding policy options and analytic methods. They merit special recognition for their efforts:

Nelda McCall
Laguna Research Associates

Arlene Ash
Boston University

Richard Scheffler
University of California, Berkeley

Pete Welch
The Urban Institute

Bill Thomas
University of Michigan

Finally, a number of KP staff in the Northwest Region, Northern California Region, and Central Office contributed to the papers presented in this volume. They are acknowledged in each paper.

REFERENCES

Enthoven, A.C. (1988). *Theory and Practice of Managed Competition in Health Care Finance.* Prof. D. F. de Vries Lectures in Economics (Vol. 9). Amsterdam: North-Holland.

Health Insurance Association of America (HIAA). (1990). *Source Book of Health Insurance Data, 1990.* Washington, DC: HIAA.

Kramon, G. (1991). "Medical Insurers Vary Fees to Aid Healthier People." *New York Times* (March 24), pp. 1,14.

PART I

ADJUSTING FOR RISK UNDER MULTI-OPTION HEALTH BENEFIT PROGRAMS: POLICY ISSUES AND OPTIONS

CAN RISK-ASSESSMENT TOOLS BE FEASIBLY USED IN THE HEALTH BENEFIT MARKETPLACE?

Richard V. Anderson

INTRODUCTION

Employers are seeking to better manage their employee health benefit programs with the help of tools to assess employee health risk. Such tools may be used to measure selection bias, to establish employer contribution levels made on behalf of employees, to set targets for reasonable premium rates, or to determine comparative value between competing health plans or systems. It is critically important that risk assessments be sound and fairly applied. Without good tools, employers may make decisions that conflict with their management objectives and self-interest. Employees and plans may not be treated fairly and there may be unwarranted conclusions about which plan choices offer the most value. Indeed, it may not be possible to successfully manage the offering to employees of choices between competing health benefit plans or to demonstrate that competition works.

A key question is whether it is feasible and practical for employers to effectively use such tools. This question is first examined by considering current

Advances in Health Economics and Health Services Research, Vol. 12, pages 3-18.
Copyright © 1991 by JAI Press Inc.
All rights of reproduction in any form reserved.
ISBN: 1-55938-241-4

applications of risk assessments by employers. This paper discusses what one major employer did, the reasons for doing so, and implications. Concerns are raised about methodological limitations and implications to the various stakeholders. Following this, the paper discusses the properties of proper risk-assessment methods and draws some related conclusions. Finally, observations are made about the implications to choice and competition if adequate risk-assessment tools cannot be developed.

RISK ASSESSMENT AND SELECTION BIAS

Risk has various meanings, depending upon the context in which it is used. The Health Insurance Association of America defines risk as the probable amount of loss foreseen by an insurer in issuing a contract (Health Insurance Association of America, 1979). In the insurance industry, the context usually is risk management, which involves identifying and evaluating various forms of risk (chance of loss) and using various means to deal with those risks. A common means is to transfer it from one party to another—for example, to transfer the risk of health insurance loss to the insurance company in return for the payment of a group insurance premium.

Risk usually is considered in a broader context by employers who offer a choice of different levels of benefits or plans to employees. For some the focus is the expected cost of employees in a future period, while others may want to know about expected propensity to consume resources or services, whether or not actual costs may occur. Usually, risk is considered in relative terms—for example, the expected cost of one population compared to another. And predictions usually are based on extrapolations of past data for individuals or populations whose characteristics are considered to be representative.

Risk assessment is simply the analysis of risk for various purposes. One approach widely used by employers is to actuarially predict future costs for employees who belong to different plans, based on proxies for risk such as costs by age and gender. Assuming that past cost-relationships are applicable and knowing the numbers of employees in each plan who are expected to be in each age/gender class, one can easily calculate the expected average risk of employees in one plan relative to those in another.

In theory, there is only one right answer to the question of what is the relative risk of one person or population compared to another. One might envision a perfect method that always will give the same result. However, in reality risk-assessment methods used by employers have generally been crude and have had low predictive power.

Much of employers' interest in risk assessment has been driven by their concern about selection bias. This happens when risks are not randomly distributed among various populations, as may happen when an employer permits employees to choose between several health benefit plan options. If a disproportionate number of higher risk persons enroll in one of the plan choices, that plan is said to have adverse selection. In contrast, other plans which predominantly have lower risk persons are said to benefit from favorable selection. Selection bias can create significant problems for employers who offer a choice of plans. It can complicate efforts to analyze the determinants of cost in various plan choices, can compromise employers' ability to offer fair choices to employees and, under some circumstances, can increase employers' overall costs. A broad overview of selection bias, including a literature review, may be found in recent published work by Wrightson (1990).

HOW ARE RISK ASSESSMENTS BEING USED BY EMPLOYERS?

Employers have many reasons for assessing risk. Some want to know whether one plan offered to employees costs more than another plan, after controlling for differences in risk. Others want to have fair yardsticks for determining the reasonableness of plan premium rates or for setting targets for rate negotiation. Yet others want to make contributions toward employee benefits that are differentiated based on risk.

A case is presented below to illustrate one employer's use of risk assessment to adjust employer contributions made on behalf of employees. The case is examined from the perspectives of two of the major stakeholders, the employer and one of the participating plans.

A large, national employer (the Company) became convinced significant selection bias was occurring among employees who were enrolled in various health plans. The Company decided to risk-adjust contributions to help compensate for selection bias.

The Setting

The Company offered the choice of a self-funded indemnity plan (the Traditional Plan) and nearly 150 HMOs of various types in various locations. The Traditional Plan allowed free choice of physicians but required significant deductibles and copayments for covered services. HMOs generally restricted the choice of providers and covered most services with no deductibles and minimal or no copayments. The Company made full contributions for employees who were enrolled in the Traditional Plan. That is, such employees were not required to have payroll deductions to cover part of the cost. For those enrolled in HMOs, employer contributions were based on average Traditional Plan costs. Contributions varied by the size of an employee's family and were adjusted for payment differences in different geographic areas. If an HMO's premium rates were lower than the Traditional Plan payments, there was no sharing of premium costs for employees who were enrolled in the HMO. If higher, payroll deductions were required to make up the difference.

One of the HMOs was a large group practice prepayment plan (the GPPP) that had locations in many of the nation's largest metropolitan areas. Since first being offered by the Company in the mid 1970s, the GPPP's enrollment in the group had increased steadily. By March of 1990, nearly 21,000 members (employees and their dependents, Medicare excluded) had joined through the Company. There were 11,100 members in the GPPP's Region A and 4,000 members in Region B. Information on 1990 premium rates for Regions A and B is given in Table 1.

Each region used a method of determining premium rates called Adjusted Community Rating,[1] or ACR, that was designed to reflect the region's expected costs for the group in the forthcoming contract period. As shown in the table, these were three-tiered rates, varying by the number of dependents. There were no employee payroll deductions for Region A and modest payroll deductions for Region B.

The Employer's Perspective

The Company had experienced persistently high increases in overall health benefit costs during the decade of the 1980s. Moreover, the number of HMO choices had proliferated and there was concern about the small number of employees enrolled in many of the plans and about related administrative costs

Table 1. 1990 Monthly Premium Rates and Payroll Deductions

	Employee Only	*Employee Plus One Dependent*	*Employee Plus Two or More Dependents*
Region A			
Premium Rate	$128.09	$256.18	$340.74
Employee's Share	-0-	-0-	-0-
Region B			
Premium Rate	$116.12	$225.27	$300.76
Employee's Share	2.27	3.89	6.19

and complexity. The average age of employees enrolled in various plans differed significantly. Generally, employees enrolled in HMOs were younger than those in the Traditional Plan.

The Company was committed to maintaining choice among plans for employees but wondered if selection bias was impairing the ability to achieve this in a fair, cost-effective manner. The employer suspected favorable selection for HMOs and believed this was happening because employees with strong physician ties were not willing to change from the Traditional Plan if it meant switching doctors. The employer reasoned that those with strong physician ties were more likely to be higher risk, higher cost persons. Alternatively, younger, healthier employees with no physician ties were expected to be relatively more attracted to HMOs. Assuming significant and progressive adverse selection against the Traditional Plan, the employer suspected this was leading to higher costs each year, out of proportion to general inflation. Considering that Traditional Plan costs were the basis for contributions toward HMOs, the employer suspected that the HMOs' payments were higher than they should be, especially if HMOs added benefits to take full advantage of available employer contributions. The employer wondered if offering HMOs had resulted in higher, rather than lower, costs.

The Plan's Perspective

Growth had been stable and predictable, important considerations for a plan that must organize and provide services in return for prospectively fixed payments from a group. There were few signs of trouble. Relations generally were good with the Company, and GPPP members appeared to be quite satisfied, especially with their low levels of out-of-pocket costs for care.

Conducting a Risk Assessment

A consultant was engaged to conduct a risk-assessment study for the Company. Objectives were to identify whether there were, in fact, significant selection bias problems and, if so, what to do about them. The consultant had a reputation for being experienced in risk-assessment work and a long-standing record of good service with the Company.

The central research question framed by the consultant was, "What would the Company's cost be if everyone were enrolled in the Traditional plan?" This was felt to be the appropriate yardstick for making comparisons among plans and for determining maximum contributions toward HMOs. The consultant sought to identify predictors of Traditional Plan equivalent claims-costs for persons who were enrolled in HMOs. The objective was to define homogeneous classes of employees where, for each class, it should be expected that all employees would have the same Traditional Plan cost in the absence of HMOs.

Using the Traditional Plan's claims data base, the consultant calculated a set of actuarial factors which represented relative incurred costs for certain demographic classes of Traditional Plan employees (that is, by age and family status of employee). Claims files were purged of information pertaining to retirees. The consultant recognized the importance of adjusting for differences in the costs of care in different geographic localities and sought to take this into account.

The consultant knew that employee age and family status, by themselves, were relatively poor predictors of health care costs. A risk assessment based solely on these variables would ignore the substantial variation in health status and costs of care within age and family status categories. To increase predictive power, the consultant sought a proxy measure for health status that could be determined from the available claims data and settled upon a variable that represented the "prior use" of "switchers" into HMOs. The consultant hypothesized that those who had recently joined HMOs were probably similar in health status to those already in HMOs. If so, one could look at the prior claims experience of the recent switchers under the Traditional Plan and compare this with the experience of those who stayed in the Traditional Plan. By inference, after adjusting for demographic differences between the switchers and the Traditional Plan stayers, any remaining difference would be assumed to represent the effects of health status. Table 2 provides a summary of the formula developed by the consultant to determine the Traditional Plan equivalent cost for employees in HMOs.

Under the formula, three relative cost factors were to be developed for each HMO, representing differences from the Traditional Plan in age, health status, and geographic costs. The product of these factors multiplied by the unadjusted average Company contribution for Traditional Plan employees would yield the adjusted contribution for an HMO. Separate calculations of contributions were to be made for employees with no dependents, employees with one dependent, and employees with two or more dependents.

The consultant had to make many simplifying assumptions. The large number of individual HMOs and the small enrollment in many of them precluded having credible data for every plan. Because of this and other data limitations, the consultant combined data for HMOs of different types and sizes. The same health status adjuster was used for all HMOs.

The consultant calculated risk-adjusted contributions for each HMO and presented these to the Company. The average risk-adjusted cost of enrollees in HMOs, based on the product of the three relative costs factors, was about 55% of the average Traditional Plan cost. Most of the lower HMO risk was attributed to the health status factor. The consultant proposed that these results

Table 2. Formula for Calculating the Adjusted Employer Contribution

The formula is:

$$C = A \times H \times G \times T$$

Where,

C =	Risk-adjusted employer contribution (applicable to the HMO)
A =	Age factor (representing relative differences in HMO and Traditional Plan costs due to age differences)
H =	Health status factor (representing relative differences in HMO and Traditional Plan costs due to health status differences)
G =	Geographic factor (representing relative differences in HMO and Traditional Plan costs due to geographic differences)
T =	Traditional plan average employer contribution

Separate calculations are made for employees only, employees with one dependent, and employees with two or more dependents.

should be considered as the "appropriate" maximum contributions for the Company to make toward the cost of HMOs in 1991.

Looking ahead to 1991

The GPPP's Regions A and B submitted their proposed premium rates for the 1991 contract year (effective January 1). The Company compared these rates with the adjusted contributions calculated by the consultant. The rates, contributions, and resulting employee payroll deductions that would be required to make up the difference are given in Table 3. For reference, the 1990 actual employee payroll deductions also are shown.

The proposed rates and employer contributions would have created striking changes in employee payroll deductions. An employee with two or more dependents enrolled in Region A would immediately face a payroll deduction of more than $107, compared with no payroll deduction in 1990. In Region B, an employee in the same category would be subject to an increase from about $6 to $112. No payroll deductions were to be required for employees in the Traditional Plan in 1991.

Table 3. 1991 Initially Proposed Premium Rates and Contributions

	Employee Only	*Employee Plus One Dependent*	*Employee Plus Two or More Dependents*
Region A			
Premium Rate, 1991	$148.33	$296.66	$394.56
"Appropriate" Employer Contribution	119.49	233.62	287.07
Employee's Share	28.84	63.04	107.49
Compare with Employee's Share, 1990	-0-	-0-	-0-
Region B			
Premium Rate, 1991	$136.13	$264.09	$352.58
"Appropriate" Employer Contribution	100.31	196.12	240.98
Employee's Share	35.82	67.97	111.60
Compare with Employee's Share, 1990	2.27	3.89	6.19

The Employer's Perspective

It was clear to the Company that the immediate imposition of such substantial payroll deductions would be disruptive for employees in HMOs and would likely lead to reduced employee satisfaction and terminations from HMOs. The Company was anxious not to alienate employees and was troubled about the implications to the Company's HMO strategy. Heretofore, the Company had encouraged enrollment in HMOs, believing they were a key to achieving cost containment. Now, the Company was not so sure. The consultant's study seemed to imply that in most cases, the Traditional Plan was the less costly alternative. If so, this meant that the Company would pay less, rather than more, if HMOs were eliminated.

The Company recognized the practical limitations in the risk-assessment method used by the consultant. Nevertheless, believing there was significant selection bias, the company felt the need to adjust employer contributions for 1991. The Company decided on a two-pronged course of action. First, HMOs would be encouraged to reconsider the size of their proposed 1991 rate increases. In part, to accomplish this, they would be encouraged to adopt modest copayments as an offset to rates. Second, the Company would seek to mitigate the immediate effect on employees by deferring about half of the indicated risk adjustment. This would permit more time to validate results and to consider other alternatives.

In late 1990, the Company and consultant met with the GPPP to discuss the study results and related proposals.

The Plan's Perspective

The GPPP reacted with concern. The increases in employee payroll deductions based on the risk-adjustment method were alarming and would surely translate to major reductions in enrollment. There was little room to revise rates. Each Region had already announced its basic rate increase for all groups—an increase predicated on revenue necessary to meet largely fixed costs for 1991. For legal and policy reasons, each region's rating system had to be uniformly and consistently applied to all membership groups.[2] A reduction in the basic rate granted to one employer would have to be translated to a downward reduction for all. This would mean insufficient revenue to meet budgeted costs for 1991, with little room to make up the difference. Even without revisions to rates, there would likely be a shortfall in revenue from reductions in enrollment (due to the high payroll deductions).

There were major concerns about the validity of the consultant's risk assessment. For one thing, the method was relatively crude (for example, variables such as gender, which might have been used, were not). Moreover, the formula itself was flawed in that the terms were not mutually exclusive and thus should not have been multiplied together.

Strong objections were raised about the use of switcher experience as the basis for determining the health status adjuster for HMOs and about the underlying assumption that all HMO enrollees had the same health status risk. The view was expressed that risk differences should be expected for enrollees in HMOs of different types, sizes, and levels of maturity. In some mature HMOs, little switching occurred from year to year; in others, recent switchers accounted for a high proportion of current enrollment. Under any circumstance, recent switchers were felt to be nonrepresentative of either HMO or Traditional Plan enrollees. And it was assumed that the cost experience of recent switchers should increase with time to more closely approximate the average HMO experience (that is, "converge to the mean").

More fundamentally, the size of the risk-adjusted cost differential between HMO enrollees and those in the Traditional Plan (calculated under the formula to be about 45%) was enormous and did not appear to be plausible. The rates charged by both Regions A and B reasonably reflected the expected costs of providing covered benefits to the Company; that is, the rates were a projection of the Company's own experience in the plan. Yet these rates were much higher than the calculated "appropriate" contribution maximums. Even though GPPP benefits were broader than those in the Traditional Plan, this could not account for a 45% difference. If one believed the data, not only were there no apparent savings to the Company from Regions A and B, but the added cost appeared to be substantial.

Next Steps

Both regions agreed to make modest revisions in rates within legal and policy constraints. Region A achieved a downward revision by substituting increased office visit copayments for prepayment. Region B realigned its rates, achieving reduced rates for single employees and for employees with one dependent by imposing a compensating increase in the rate for employees with two or more dependents. Meanwhile, the Company reconsidered its method for calculating geographic adjusters and revised them. Also, the Company agreed to contribute at least the levels of payments made for HMOs in 1990. Plan rates and employer contributions were disclosed to employees and they were given an opportunity to change plans at the annual open enrollment period.

What Finally Happened

Final 1991 rates and contributions are given in Table 4. The revisions resulted in relatively low employee payroll deductions for Region A, compared to those that were initially calculated On the other hand, while payroll deductions were reduced for Region B, they remained substantial, especially for employees with one or more dependents. The Company did not impose payroll deductions for employees in the Traditional Plan.

Table 4. 1991 Final Premium Rates and Contributions

	Employee Only	*Employee One Dependent*	*Employee Plus Two or More Dependents*
Region A			
Premium Rate, 1991	$142.65	$277.41	$369.11
Employer Contribution	141.52	275.21	366.19
Employee's Share	1.13	2.20	2.92
Region B			
Premium Rate, 1991	$128.25	$256.50	$359.10
Employer Contribution	117.27	228.02	303.41
Employee's Share	10.88	28.48	55.69

Table 5. Company Enrollment by Plan, 1990 and 1991[1]

	March 1990	*March 1991*	*Change*
Region A			
Number of subscribers[2]			
Employee Only	1,024	874	(150)
Employee + one dependent	851	729	(122)
Employee + two or more	2,011	1,893	(118)
Number of members[3]	11,.091	10,424	(667)
Region B			
Number of subscribers[2]			
Employee Only	278	223	(55)
Employee + one dependent	330	250	(80)
Employee + two or more	770	511	(259)
Number of members[3]	4,014	2,748	(1,266)

Notes: [1] Excludes Medicare beneficiaries.
[2] Analogous to the number of employees.
[3] Includes subscribers, spouses, and child dependents.

As shown in Table 5, Region B suffered a significant decline in enrollment from 1990 to 1991, following the open season change, with a net decrease of 1,266 members in the group from March 1990 to March 1991 (a 32% reduction). Most of this change was attributed to the large increase in payroll deductions. Region A also had a loss of members, but in relative terms it was much lower than what Region B experienced.

Both the Company and the GPPP continued to be troubled about methodological deficiencies in the study and the implications of the findings. Both agreed it would be fair to risk-adjust employer contributions if sound methods were used. Both concurred that much better methods were needed. And both committed themselves to continue to work together to try to achieve improvements.

IMPLICATIONS

This case illustrates several points:

1. *High Stakes.* First, the stakes are high for the various stakeholders. An inadequate risk assessment could result in an employer making an erroneous judgment about the relative cost-effectiveness of plans that are offered to employees. This could lead the employer to restrict or eliminate some plans

that actually deliver cost savings. And it could lead to unwarranted encouragement of inefficient plans.

Furthermore, this could subvert an employer's objective to achieve greater equity in contributions made on behalf of employees. Improper adjustments for differences in risk could lead to unintended subsidies for some employees made at the expense of others. The degree of cost sharing dictated by an unsound method might make it prohibitively expensive for some employees to remain in their plan of choice.

2. *Limitations in Data and Methods.* The case also illustrates the challenges employers face to overcome data and methodological limitations. Most employers are simply too small or do not have sufficient resources to carry out valid risk assessments. Many larger employers do not maintain data for employees in routine administrative files and therefore cannot conduct even a baseline risk assessment. That is, they cannot produce timely information on employee eligibility in each plan, differentiated by age, gender, and number of dependents. Also, they cannot relate the available employee data to information on their employees' health care costs. Other employers have better data on employee attributes but none on their own company costs. They may resort to using actuarial tables developed for other purposes, raising questions about applicability of results.

The Company in this case was large enough to have credible data and had reasonably good integration of employee administrative records with health claims data bases. And efforts were made to take into account employee health status in addition to commonly used demographic variables. Yet, simplifying assumptions were used that cast doubt on the study results—for example, that all HMOs have the same average health risk for persons enrolled through the Company, and that the prior fee-for-service experience of recent switchers is representative of the average risk for all of the Company's enrollees in an HMO.

Risk-assessment methods of the type commonly used by larger employers (for example, actuarial methods that consider only employee age, gender, and number of family dependents) tend to understate the effects of outliers (for example, catastrophic costs incurred by a few persons), leading to systematic bias if outliers are not evenly distributed among enrollees in different plans. A consequence is that the variation in predicted average costs for groups tends to be less than the variations in their actual average costs. Moreover, if there is systematic bias in outlier effects, projected differences in relative risk between plans could be either over- or under-stated.

Better methods are available but are seldom tried. They require better indicators of risk and better sources of data than are generally available to most employers. Some methods are designed to take into account what happens after persons join HMOs. These methods may involve projecting future costs for different subsets of employees—for example, those who newly join, those who stay, and those who leave. They may incorporate variables (for example, prior hospitalizations for treatment of high cost, chronic conditions) that are highly predictive of future costs for individuals. Other methods seek to take into account data obtained through surveys of self-assessed health status. But even the few employers who understand such methods may judge them to be too costly or otherwise unfeasible.

3. *Tenuous Stakeholder Relationships.* Risk assessment can be extremely complicated and may be difficult to justify under the best of conditions, let alone when stakeholder relationships are tenuous. In this case, the Company and the GPPP sought to work collaboratively, even though there were strong differences in points of view about the adequacy of methods used and the validity of findings. Both sides were open-minded and willing to share information. A compromise was reached with the promise of working together to achieve refinements.

In other cases, however, the stakeholders are at odds and are unwilling to cooperate in work on risk assessments. An employer may not be willing to discuss objectives or to disclose the results of studies with participating plans, especially if there are a large number of them and if some of them are perceived to be the source of problems. This may be complicated by the tendency of some consultants to regard their risk-assessment work as proprietary. They may not be willing to open their "black boxes" to public scrutiny, even for paying clients.

Some employers have little trust in HMOs, believing they are prone to practices such as "shadow pricing" (that is, pricing that takes full advantage of available employer contributions) and "skimming" (that is, targeted efforts to only enroll lower risk persons). Conversely, HMOs may distrust employers' motives, reflecting concerns about discriminatory practices. Neither side may be willing to share sufficient data. Relationships may be complicated by active involvement of other stakeholders—for example, unions and patients.

In short, all stakeholders may not be fully informed and may not be given an opportunity to contribute to problem resolution.

4. *Conceptual Framework.* Having the right conceptual framework for risk assessment is important. The research question framed by the consultant in the case was, "What would happen to costs if all employees were enrolled in the traditional fee-for-service plan?" This is often the context when employers conduct risk assessments. Fee-for-service yardsticks are used to define a point of indifference from the employer's perspective. If a plan is perceived to cost less, it may be promoted. If its cost is higher, the plan may be terminated. It can be argued that the fee-for-service equivalent cost is an inadequate yardstick for measuring what might be achieved with better management of costs.

An employer interested in cost containment might frame a different research question—such as, "What would it cost if all employees were enrolled in well-managed, efficient plans?" This would suggest a different method of risk assessment or, at least, the use of different sources of data. One could argue that this question is more in keeping with the employer's objective.

CRITERIA FOR PROPER RISK ASSESSMENTS

What are the properties of a good risk-assessment method? Evaluation criteria include validity, degree of bias, stability, practicality, and acceptability. Here are some questions by which to judge these criteria.

1. *Validity.* Does the method measure what it is supposed to measure? For example, if the method is designed to accurately predict future health care costs for a population, does it accomplish this? Is the overall mean prediction error small? Has the method been thoroughly tested?
2. *Degree of Bias.* Does the method accurately predict for defined subgroups of a population—for example, for young as well as old, for males as well as females, or for high cost cases as well as low? If not, is the prediction bias significant? Are predicted differences consistently greater than or less than actual differences? Is the degree of bias tolerable?
3. *Stability.* Does the method perform consistently over time? Are the same results obtained if the method is used for similar populations? Would the application of results cause disruptions and dislocations?
4. *Practicality.* Can the method be implemented? Are data and systems requirements practical and affordable? Can the job be accomplished with available analytical resources? Does evaluation require expensive consulting support?
5. *Acceptability.* Does the method meet the test of reasonableness? Are results consistent with intuitive expectations? Will key stakeholders be likely to agree that the method is fair?

CONCLUSIONS

Feasibility

Most employers currently are unable to conduct proper risk assessments. Many do not have the data, resources, or inclination to carry out the necessary work. Moreover, as a rule of thumb, it is probably a waste of time for employers with less than 250-500 employees to try to measure the relative risk of various employee subsets. Errors in prediction, reflecting lack of credible data, are too great to have general applicability for smaller employers. However, it should not be viewed as beyond the reach of larger employers to conduct proper risk assessments. With modest investments in data and the means for proper analysis, it should be feasible for them to develop this capability. Considering the stakes, many will conclude that such investments are well worth it.

Acceptable Methods

Employers and their consultants should use fair and proper methods in risk assessments and applications. Methods should be made explicit and should be reproducible by others.

To be minimally acceptable, methods of risk assessment should take into account differences in age, gender, number of family dependents, and retiree status of employees. Methods may be improved by adding other predictor variables such as employment status, income, absenteeism, disability, prior hospitalization, and functional health status. As emphasized above, methods should be valid, unbiased, stable, administratively practical, and acceptable to stakeholders.

It is not valid to assume that the "prior experience" of recent "switchers" into HMOs is representative of either their expected future experience or the average experience of all HMO enrollees. Moreover, it is not valid to assume that all HMOs have the same-risk enrollees, regardless of plan type, maturity, size, etc.

Risk assessments should be independently applied to a group or plan if it has credible data. If not, data may be pooled, but only if the groups or plans have reasonably similar characteristics.

Implications for Public Policy

Perhaps the most important issues raised here have to do with the viability of individual choice for employees and the effectiveness of competition among health plans. Many employers have given strong support to the concept of "dual choice" whereby employees are periodically given the right to choose among competing health benefit plans or systems.[3] This concept is embodied in the federal HMO Act, which generally requires employers with 25 or more employees to include a qualified HMO as one of the choices available to employees.

Selection bias can create significant problems when employers offer a choice of different health benefit plans to employees. Without proper assessment tools, an employer may not be able to accurately identify the degree of the problem, find a proper remedy, and maintain effective choice of plans. The result may be unfair competition and an inability for the employer to take advantage of opportunities to save.

Some employers have reached the conclusion that selection bias is an insoluble problem, either because it cannot be adequately measured or because there are inadequate means to address identified problems. They have eliminated choice between competing plans and have resorted to exclusive arrangements with organizations for the provision of health benefits to employees. Such arrangements render moot the question of whether there is selection bias. All employees may have the same benefits and the same employer contributions. With no choice and no competition between plans, there is little need for risk-assessment tools.

The health care marketplace is in flux. Some are convinced that competition and choice can be effectively managed with the right tools and that such tools are feasible. They believe that proper risk assessments and applications such as risk adjustment of employer contributions are preferable to more drastic actions which would involve limiting or terminating cost-effective plans. Others have given up on competition and choice. Which strategy will predominate is a critically important public policy question.

NOTES

1. Adjusted Community Rating (ACR) is a permissible method of community rating for qualified HMOs under the federal Health Maintenance Act as amended in 1988 (Pub.L.No. 100-517). Under ACR, an HMO may determine premium rates for an employer group based on the anticipated revenue requirements for that group. Generally, this involves extrapolating from a group's prior patterns of utilization to project revenue required to cover future costs for services provided to enrollees in the group during a future contract period. If a group's utilization is consistently lower than the average for the plan, its rates under ACR will be lower than the average. Under the more conventional form of community rating, a lower utilizing group has the same rate as other groups (all other things being equal). This has led some employers to conclude that when there is selection bias in favor of HMOs, community rating results in paying more than would be incurred under fee-for-service alternatives. In part, ACR ameliorates this concern. The employer's ACR payment to the HMO will reflect the HMO's cost for the group. Thus, the lower the group's risk in an HMO, the lower the rate.
2. Federal HMO Act provisions require a plan that uses Adjusted Community Rating (ACR) to base all groups' rates on the same community rate, before adjusting for differences in their utilization, all other things being equal (including benefit levels and dates of contract renewal). The Act does not permit granting discounts to individual groups.
3. The dual choice concept is believed to have originated in the San Francisco Bay Area during the 1940s and 1950s when it became common for pooled health and welfare trust funds to provide individual beneficiaries a choice between a group practice prepayment plan such as Kaiser Permanente and a fee-for-service plan such as Blue Cross, Blue Shield, or an insurance company. (Yedidia, 1959). The concept gained public recognition when it became embodied in the employer mandate provisions of the HMO Act of 1973 (Pub. L. No. 93-222). A key provision of the Act required employers to make equal contributions to HMOs that were no less than the contributions made toward other health plans which were offered. Much of the employer concern about increased costs when selection bias is present reflects this provision.

REFERENCES

Health Insurance Association of America. (1979). *A Course in Group Life & Health Insurance* (p. 305). Chicago, New York, and Washington, DC: Health Insurance Association of America.

Wrightson, C. W., Jr. (1990). *HMO Rate Setting & Financial Strategy* (pp. 245-292). Ann Arbor, MI: Health Administration Press.

Yedidia, A. (1959). "Dual Choice Programs." *American Journal of Public Health* 49(11):1475.

SOME EVIDENCE REFUTING THE HMO "FAVORABLE SELECTION" HYPOTHESIS:

THE CASE OF KAISER PERMANENTE

Nancy P. Gordon and George A. Kaplan

INTRODUCTION

Many health services researchers and benefit specialists believe that health maintenance organizations (HMOs) experience favorable selection of enrollees. Favorable selection is said to occur if, after adjusting for factors used to set rates (generally demographic characteristics), HMO enrollees have lower average health care costs or are healthier than people covered by alternative types of health plans (Hellinger, 1987). Evidence regarding this selection bias issue is conflicting. Several studies have shown that HMO enrollees do not differ significantly in health status from people covered by conventional health insurance plans (Welch, Frank and Diehr, 1984; Grazier et al., 1986; Lairson and Herd, 1987). Yet, many studies of health plan choice have also shown that HMO joiners tend to have significantly lower prior health service use than those

Advances in Health Economics and Health Services Research, Vol. 12, pages 19-39.
Copyright © 1991 by JAI Press Inc.
All rights of reproduction in any form reserved.
ISBN: 1-55938-241-4

who remain in conventional plans (Roghmann, Sorenson, and Wells, 1977; Luft, 1981; Jackson-Beeck and Kleinman, 1983; Buchanan and Cretin, 1986). Some evidence suggests that past health service utilization is one of the best predictors of future utilization (Mullooly and Freeborn, 1979; Hellinger, 1987). Based on a study of utilization by people randomized into HMO or conventional fee-for-service (FFS) care, Manning et al. (1984) suggest that prepaid group practices have a less expensive practice style than FFS, primarily because they try to avoid hospitalizations. However, since many of these studies were conducted before conventional plans began to reduce their hospitalization costs because of DRG guidelines and a trend toward outpatient surgery, the differences in cost of care observed in earlier studies may no longer hold.

We tested the hypothesis that favorable selection was occurring for the Kaiser Permanente Medical Care Program (KPMCP), the largest prepaid group practice model HMO in California, using data from state- and county-level probability sample health surveys conducted by the California Department of Health Services in 1989, the Behavioral Risk Factor Surveillance Survey and the Alameda County Chronic Disease Surveillance Survey. In this paper we summarize the results of our analyses that compare the sociodemographic characteristics, self-reported health status, health practices, and use of selected health care services of adults covered by the Kaiser Permanente health plan with adults covered by another private health insurance plan, and then discuss their implications.

CALIFORNIA BEHAVIORAL RISK FACTOR SURVEILLANCE SURVEY

Methods

The California Behavioral Risk Factor Surveillance Survey (CALBRFSS) is a telephone interview survey covering health risk behaviors, chronic disease conditions, and preventive health practices. The survey has been conducted continuously for the State of California since January 1984 by the Chronic Diseases Branch, California Department of Health Services (California Department of Health Services, 1990a). CALBRFSS respondents are a probability sample of noninstitutionalized adults living in residences with telephones. Telephone numbers are randomly selected using the Waksberg method, a three-stage cluster sampling technique with random-digit dialing, which is designed to generate a random sample of California telephone numbers, including unlisted and new subscribers (Waksberg, 1978). At the last stage, a household member aged 18 or older is randomly selected for interview. Interviews are completed with only the target respondent and are conducted in either English or Spanish. During 1989, interviews were completed for 82.8% of eligible adults who were identified through these procedures. The CASRO (Council of American Survey Research Organizations) response rate, which is more conservative in that it includes in the denominator a fraction of numbers for which there was no answer, was 64.2%. Data from respondents were weighted to reflect the estimated age-, sex-, and race-ethnic composition of the 1989 California adult population, using population estimates obtained from the California Department of Finance (CDOF). The distributions of household income and educational level data in the weighted CALBRFSS sample are comparable to CDOF estimates for the California population, even though these variables were not specifically adjusted for.

Source of health care coverage was assessed with a series of eight questions (see Appendix). All respondents were asked whether they were covered by Medicare, Medi-Cal (the California Medicaid equivalent), major medical insurance, a health maintenance organization (HMO), an indemnity-type plan, another type of plan, or a combination of plans. When individuals indicated that they were covered by a private health insurance plan, they were asked the name of their health plan (or the plan they used most often if they had multiple coverage). Respondents who did not indicate having any of the types of health insurance plans mentioned were asked a follow-up question to ascertain whether they paid for most of their doctor bills themselves (as opposed to getting care from a "free" or county clinic) in order to be sure that they really did not have any outpatient health coverage. Based on health care information supplied, six categories of outpatient insurance types were developed: HMO, conventional plan (for example, indemnity or self-insured employer plan), VA/Military, Medicare (with or without supplemental insurance), Medi-Cal only, and No Outpatient Insurance Coverage. Approximately 10% of those in the no outpatient coverage category had major medical coverage. Approximately 2% of the study sample (or 1% using unweighted data) did not supply sufficient information to categorize health plan type.

The study sample was restricted to respondents aged 65 years or under ($n = 1{,}599$), the population typically receiving health care coverage through their place of employment or professional affiliations. Respondents who reported that their primary source of health care coverage was a non-Kaiser HMO, a conventional indemnity plan or preferred provider plan, or Medicare supplement plan were categorized as "Non-Kaiser Privately Insured" (Non-Kaiser). Respondents without private health insurance (that is, non-CHAMPUS military source, Medi-Cal, Medicare without supplemental plan, and no outpatient insurance) were excluded from the analysis. The approximately 1% of the sample with major medical insurance but no outpatient coverage was also excluded.

Data were analyzed using the crosstabs procedure from the Research Triangle Institute SUDAAN statistical software package for personal computer (Research Triangle Institute, 1990). This software, which was specially developed for analysis of weighted data obtained from complex multistage sampling designs, calculates the sample design effect and adjusts sample variance upward when computing standard errors and significance tests.

Kaiser Permanente was named as the primary source of outpatient health coverage by 20.3% of the study sample, after the data were weighted to reflect the age-sex-race composition of the 1989 California population. The remaining 79.7% reported coverage by another HMO (19.5%), a traditional indemnity plan or preferred provider network (56.3%), CHAMPUS (1.8%), or another type of plan offered through their employer or institution (2.1%).

Results

Sociodemographic Characteristics

The Kaiser and non-Kaiser groups were highly similar in terms of sex, age, educational attainment, self-reported household income, and marital status, (Table 1). However, compared to the non-Kaiser group, the Kaiser group had both a significantly higher proportion of minorities (45.4% vs.30.7%, $p < .001$) and a significantly higher proportion of people who were currently employed (82.6% vs. 73.9%, $p < .01$).

Health Characteristics

The two groups had similar health profiles based on self-reported health indicators (Table 2). Over 85% of both groups considered their health to be good or excellent (87.3% of the Kaiser group, 89.1% of the non-Kaiser group). The two groups did not differ significantly in prevalences of self-reported chronic health conditions (arthritis, asthma, back trouble, frequent headaches, heart problems, kidney/bladder trouble, liver trouble, stroke, diabetes, high blood pressure) or health risks (elevated cholesterol, smoking, obesity, and chronic drinking).

Use of Preventive Health Screening Services

While the survey did not collect data about overall health care utilization during the previous year, respondents were asked to indicate how long it had been since they had received a routine health checkup and various cancer detection procedures. The Kaiser and non-Kaiser groups had similar proportions of men and women reporting routine screening procedures (health checkup, digital rectal exam, fecal occult blood test, Pap smear, and mammogram) within the past year (Table 3).

Table 1. A Comparison of the Sociodemographic Characteristics of California Residents Ages 18 to 65 with Different Sources of Outpatient Health Coverage: Kaiser Permanente versus Other Private Health Insurance[1]

Sociodemographic Characteristics	*Kaiser Permanente Health Plan Members*[2] % (*SE*)		*Non-Kaiser Private Coverage*[2] % (*SE*)	
Sex				
Male	52.2	(3.1)	49.9	(1.6)
Female	47.8	(3.1)	50.1	(1.6)
Age				
18-44 years	64.9	(3.2)	68.1	(1.5)
45-65 years	35.1	(3.2)	31.9	(1.5)
Age by Sex				
Male 18-44 years	33.6	(2.9)	35.0	(1.5)
Male 45-65 years	18.6	(2.7)	14.9	(1.2)
Female 18-44 years	31.3	(2.8)	33.1	(1.4)
Female 45-65 years	16.5	(2.5)	17.0	(1.2)
Race/Ethnicity				
White, non-Hispanic[3]	54.6	(3.2)	69.3	(1.6)
Nonwhite or Hispanic	45.4	(3.2)	30.7	(1.6)
Black, non-Hispanic	13.3	(2.2)	4.1	(0.7)
Hispanic	19.7	(2.7)	17.3	(1.2)
Asian	11.0	(2.2)	7.7	(1.1)
Other	1.3	(0.9)	1.6	(0.4)
Education				
12th grade or less	35.9	(3.1)	32.5	(1.5)
Some post-high school education/training	32.0	(2.9)	33.5	(1.5)
College graduate	32.2	(3.0)	34.0	(1.5)
Income				
Less than $20,000	18.7	(2.6)	19.1	(1.3)
$20,000-$34,999	29.9	(2.9)	26.1	(1.4)
$35,000-$50,000	18.5	(2.4)	21.0	(1.3)
Over $50,000	28.4	(2.8)	28.1	(1.4)
(unknown)	4.5		5.7	
Employment Status[4]				
Employed by other	75.2	(2.6)	64.1	(1.5)
Self-employed	7.4	(1.4)	9.8	(0.9)
Not employed	17.4	(2.4)	26.2	(1.5)
Marital Status				
Single	34.1	(2.9)	34.2	(1.5)

Notes: SE = Standard error.

[1] From the 1989 California Behavioral Risk Factor Survey, based on self-reported interview data for adults ages 18-65, weighted to the age-, race- and sex-specific distribution of the 1989 California population (California Department of Health Services, 1990).

[2] Group denominators for the percentages are as follows: Kaiser, $n = 346$ (unweighted $n = 324$); non-Kaiser with private insurance, $n = 1{,}178$ (unweighted $n = 1{,}275$).

[3] Difference significant at: $p < .001$.

[4] Difference significant at: $p < .01$.

Table 2. A Comparison of the Health Characteristics of California Residents Ages 18 to 65 with Different Sources of Outpatient Health Coverage: Kaiser Permanente versus Other Private Health Insurance[1]

Health Characteristics	*Kaiser Permanente Health Plan Members*[2] % (*SE*)		*Non-Kaiser Private Coverage*[2] % (*SE*)	
Overall Health				
Good or Excellent	87.3	(2.0)	89.1	(1.0)
History of chronic conditions[3]				
Arthritis	13.1	(2.3)	13.1	(1.1)
Asthma	7.5	(1.6)	7.7	(0.8)
Back trouble in past year	17.5	(2.4)	18.6	(1.2)
Frequent headaches in past year	13.2	(2.0)	12.7	(1.0)
Heart problems	6.8	(1.6)	6.9	(0.9)
Kidney/bladder trouble	9.4	(1.8)	10.8	(0.9)
Liver trouble	3.6	(1.1)	1.9	(0.4)
Stroke	1.2	(0.6)	1.0	(0.3)
Cancer	3.4	(1.2)	3.1	(0.5)
Diabetes	4.2	(1.4)	3.3	(0.6)
High blood pressure[4]	19.2	(2.5)	14.2	(1.1)
Chronic Health Risks				
Elevated cholesterol[5]	10.6	(2.2)	8.2	(0.9)
Current smoker	19.4	(2.4)	19.4	(1.2)
Overweight[6]	19.5	(2.5)	15.7	(1.2)
Chronic drinker (> 60 drinks/mo.)	3.1	(1.1)	4.3	(0.7)

Notes: SE = Standard error.

[1] From the 1989 California Behavioral Risk Factor Survey, based on self-reported interview data for adults ages 18-65, weighted to the age-, race- and sex-specific distribution of the 1989 California population (California Department of Health Services, 1990).

[2] Group denominators for the percentages are as follows: Kaiser, n = 346 (unweighted n = 324); non-Kaiser with private insurance, n = 1, 178 (unweighted n = 1,275).

[3] "I'm going to read you a list of medical conditions and physical ailments that usually last some time. Please tell me if you have ever experienced this problem or been told by a medical doctor that you have this problem." (*Note:* missing responses coded as not having the condition.)

[4] "Have you ever been told by a doctor, nurse, or other health professional that you have high blood pressure?" (*Note:* missing responses coded as not having high blood pressure.)

[5] "Are you now under the advice of a doctor to reduce your cholesterol?"

[6] Body Mass Index (BMI) of 27.8 or higher for males and 27.3 or higher for females (≥ 85th percentile of BMIs for the reference population in the second National Health and Nutrition Examination Survey.)

Table 3. A Comparison of the Preventive Health Service Use by California Residents Ages 18 to 65 with Different Sources of Outpatient Health Coverage: Kaiser Permanente versus Other Private Health Insurance[1]

Preventive Health Service Use	*Kaiser Permanente Health Plan Members*[2] % (*SE*)	*Non-Kaiser Private Coverage*[2] % (*SE*)
Screening Procedures Within the Past Year		
Routine physical exam	66.7 (2.9)	65.0 (1.5)
Digital rectal exam[3]	33.5 (3.1)	27.4 (1.4)
Blood stool tests	20.8 (2.6)	15.5 (1.2)
Pap smear (*all women*)[5]	68.6 (4.0)	73.8 (1.9)
Mammogram (*all women*)[6]	37.2 (4.4)	30.0 (2.0)

Notes: SE = Standard error.

[1] From the 1989 California Behavioral Risk Factor Survey, based on self-reported interview data for adults ages 18-65, weighted to the age-, race-, and sex-specific distribution of the 1989 California population (California Department of Health Services, 1990).

[2] Approximate group denominators for the percentages are for digital rectal exam, routine physical exam, and blood stool test, Kaiser, $n = 346$ (unweighted $n = 324$); non-Kaiser with private insurance, $n = 1{,}178$ (unweighted $n = 1{,}275$); Pap smear and mammogram: Kaiser, $n = 165$ (unweighted $n = 165$); non-Kaiser, $n = 597$ (unweighted $n = 678$).

[3] Digital rectal exams are not recommended by the U.S. Preventive Services Task Force as a routine cancer screening procedure for low-risk men and women under the age of 40.

[4] Blood stool tests are not recommended by the U.S. Preventive Services Task Force as a routine cancer screening procedure for low-risk men and women under the age of 50.

[5] Pap smears are not recommended by the U.S. Preventive Services Task Force for women who have had a hysterectomy.

[6] Mammography is not recommended by the U.S. Preventive Services Task Force as a routine breast cancer screening procedure for low-risk women under the age of 40.

ALAMEDA COUNTY CHRONIC DISEASE SURVEILLANCE SURVEY

Methods

The Alameda County Chronic Disease Surveillance Survey (ACCDSS) study sample was also selected using a Waksberg-type three-stage cluster design with random digit dialing. The survey was conducted by the Human Population Laboratory of the California Department of Health Services

(California Department of Health Services, 1990b). For these analyses, the sample was restricted to respondents aged 65 years or under who indicated that they had some type of health insurance or health plan that paid for at least some of their visits to the doctor when they were ill ($N = 1{,}003$). People who indicated that they received Medi-Cal were excluded from this sample since it was unlikely that they also had private insurance. Medicare recipients were not likely to influence outcomes since age was restricted to 65 years or under. Kaiser Permanente members were identified from the question, "Do you have the Kaiser plan?" Data were weighted to reflect the estimated age, sex, and racial composition of the adult population in Alameda County in 1989. Based on the weighted data, approximately 43.6% of the respondents were covered by the Kaiser Health Plan. We estimate, based on 1989 CALBRFSS data, that about 20% of the non-Kaiser privately insured group were covered by other HMOs. Data were analyzed using the crosstabs and regression procedures from the Research Triangle Institute SUDAAN statistical software package for personal computer.

Results

Sociodemographic Characteristics

The average age of men and women in the Kaiser group was slightly higher than that of the non-Kaiser group (39.2 years versus 37.1 years). This age difference shows up most dramatically among males, with the Kaiser group having approximately 10% fewer males under the age of 45 as compared to the non-Kaiser group (average age for males was 39 years versus 36.1 years, and for females, 39.3 years versus 38 years). The Kaiser group also had a higher proportion of minorities (48.4% versus 34.9%, $p < .001$), particularly Blacks and Hispanics. Finally, the Kaiser group did not appear to be as well-educated, with 36.2% versus 26.8% of respondents reporting completion of 12 or fewer school years and 30.3% versus 42.1% reporting completion of a college degree ($p < .001$). No statistically significant differences were observed in the distributions of household income level, employment status, marital status, and sex (Table 4).

Health Characteristics

The Kaiser group did not differ from the non-Kaiser group on self-rating of general health status, with more than 90% of both groups reporting that their health was good or excellent (Table 5). No statistically significant differences between the two groups were observed in the prevalences of most chronic health problems (heart trouble, stroke, cancer, lung disease, asthma, diabetes, high blood pressure, arthritis, back pain, muscle/joint pain, ulcer,

Table 4. A Comparison of the Sociodemographic Characteristics of Alameda County Residents Ages 18 to 65 with Different Sources of Outpatient Health Coverage: Kaiser Permanente Members versus People with Coverage for at Least Some Doctor Office Visits (Excluding Medi-Cal Recipients)[1]

Sociodemographic Characteristics	*Kaiser Permanente Health Plan Members*[2] % (*SE*)		*Non-Kaiser with Outpatient Coverage*[2] % (*SE*)	
Sex				
Male	45.3	(2.8)	50.0	(2.4)
Female	54.7	(2.8)	50.0	(2.4)
Age[3]				
18-44 years	65.8	(2.6)	73.6	(2.1)
45-65 years	34.2	(2.6)	26.4	(2.1)
Age by Sex[3]				
Male 18-44 years	29.2	(2.6)	38.8	(2.4)
Male 45-65 years	16.1	(2.0)	11.4	(1.6)
Female 18-44 years	36.6	(2.6)	34.8	(2.3)
Female 45-65 years	18.1	(2.1)	15.0	(1.7)
Race/Ethnicity[4]				
White, non-Hispanic	51.6	(2.7)	65.1	(2.4)
Nonwhite or Hispanic	48.4	(2.7)	34.9	(2.4)
Black, non-Hispanic	15.9	(1.8)	9.6	(1.5)
Hispanic	18.6	(2.3)	11.1	(1.6)
Asian	11.7	(2.1)	10.3	(1.6)
Other	2.2	(0.8)	3.9	(1.2)
Education[5]				
12th grade or less	36.2	(2.7)	26.8	(2.2)
Some post-high school education/training	33.5	(2.5)	31.1	(2.3)
College graduate	30.3	(2.5)	42.1	(2.4)
Income				
Less than $20,000	16.8	(2.1)	17.0	(2.0)
$20,000-$34,999	29.0	(2.5)	25.4	(2.1)
$35,000-$50,000	23.6	(2.3)	20.0	(1.9)
Over $50,000	27.4	(2.5)	32.3	(2.2)
Unknown	3.2		5.2	
Employment Status				
Work for wages/self	78.7	(2.5)	82.9	(1.9)
Marital Status				
Single	42.7	(2.7)	46.2	(2.4)

Notes: SE = Standard error

[1] From the 1989-90 Alameda County Chronic Disease Survey, based on self-report interview data of adults ages 18-65, weighted to the estimated age-, race-, and sex-specific distribution of the 1989 Alameda County population (California Department of Health Services, 1990b).

[2] Group denominators for the weighted percentages are: Kaiser, $n = 444$; non-Kaiser, $n = 554$.

[3] Difference significant at $p < .05$.

[4] Difference significant at $p < .001$.

[5] Difference signifiсnt at $p < .01$.

Table 5. A Comparison of the Health Characteristics of Alameda County Residents Ages 18 to 65 with Different Sources of Outpatient Health Coverage: Kaiser Permanente Members versus People with Coverage for at Least Some Doctor Office Visits (Excluding Medi-Cal Recipients)[1]

Health Characteristics	*Kaiser Permanente Health Plan Members*[2] % (*SE*)		*Non-Kaiser with Outpatient Coverage*[2] % (*SE*)	
Overall Health				
Good or Excellent	93.1	(1.2)	90.2	(1.5)
History of chronic conditions[3]				
Heart trouble (any)	10.5	(1.5)	11.3	(1.5)
Angina	2.7	(0.8)	3.4	(0.9)
Myocardial infarction	1.5	(0.6)	1.0	(0.4)
Other heart problems	8.3	(1.3)	9.3	(1.3)
Stroke (CVA or major)	1.0	(0.5)	0.9	(0.4)
Cancer	4.4	(1.0)	3.5	(0.9)
Respiratory problems (lung/asthma)	13.4	(1.9)	15.5	(1.9)
Lung disease	4.3	(1.2)	5.2	(1.3)
Asthma	10.9	(1.7)	12.3	(1.7)
High blood pressure	15.4	(1.9)	13.7	(1.7)
Diabetes	2.5	(0.9)	3.1	(0.8)
Arthritis	11.5	(1.6)	13.4	(1.7)
Frequent pain in past year:	51.4	(2.7)	46.6	(2.4)
Back pain	28.4	(2.5)	27.2	(2.2)
Muscle/joint pain	24.1	(2.3)	23.8	(2.1)
Headaches[4]	25.8	(2.4)	18.0	(1.8)
Ulcer	5.9	(1.3)	6.3	(1.1)
Environmental smell/ chemical sensitivity[5]	21.4	(2.3)	18.8	(1.9)
Injury requiring treatment in past year	25.0	(2.4)	21.2	(2.0)
Chronic Health Risks				
Current smoker	19.2	(2.0)	19.9	(1.9)
Hearing problem[4]	11.2	(1.8)	6.8	(1.2)
Elevated cholesterol	13.7	(1.8)	14.2	(1.7)
Obesity[6]	17.9	(2.1)	14.3	(1.7)

(*continued*)

Table 5. (Continued)

Sociodemographic Characteristics	*Kaiser Permanente Health Plan Members*[2] % (*SE*)		*Non-Kaiser with Outpatient Coverage*[2] % (*SE*)	
Currently, or in past, has often been exposed to solvents, heavy metals, chemical acids, radioactive materials, heavy dust/asbestos, or pesticides	32.4	(2.5)	32.5	(2.3)

Notes: SE = Standard error.

[1] From the 1989-90 Alameda County Chronic Disease Survey, based on self-report interview data for adults ages 18-65, weighted to the estimated age-, race-, and sex-specific distribution of the 1989 Alameda County population (California Department of Health Services, 1990b).

[2] Group denominators for the weighted percentages are: Kaiser, $n = 444$; non-Kaiser, $n = 554$.

[3] "Has a doctor or other health professional ever told you that you have/had [type of health problem]?" (*Note:* missing responses coded as not having the condition; in most cases, less than 1% of responses were missing.)

[4] Difference significant at $p < .05$.

[5] "Are you made sick by smells or chemicals you encounter that do not seem to bother most other people?"

[6] Defined as a Body Mass Index (BMI) of 27.8 or higher for males and 27.3 or higher for females (≥ 85th percentile of BMIs for the reference population in the second National Health and Nutrition Examination Survey).

environmental/chemical sensitivity) or injury in the past year that required medical treatment, nor for health risks (smoking, obesity, and exposure to hazardous materials). The only statistically significant differences found were the Kaiser group's higher rates of frequent headaches in the past year (25.8% versus 18%, $p < .05$) and hearing problems (11.2% versus 6.8%, $p < .05$).

Health Services Utilization

Less than 10% of the people in both the Kaiser and non-Kaiser groups reported a hospitalization of at least one night during the previous 12 months (Table 6). The men and women in the two groups had comparable average rates of hospitalization (about 0.11 per person). Hospitalizations for childbirth are included in these totals, which may account for the higher hospitalization rates of women aged 18-44 as compared to those for women over age 44.

Table 6. A Comparison of Health Care Use by Alameda County Residents Ages 18-65 with Different Sources of Outpatient Health Coverage: Kaiser Permanente Members versus People with Coverage for at Least Some Doctor Office Visits (Excluding Medi-Cal Recipients)[1]

	Men		*Women*	
Health Service Use	*ages 18-44*	*ages 45-65*[2]	*ages 18-44*	*ages 56-65*[2]
Number of hospitalizations of ≥ 1 night in past 12 months[3]				
Kaiser members				
None (% SE)	96.3 (1.8)	87.2 (5.0)	86.8 (3.0)	96.1 (3.9)
1 or more (% SE)	3.7 (1.8)	12.8 (5.0)	13.2 (3.0)	3.9 (1.8)
Total (Mean SE)	.09 (.04)	.15 (.06)	.16 (.04)	.06 (.03)
Non-Kaiser members				
None (% SE)	93.1 (2.2)	91.2 (6.8)	89.5 (2.3)	94.8 (2.4)
1 or more (% SE)	6.9 (2.2)	8.8 (6.8)	10.5 (2.3)	5.2 (2.4)
Total (Mean SE)	.12 (.04)	.11 (.07)	.12 (.03)	.05 (.02)
Number of illness-related doctor visits in the past 12 months[4,5]				
Kaiser members				
0-1 (% SE)	68.6 (4.7)	78.4 (5.2)	57.9 (4.5)	73.1 (5.1)
2-5 (% SE)	27.3 (4.4)	15.8 (4.5)	34.8 (4.4)	21.7 (4.7)
6-10 (% SE)	3.4 (2.3)	3.6 (2.1)	5.6 (2.4)	2.1 (1.6)
11-20 (% SE)	0.6 (0.6)	2.2 (2.2)	1.3 (0.8)	2.6 (1.8)
> 20 (% SE)	0.0 (—)	0.0 (—)	0.3 (.03)	0.6 (0.6)
Total (Mean SE)	1.4 (0.2)	1.1 (0.3)	2.0 (0.3)	1.9 (0.5)
Non-Kaiser members				
0-1 (% SE)	73.1 (3.6)	62.8 (7.5)	53.5 (4.0)	47.4 (5.9)
2-5 (% SE)	20.7 (3.6)	20.7 (5.4)	35.8 (3.8)	36.5 (6.1)
6-10 (% SE)	2.5 (1.1)	13.3 (7.1)	8.3 (2.2)	5.2 (2.4)
11-20 (% SE)	1.3 (1.0)	3.3 (2.0)	1.7 (0.9)	5.4 (2.3)
> 20 (% SE)	2.3 (1.3)	0.0 (—)	0.9 (0.5)	5.5 (2.9)
Total (Mean SE)	2.3 (0.7)	2.3 (0.6)	2.5 (0.3)	4.3 (1.0)

Notes: SE = Standard Error.

[1] From the 1989-90 Alameda County Chronic Disease Survey, based on self-report interview data of adults ages 18-65, weighted to the estimated age-, race-, and sex-specific distribution of the 1989 Alameda County population (California Department of Health Services, 1990b).

[2] Group denominators for the age-sex specific data are as follows:

Kaiser: men 18-44, n = 117; men 45-65, n = 77; women 18-44, n = 156; women 45-65, n = 85; Non-Kaiser: men 18-44, n = 195; men 45-64, n = 65; women 18-44, n = 213; women 45-65, n = 89.

[3] "How many different times were you in the hospital at least overnight in the past 12 months?"

[4] "During the past 12 months, how many times did you see a doctor about your health when you were not feeling well?"

[5] Kaiser versus Non-Kaiser differences in illness-related doctor visit rates for Men 18-44 and Women 45-65 significant at $p < .05$.

Illness-related doctor visits during the previous 12 months were examined separately for men and women overall and by 18-44 and 45-65 year-old age groups. It should be noted that these visit data do not reflect total doctor office visits during the year—that is, they do not include visits for routine wellness checks or follow-up care for chronic health problems, such as high blood pressure or diabetes. Overall, Kaiser women averaged 1.96 (s.e. 0.24) visits as compared to non-Kaiser women's 3.04 (s.e. 0.37) visits, a difference statistically significant with $p < .01$. This was primarily a result of very high utilization by approximately 10% of the non-Kaiser women aged 45-65. Kaiser men had a lower average number of illness-related visits than non-Kaiser men, 1.3 (s.e. 0.16) versus 2.27 (s.e. 0.58), respectively, but the difference was not statistically significant. Because these means may be unduly influenced by the extremely high utilization of a small percentage of respondents, the distribution of visits by sex and age group is also shown. Approximately 39% of respondents in both the Kaiser and non-Kaiser groups reported no illness-related visits during the previous 12 months, and the majority had less than two visits. Non-Kaiser men aged 18-44 and non-Kaiser women aged 45-65 were significantly more likely than their Kaiser counterparts to report making more than 10 illness-related visits (3.6% versus 0.6% and 10.9% versus 3.2%, respectively) during the year, and non-Kaiser men aged 45-65 also had greater percentages reporting more than one such visit than Kaiser men in that age group.

Multiple linear regression models were used to test the relationship of Kaiser membership to illness-related doctor visits for each sex separately, controlling for age (18-44 versus 45-65), race (white versus minority), and capping number of visits at 21 to counter the influence of the few very high utilizers (Table 7). As was expected, Kaiser membership was a significant predictor for women ($p < .01$), but not for men. However, neither age (45-65 versus 18-44, or 35-44, 45-54, and 55-65 versus 18-34) nor race were significant independent predictors, and these models explained less than 1% of the variance in illness-related visits. When several self-reported health indicators were added into the models (in good or excellent health, injury during the past year, chronic back pain during the past year, frequent muscle/joint pain or arthritis during the past year, and a history of respiratory problems such as asthma or emphysema), Kaiser women still had a significantly lower average visit rate ($p < .02$), although the difference was attenuated somewhat from the first model; the difference for men became borderline significant ($p < .10$). These more inclusive models explained a significantly greater amount of the variance in illness-related utilization, 27% for women and 19% for men. None of the other health indicators tested (cancer, heart problems, stroke, diabetes, and high blood pressure) added significantly to the explanatory model. This may have been due to the low prevalence of the severe health problems in the sample population and the fact that most respondents probably did not consider visits for diabetes and high blood pressure as seeing a doctor about their health when they "were not feeling well."

Table 7. Multiple Linear Regression Models Predicting Illness-Related Doctor Visits by Alameda County Residents Ages 18-65 with Different Sources of Outpatient Health Coverage: Kaiser Permanente Members versus People with Coverage for at Least Some Doctor Office Visits (Excluding Medi-Cal Recipients)[1,2]

Independent Variables	*B Coeff.*	*(SE)*	*p-value*
Women: Model 1, $R^2 = .021$			
(Intercept = 2.455)			
Age (1 = 45-65, 0 = 18-44)	0.573	(0.439)	.193
Race (1 = nonwhite, 0 = white)	0.315	(0.372)	.397
Coverage (1 = Kaiser, 0 = non-Kaiser)	-0.965	(0.350)	.006
Women: Model 2, $R^2 = .269$			
(Intercept = 5.478)			
Age (1 = 45-64, 0 = 18-44)	0.158	(0.323)	.626
Race (1 = nonwhite, 0 = white)	-0.026	(0.293)	.930
Health (1 = good/excellent 0 = fair/poor)	-4.217	(0.878)	.000
Respiratory problems (1 = yes, 0 = no)	0.959	(0.564)	.090
Injury requiring MD care (1 = yes, 0 = no)	2.175	(0.481)	.000
Frequent back pain (1 = yes, 0 = no)	1.212	(0.352)	.001
Coverage (1 = Kaiser, 0 = non-Kaiser)	-0.637	(0.279)	.023
Men: Model 1, $R^2 = .008$			
(Intercept = 1.844)			
Age (1 = 45-65, 0 = 18-44)	0.169	(0.437)	.699
Race (1 = nonwhite, 0 = white)	-0.024	(0.416)	.954
Coverage (1 = Kaiser, 0 = non-Kaiser)	-0.587	(0.364)	.107
Men: Model 2, $R^2 = .196$			
(Intercept = 4.833)			
Age (1 = 45-64, 0 = 18-44)	-0.175	(0.305)	.565
Race (1 = nonwhite, 0 = white)	-0.225	(0.336)	.504
Health (1 = good/excellent) 0 = fair/poor)	-3.737	(1.302)	.004
Respiratory problems (1 = yes, 0 = no)	1.644	(0.761)	.031
Injury requiring MD care (1 = yes, 0 = no)	0.585	(0.405)	.149
Frequent back pain (1 = yes, 0 = no)	0.991	(0.471)	.036
Coverage (1 = Kaiser, 0 = non-Kaiser)	-0.580	(0.311)	.063

Notes: SE = Standard error.

[1]From the 1989-90 Alameda County Chronic Disease Survey, based on self-report interview data of adults ages 18-65, weighted to the estimated age-, race-, and sex-specific distribution of the 1989 Alameda County population (California Department of Health Services, 1990b).

[2]"During the past 12 months, how many times did you see a doctor about your health when you were not feeling well?"

Table 8. A Comparison of Preventive Health Service Use by Alameda County Residents Ages 18-65 with Different Sources of Outpatient Health Coverage: Kaiser Permanente Members versus People with Coverage for at Least Some Doctor Office Visits (Excluding Medi-Cal Recipients)[1]

Procedure Done in Past Years	*Kaiser Permanente Health Plan Members*[2] % (*SE*)		*Non-Kaiser with Outpatient Coverage*[2] % (*SE*)	
Routine physical exam	50.8	(2.7)	48.7	(2.4)
Cholesterol check	35.8	(2.6)	36.0	(2.3)
Blood pressure check	83.3	(2.0)	81.7	(1.9)
Pap smear (*all women*)[3]	66.7	(3.6)	66.3	(3.1)
Mammograms (*all women*)[4,5]	23.8	(3.1)	15.9	(2.3)

Notes: SE = Standard error.

[1] From the 1989-90 Alameda County Chronic Disease Survey, based on self-report interview data of adults ages 18-65, weighted to the estimated age-, race-, and sex-specific distribution of the 1989 Alameda County population (California Department of Health Services, 1990b).

[2] Group denominators for the percentages: Kaiser, $n = 444$ (women $n = 207$); non-Kaiser, $n = 555$ (women $n = 302$).

[3] Rates for all women ages 18-65. Pap smears are usually not recommended for women who have had a hysterectomy.

[4] Rate for all women ages 18-65. Screening mammograms are usually not recommended for women under the age of 40.

[5] Difference significant at $p < .05$.

In terms of routine health screening procedures, the Kaiser and non-Kaiser groups had similar percentages of people reporting that they had received routine physical exams, cholesterol checks, blood pressure checks, and Pap smears within the past year, but Kaiser women had significantly higher mammogram rates (Table 8). Although this may be a result of slightly more Kaiser than non-Kaiser women being 40 years of age or older (screening mammography is not recommended for women under 40), mammography rates were substantially higher for women aged 40 and over with Kaiser coverage than non-Kaiser coverage (47.3% versus 34.9%).

Respondents were asked to report the extent to which their health coverage paid for hospital bills, doctor visits, routine checkups/preventive services, and prescriptions (Table 9). Compared to the group of respondents covered by non-Kaiser plans, the Kaiser group had significantly higher percentages reporting that their health plan covered all or most of their doctor visits (93.8% versus 77.1%, $p < .001$), routine and preventive care (87.8% versus 60.0%, $p < .001$), and prescription medications (70.5% versus 57.1%, $p < .001$).

Table 9. A Comparison of the Perceptions of What Their Health Plan Covers, Alameda County Residents Ages 18-65 with Different Sources of Outpatient Health Coverage: Kaiser Permanente Members versus People with Coverage for at Least Some Doctor Office Visits (Excluding Medi-Cal Recipients)[1]

Perceptions Of Coverage	*Kaiser Permanente Health Plan Members*[2] % (*SE*)		*Non-Kaiser with Outpatient Coverage*[2] % (*SE*)	
Percentage who say that their health plan covers all or most of the costs of their:				
Hospital bills	90.6	(1.7)	83.6	(2.0)
Doctor visits for illness care[3]	93.8	(1.4)	77.1	(2.2)
Routine checkups/ preventive services[3]	87.7	(2.1)	60.0	(2.4)
Prescription medications[3]	70.5	(2.5)	57.1	(2.5)

Notes: SE = Standard error.

[1] From the 1989-90 Alameda County Chronic Disease Survey, based on self-report interview data of adults ages 18-65, weighted to the estimated age-, race-, and sex-specific distribution of the 1989 Alameda County population (California Department of Health Services, 1990b).

[2] Group denominators for the percentages are: Kaiser, $n = 444$; non-Kaiser, $n = 555$.

[3] Difference significant at $p < .001$.

DISCUSSION

The results of our analyses of data from probability sample surveys of state (the 1989 California Behavioral Risk Factor Surveillance Survey) and county (1989 Alameda County Chronic Disease Surveillance Survey) populations indicate that, as a group, 18 to 65-year-olds covered by the Kaiser Permanente Medical Care Program are highly comparable to those covered by other sources of private outpatient health insurance in terms of sociodemographic and self-reported health characteristics. Thus, based on health characteristics alone, there is no evidence for "favorable selection" by the Kaiser HMO in this particular population. This finding replicates the results of the studies by Luft (1981); Welch, Frank, and Diehr (1984); and Grazier et al. (1986).

The Kaiser and non-Kaiser samples were highly comparable in their use of preventive health services. In both studies, the proportions of respondents in both groups who reported that they had received a routine physical examination, blood pressure check, and cholesterol check in the past year did not differ significantly although women in the Kaiser group were more likely to report having had a mammogram in the past year. This suggests that there was not a greater propensity for Kaiser members to receive preventive screening services than for those covered by other plans. However, in recent years, it has become more difficult to assign costs of preventive care to health plans for the first three procedures because they can take place outside of a doctor's office (for example, through worksite- or community-based programs). Since 40% of the non-Kaiser respondents in the Alameda County study indicated that their health plan did not cover the costs of routine/preventive care, the comparability of percentages receiving preventive services in the past year should not be equated with comparable cost outlays for preventive health care by the different types of health insurers.

We want to point out that most cancer screening procedures, Pap smear being the exception, are not recommended for low-risk people under the age of 40 or 50. Consequently, the data presented in this report should not be extrapolated for use as an indicator of quality of cancer prevention activities in the Kaiser Permanente Medical Care Program as compared to other health plans. The higher-than-expected percentages of 18 to 65-year-old adults reporting a routine checkup within the past year suggest that some respondents may have interpreted the term as any type of checkup, such as for diagnosis of illness, as opposed to a comprehensive wellness exam.

In our analysis of the Alameda County data, we found some evidence for "favorable selection" among women, but not among men, using the average number of illness-related outpatient visits during the previous 12 months as a criterion. We do not know why this was the case, although re-analysis of the self-reported health data by sex suggested that non-Kaiser women were somewhat less healthy than the Kaiser women. Unfortunately, the Alameda survey did not ask about total number of doctor office visits during the past year for any reason, including follow-up or monitoring of chronic health problems. It is possible that some types of visits considered to be illness-related by people who have to submit claims for reimbursement may have been considered to be health maintenance visits by Kaiser members, who were more likely than their counterparts to indicate that their plan covered routine/preventive services. It is also possible that the combination of the HMO's health maintenance care, the self-care orientation conveyed to members, the telephone advice nurse service, and appointment nonavailability kept Kaiser members' illness-related visits lower than their non-Kaiser counterparts, especially for self-limiting conditions. Finally, fee-for-service practitioners may be more likely to encourage patients to return for follow-up visits in order to generate revenue. No differences were found in average number of hospitalizations during the previous year; however, we have no information about average length of stay or about the reasons for hospitalizations that did occur.

We acknowledge that this study has several limitations. First, neither of the two surveys whose data we used for these analyses was specifically designed to examine the "HMO favorable selection" issue. Thus, while we feel that we had good information about the sociodemographic and health characteristics of the respondents, our information about their health service utilization during the previous year was very limited and based entirely on self-report. Second, the overall size of the two survey samples, after eliminating respondents over age 65 and those with no private health care coverage, did not allow for more refined subgroup analyses (for example, comparison of the characteristics and utilization patterns for the Kaiser and non-Kaiser groups in different age-sex groups). Third, neither of the surveys contained questions about the health status and utilization histories of the families of the respondents. Lairson and Herd (1987) have suggested that "favorable selection" for HMOs may be more a function of the size and health of the individual's family than the individual per se.

Finally, the non-Kaiser insured group comprised people with diverse types of health care coverage—Independent Practice Association (IPA) and group model HMOs, conventional indemnity plans, preferred provider organizations (PPOs), self-insured employer plans, union-affiliated plans, and so forth, rather than conventional indemnity plans alone—although approximately 80% of the group were covered by a conventional plan. We do not know the extent to which inclusion of HMO and PPO subscribers in the non-Kaiser group mitigated against our finding significant between-group differences in health indicators and utilization rates. However, a separate parallel analysis of the CALBRFSS data comparing HMO enrollees versus conventional plan subscribers arrived at the same results. Because of the nature of the ACCDSS health care coverage questions, we were unable to separate HMO enrollees from conventional plan holders in order to make a cleaner comparison of the association of health care coverage with hospitalizations and illness-related outpatient visits during the previous year.

Further studies in this new cost-containment era are needed to help resolve the question of whether prepaid health plans experience "favorable selection" based on an individual's health status and propensities to use health services, or whether the less hospital-based and more self-care and prevention-oriented practice styles associated with prepaid health plans are what really account for more "favorable costs."

APPENDIX

Health Care Coverage Questions on the Surveys

California Behavioral Risk Factor Surveillance Survey Questions:

Now I'd like to ask you a few questions about your health care coverage, which you use when paying hospital bills, doctor bills, or clinic bills. We are interested in the relationship between different kinds of health care coverage and use of preventive services.

Are you covered by any of the following kinds of health care plan?

Medicare? (*available to adults over the age of 62 or on social security*)

Medi-Cal? (*available to low-income Californians, for example, those on SSI, AFDC*)

Major medical insurance, which pays for hospital stays?

A health maintenance organization, or HMO, for example, Kaiser, Maxicare or Foundation, which allows you to see doctors for no fee or a small fee at each visit?

A health insurance plan, such as Blue Cross or Aetna, which pays a percentage of each doctor bill for routine care while you are responsible for the rest?

Any other type of plan, for example, the military or student health?

(*If has a health plan*): What is the name of your health plan?

(*If more than one health plan*): What is the name of the plan you use most often?

(*If no apparent health care coverage*): Does this mean you pay all the costs each time you see a doctor for routine office care?

Is there one doctor you usually go to who knows your medical history?

Alameda County Chronic Disease Surveillance Survey Questions:

Do you have any kind of health insurance or medical care plans, including Medi-Cal or Medicare?

Do you have the Kaiser plan?

Do you have Medi-Cal?

Do you have Medicare?

Does your health care plan cover all, most, some, or none of your hospital bills?

Does your health care plan cover all, most, some, or none of your doctor visits?

Does your health care plan cover all, most, some, or none of your prescriptions?

Does your health care plan cover all, most, some, or none of your check-ups or other preventative services?

How many different times were you in the hospital at least overnight in the past 12 months?

During the past 12 months, how many times did you see a doctor about your health when you were not feeling well?

ACKNOWLEDGMENTS

We wish to acknowledge the cooperation of William E. Wright, PhD, Chief, Cancer Surveillance Section, Chronic Diseases Branch, California Department of Health Services (CDHS), in making the 1989 California Behavioral Risk Factor Surveillance Survey (CALBRFSS) data available to us for this study. Laurence Parker, PhD, helped develop and test the CALBRFSS health care coverage questions. CALBRFSS data collection was supported in part by funds from Cooperative Agreement No. U58/CCU900590-07 between the Centers for Disease Control, U.S. Public Health Service, and the Cancer Surveillance Section, CDHS, and in part by the Northern California Cancer Center (health care coverage questions). The Alameda County Chronic Disease Surveillance Survey was supported in part by funds from the Comprehensive Environmental Response, Compensation, and Liability Act trust fund through an interagency agreement with the Agency for Toxic Substances and Disease Registry, U.S. Public Health Service; Centers for Disease Control, U.S. Public Health Service; and the California Department of Health Services. The findings and conclusions reported here are solely the responsibility of the authors.

REFERENCES

Buchanan, J. and S. Cretin. (1986). "Risk Selection of Families Electing HMO Membership." *Medical Care* 24(January):39-51.

California Department of Health Services (CDHS), Chronic Diseases Branch. (1990a). *California Behavioral Risk Factor Surveillance Survey 1989*. Sacramento, CA: Chronic Diseases Branch, CDHS.

California Department of Health Services (CDHS), Human Population Laboratory (1990b). *Alameda County Chronic Disease Surveillance Survey*. Berkeley, CA: Human Population Laboratory, CDHS.

Grazier, K., W. Richardson, D. Martin, and P. Diehr. (1986). "Factors Affecting Health Plan Choice." *Health Services Research* 20(February):659-682.

Hellinger, F.J. (1987). "Selection Bias in Health Maintenance Organizations: Analysis of Recent Evidence." *Health Care Financing Review* 9(Winter):55-63.

Jackson-Beeck, M. and J. Kleinman. (1983). "Evidence for Self-selection among Health Maintenance Organization Enrollees." *Journal of the American Medical Association* 250(November):2826-2829.

Lairson, D.R. and J.A. Herd. (1987). "The Role of Health Practices, Health Status, and Prior Health Care Claims in HMO Selection Bias." *Inquiry* 24:276-84.

Luft, H. (1981). *The Operations and Performance of Health Maintenance Organizations*. Washington, DC: U.S. Government Printing Office.

Manning, W.G., A. Lubowitz, G. Goldberg, and W. Rogers (1984). "A Controlled Trial of the Effect of Prepaid Group Practice on Use of Services." *New England Journal of Medicine* 310 (June):1505-1520.

Mullooly, J. and D. Freeborn. (1979). "The Effect of Length of Membership upon Utilization of Ambulatory Care Services: A Comparison of Disadvataged and General Membership Populations in a Prepaid Group Practice." *Medical Care* 17:922.

Research Triangle Institute (1990). *Software for SUrvey DAta ANalysis (SUDAAN) Version 5.30 for IBM Personal Computers and Compatibles*. Research Triangle Park, NC: Research Triangle Institute.

Roghmann, K.K., A.A. Sorenson, and S.M. Wells. (1977). *A Cohort Analysis of the Impact of Three Health Maintenance Organizations on Inpatient Utilization* (Final Report. Contract No. 100-77-0021). Prepared for the Department of Health, Education, and Welfare. Washington, DC: U.S. Government Printing Office.

Waksberg, J. (1978). "Sampling Methods for Random Digit Dialing." *Journal of the American Statistical Association* 73:40-46.

Welch, W.P. (1985). "Health Care Utilization in HMO's: Results from Two National Samples. *Journal of Health Economics* 4:293-308.

Welch, W. P., R. G. Frank, and A. Diehr. (1984). "Health Care Costs in Health Maintenance Organizations: Correcting for Self-Selection." In R. M. Scheffler and L. F. Rossiter (Eds.), *Advances in Health Economics and Health Services Research* (Vol. 5, pp. 95-128). Greenwich, CT: JAI Press.

ADJUSTING HEALTH BENEFIT CONTRIBUTIONS TO REFLECT RISK

Mark C. Hornbrook and Michael J. Goodman

INTRODUCTION

A competitive market for health insurance involves voluntary choices by informed consumers among multiple offerings. Health plans operating in such markets face incentives to process claims as efficiently as possible, to offer an acceptable quality of service, and to set prices that create and maintain market shares (Enthoven, 1989). The competitive market model offers one approach to meeting the criteria for socially efficient provision of health insurance—minimizing loading fees, defining acceptable standard benefit packages, offering a variety of insurers and products to consumers, providing no persistent excess profits to insurers, creating no unusual barriers to entry by new insurers, and offering coverage to those consumers who are willing to pay the actuarial premium plus the loading fee.

Health insurance, however, is different from typical economic goods and services, and especially from other forms of insurance. The economic model

Advances in Health Economics and Health Services Research, Vol. 12, pages 41-76.
Copyright © 1991 by JAI Press Inc.
All rights of reproduction in any form reserved.
ISBN: 1-55938-241-4

of perfect, or even workable, competition, is likely to lead to market failure because health insurance is characterized by externalities. The amount of health insurance consumed by one individual will influence the welfare of other persons. This arises through two mechanisms—interdependent preferences and selectivity in health plan choice. First, we care when others are not able to purchase health insurance because their access to medical care is inhibited (Pepper Commission, 1990). Our concern derives from a fundamental social value that no one should suffer pain, illness, or death solely because they cannot pay for necessary medical care. This principle also extends to correlation between income and health—low income persons should not be preordained to suffer lower health status strictly as a result of their position in the income distribution.

Second, selectivity in creating risk pools delimits risk sharing and is the antithesis of health insurance. Persons in pools of unhealthy persons face higher premiums for health insurance. Moreover, risk-based pricing distributes medical care according to the ability to pay rather than according to need—people who are more likely to be unhealthy must pay higher premiums. Unhealthy poor persons, therefore, are less able to purchase health insurance and must pay a disproportionate share of their incomes for it.

A well-designed insurance policy should reduce both risk to individuals and waste to the economy (Zeckhauser, 1970). Pooling functions to reduce risk to each insured person. Competition among health plans focuses on pure efficiency effects—the administrative overhead reflected in the loading fee and the waste associated with the providers' style of practice. Problems arise when competition focuses on segmenting the market according to risk—the underlying permanent health status of the insured. Insurers tend to drop or restrict offerings to high-risk groups because ability to pay tends to be inversely correlated with risk. High-risk persons face high premiums and inferior or no coverage. This type of product differentiation interferes with risk reduction for high-risk persons and may lead to the waste associated with delayed access to health care. This problem reveals the interdependence of equity and efficiency in the health insurance market—efficient health plans for low-risk persons drive out efficient health plans for high-risk persons.

Ideally, consumers should select their health plans on the basis of internal plan efficiencies rather than, say, their (healthy/sick) coworker's (or neighbor's) choice of plan. Removing the health selectivity component from variation in health insurance premiums would leave consumers facing relative prices that reflected internal plan efficiencies rather than plan enrollment and disenrollment policies. Risk-pricing (experience-rating) schemes offer private efficiency under the assumption that health care should be distributed according to the ability to pay, but they are very perverse judged by the assumption that health care should be distributed according to need.

AIMS

In this paper, we examine the theoretical and policy issues involved in compensating for health selectivity effects under dual and multiple choice health benefit programs. These effects undermine the efficiencies of a competitive market when all health plans attempt to specialize in low-risk lines of insurance. The specific aims of this paper are, first, to outline the principles for efficient and equitable sharing of the risk of health care expenses for society and to highlight the conflict between the competitive market model and socially efficient risk sharing in pluralistic health insurance markets; second, to specify alternative methods for improving the performance of health insurance markets; third, to develop a conceptual framework for classifying various types of health benefit programs; fourth, to derive the implications of selected features of health benefit programs for efficient risk sharing; fifth, to develop a taxonomy of risk-adjustment models; and, sixth, to determine the appropriate use of risk-adjustment procedures under various health benefit programs.

Any number of auspices can serve to create sufficiently large groups of consumers to serve as risk pools for underwriting health insurance. Employer-based groups represent the predominant mode in this country. Medicare, Medicaid, and state health insurance plans create publicly subsidized risk pools for disadvantaged and other special target groups. Insurance companies can offer their own existing pools of customers to underwrite new enrollees, either as individuals or as groups. In this paper, we focus primarily on employment-related health benefit programs, although many of the principles apply equally well to the risk-contracting programs under Medicare and Medicaid, where beneficiaries have a choice between a fee-for-service indemnity option and a risk contract option, as well as among multiple risk contractors.

In the next section, our assumptions about how health risk ought to be distributed are highlighted and the rationale for government intervention via regulations governing rate-setting and contribution formulas to adjust for risk differences is presented.

POLICY FRAMEWORK

Social Efficiency and Risk Sharing

We start with the assumption that the unpredictable nature of the incidence and severity of illness and injury for an individual is the essential motivation for purchasing health insurance and creating risk pools. The general theory of insurance is that an individual accepts a small, certain loss (the premium) in return for protection—an insurer's promise to pay—against a potentially large, but uncertain loss (Zeckhauser, 1970; Borch, 1990). An "insurable" event has a low probability of occurrence with a high expected loss, and the probability of a loss is *not* under the insured's control but is predictable to the insurer (Feldstein, 1988). An individual purchases health insurance for protection from unexpected financial losses from treatment for disease and injury. Health insurance is best purchased when healthy in order to keep the cost as low as possible; if insurance is purchased only when an individual is sick or expecting use in the near future, the price of insurance will be substantially higher. The social function of health insurance is to transfer the financial burden of illness and injury from the few sick to the many well.

Risk-averse consumers prefer to purchase health insurance because predictable premium payments are manageable within household budgets, and individuals gain the assurance that their incomes and wealth are protected from the high cost of medical care. If individuals choose to self-insure ("going bare"), they would have to inherit a substantial sum of money and/or save significant portions of their income to achieve the same effective level of protection provided by a typical health insurance policy. Self-insurance is expected to lead to underinsurance because individuals usually underestimate the true probability and cost of serious illness for themselves and, for most persons, their incomes and savings are not adequate to meet the high expenses associated with major surgery and/or a long stay in a critical care unit.

The larger the population base over which to spread the risk, the closer the actuarial cost per person is to the overall population mean health care expense, which is the lowest possible actuarial premium with universal coverage. Risk pooling introduces greater predictability for the insurer via the law of large numbers; the insurer is able to accurately predict future per capita expense and, therefore, is able to set a premium to assure financial success. By pooling financial risk in a series of voluntary exchanges, both the insured and the insurer are better off.

If a single risk pool is defined for the entire population of the country, then the average premium is minimized—no individual is allowed to opt out of the risk pool and true social risk sharing is realized.[1] If two risk pools are defined, insured versus uninsured, then persons can elect not to purchase insurance if they face a very low probability of high medical bills and are not extremely risk averse, thereby saving the expense of the insurance premium. Feldstein (1988) argues that the availability of this choice is efficient because it does not force healthy persons to purchase excess health insurance against their will; that is, they have the option of self-insuring and avoiding the loading fee. Higher premiums will be imposed on the insured group to the extent that low-risk individuals take themselves out of the underwriting pool. This premium increase will induce other persons at the margin to drop their insurance. If society accepts the value position that uninsured persons must take full responsibility for their choices and for all health care expenses out of their own pockets, this will result in efficient allocation of resources. If, however, seriously ill uninsured persons are provided access to health care without paying for it fully out of their pockets, they have essentially imposed a hidden tax on insured persons—the so-called "cost-shift."

Instead of mandating that uninsured persons purchase health insurance, the government could levy a tax on the uninsured equal to the expected average annual per capita health care expense for the total population and place these tax revenues in the health insurance fund. This would leave the insured group equally well-off as compared to mandatory participation in the risk pool because they are not being taxed to pay for care of the uninsured. The health insurance fund would be indifferent to individuals' choices to insure or not because its revenue would be unaffected. Since only the healthiest persons are expected not to insure, the health plan can continue to care for the sickest persons without any reduction in quality or service. This is a simple example of risk adjustment, that is, transferring dollars from one group to another, to maintain access to health care at the lowest cost per capita.

Now suppose we move to the case of multiple risk pools with voluntary choice. If each health plan faces equal risk—expected per capita expense—realized annual per capita expenses should vary across plans only by chance and by their level of efficiency in claims processing and delivery of care (holding benefits constant). This would occur naturally if enrollment were accomplished randomly via a lottery during each annual open season.[2] But with voluntary choice, some consumers will switch to cheaper options as they become available. When faced with a choice of health plans, rational consumers will select the health plan with the lowest premium, *all other things being the same.* If premiums differ for efficiency reasons, then increasing the market shares of more efficient health plans is socially desirable and stimulates competitors to search for similar efficiencies. If, on the other hand, premiums differ because of variation in risk, an unstable cost-premium spiral will emerge for adversely selected plans.

Insurers, in building risk pools (which are subsets of the population), can control their premiums by having the largest possible risk pool and by selecting individuals with the smallest probability of experiencing a significant loss. Assuming that sick persons are more likely than healthy persons to be contained in any risk pool because they are less likely to self-insure, a large risk pool increases the number of relatively healthy individuals, offsetting the small number of sick individuals. As a risk pool shrinks, the impact of a high-expense illness episode increases and raises the importance of the use of selection techniques in defining the pool.

Another way to reduce the premium for a particular insurance plan is to create a risk pool containing only the healthiest persons and set the premium based on their experience. As long as new enrollees to the pool are healthy and continuing enrollees remain healthy, the premium can remain low. This requires that marketing policies and procedures restrict access by unhealthy persons who, as a consequence, are forced to create their own, higher cost, risk pools.

Without a mechanism to compensate for or correct adverse selection, we discriminate against enrollees in high-risk plans. These enrollees are forced to consume an inferior product (because the risk pool is sicker) and, as a group, pay higher premiums so that social risk sharing is delimited. What is needed is a mechanism to measure differences in risk among health plans.

Individuals may have a fairly good idea whether they will experience a loss in any given year. Those who are less likely to experience a significant loss choose insurance with different characteristics than individuals with poor health status. Because both insurer and individual are aware of this, insurers can offer plans tailored to low risks. As this becomes increasingly prevalent, social risk sharing declines. To the extent that healthy persons do not participate in risk sharing for sick persons, the burden of medical care costs is not spread as widely as possible, and sicker persons are forced to pay a greater share of their health care expenses. (If the incidence and severity of illness were uniform across a population over a sufficiently long time, then insurance would only serve to redistribute expenses over time for each person.)

Risk-based competition among health plans focuses on skimming the healthiest persons and dumping the sickest who, ultimately, may end up unable to purchase health insurance at a price they can afford. From a social perspective, this represents market failure and requires government intervention to meet equity goals.

When health care expenses are pooled and spread over an entire population group, moral hazard is created—insured persons can influence the probability and size of loss through their decisions about using medical care. Any actor pays only a fraction of the price of cost-increasing behaviors and receives only a fraction of the benefits of cost-saving behaviors, thereby removing incentives for efficient behavior. Consumers can contribute to medical care costs by demanding unnecessary services, choosing inefficient providers, and enrolling in inefficient health plans. More than nominal deductibles and copayments are often imposed with the stated purpose of discouraging discretionary use (Abraham, 1986). This is a form of risk-sharing with users.

User fees help to moderate moral hazard by giving the insured a stake in the size of the loss. A copayment should be large enough to discourage frivolous use, but small enough not to restrict access because of inability to pay. User fees as cost-containment measures do incur a potential tradeoff between savings from reduced use and extremely high costs created by delaying necessary treatment. Diabetes, carefully managed, can be controlled far less expensively than waiting until circulatory problems require amputation or result in cardiovascular disease. Similarly, breast cancer detected early is relatively curable; if undetected until advanced stages, it is more likely to result in high health care expense and death. User fees should only be used to attack the portion of variation in health care expense that derives from consumer behavior. They should not be used strictly as a cost-containment measure in cases where the real cause of the cost problem is supply-side inefficiency, for example, provider-induced demand to maximize incomes (Evans, 1983).

Fixed copayments and deductibles have the additional drawback of violating the principle of social risk sharing by placing a portion of the risk back on the individual. Differential incomes mean that the effect of a similar copayment is not symmetric across all users. In practice, user fees limit access rather than redistributing risk because their most significant impact is on the high users with the lowest incomes. Such fees affect necessary and discretionary services alike (Siu, et al., 1986).

Health plans can contribute to overall medical care cost variation by not curbing consumers' pursuit of wasteful patterns of care and providers' prescribing of unnecessarily elaborate patterns of care, by employing wasteful claims-processing practices, by paying plan employees excessively high salaries, by making excessive payments to providers, by constructing unnecessarily elaborate facilities, by paying excessive dividends to stockholders, and by various other inefficiencies in organizing resources to supply whatever services are provided. Providers and insurers, like consumers, should face the financial implications of their own cost-influencing behaviors.

To summarize, voluntary choice of health plan creates two sources of inefficiency: moral hazard, because risk pooling shelters all actors from the true social opportunity cost of their actions; and selection bias, because health plan choice systematically discriminates among risk pools and delimits risk sharing by private insurers. Risk adjustment removes the responsibility for expense from one set of actors when the cause of the expense is beyond their control and transfers the responsibility (or at least part of it) to a more appropriate group. The purely random, exogenous component of expense variation should be spread among the entire risk pool. Measures of risk should not incorporate inefficiency on the part of consumers, providers, or insurers.

An efficient risk-sharing mechanism will assign the nonrandom, controllable components of risk attributable to each actor to that actor so that efficient behavior is encouraged. To include factors that are beyond the actors' control does not effectively encourage behavior that minimizes moral hazard; it only increases incentives for risk-avoidance and risk-evasion behaviors.

As the number of insurers increases, consistent with a competitive market structure and freedom of entry, risk pools become increasingly fragmented and the size of each risk pool shrinks. As some insurers pursue policies to create low-risk groups, higher risk populations are forced into increasingly costly alternatives; high-risk health plans become increasingly expensive, inducing more healthy enrollees to switch to lower risk health plans. Those who remain in a high-cost risk pool are much more likely to be sicker than average because they may face higher switching costs, and the increase in premium may represent a relatively small portion of their total health care expense. This creates a cost-premium spiral that eventually ends in plan and market failure (Price and Mays, 1985; Luft, Trauner, and Maerki, 1985). Social risk sharing is defeated and unnecessary switching costs are imposed on enrollees.

Varying premiums with the degree of risk serves to level the competitive playing field among health plans. From a social perspective, an insurer specializing in high-risk populations could be given special consideration in order to provide incentives for access and high quality of care for the most vulnerable groups of our society.

To summarize, we offer the following nine principles for efficient and equitable sharing of risk for health care expenses:

1. Risk should be spread among the largest possible population;
2. Where risk is assigned to an *individual* actor, it should be controllable by that actor (insurers control the ultimate underwriting risk via the operation of the law of large numbers and by use of accurate prediction models);
3. User fees should be used only to limit moral hazard, not to limit access or ration services;
4. Choice among private health plans can help achieve social efficiency by providing incentives to insurers to control costs, lower prices, and maintain quality of service;
5. Health plans enrolling sicker than average persons should be able to survive over the long run if, and only if, they are relatively efficient in caring for that population;
6. Health plans enrolling healthier-than-average persons should not reap windfall profits;
7. Inefficient health plans should become more efficient or leave the market;
8. Efficient health plans should be able to increase their market shares as long as efficiency is not threatened; and,
9. Plans with very rich benefit packages should not receive subsidies solely because they provide higher benefits.

Policy Options for Distributing Risk

A mechanism for reinsuring separate risk pools, that is, pooling health plans into larger pools, will increase the social efficiency of risk sharing. Such reinsurance increases moral hazard on the part of the insurer, however, because it also spreads the risk arising from plan inefficiencies (including poor pricing decisions). Careful attention must be paid to designing a mechanism to preserve the accountability of health plans for their own behaviors. In this section, we consider seven alternative policy options for improving the distribution of risk from a social perspective.

National Health Insurance

Rather than creating many small risk pools, with a concomitant opportunity for selectivity and selection bias, national health insurance (NHI) could offer a single nationwide risk pool in which all persons are required to participate; this is the largest pool possible. Participation could be scaled according to ability to pay via progressive financing so that no individual is restricted from participating in the risk pool. The rationale for this is that medical care is characterized by externalities such that social welfare is reduced when persons who cannot pay for medical care are left untreated when they suffer serious illness or injury. Placing low income persons in the risk pool via subsidies averts the need for point-of-service subsidies and cost-shifting. As long as aggregate administrative costs are not higher than those for private health insurance, sicker persons would be better off because they would not become trapped in a separate high-cost risk pool.

NHI requires that consumers give up their choice of risk pools and accept a national monopoly. Without the competitive discipline of the market, consumers would have to find nonmarket criteria for judging the efficiency of the national health plan. Administrative and Congressional oversight would be required to pursue efficient operations. Under NHI, all providers would face a monopsonistic payer. Such countervailing market power would likely not be acceptable to providers accustomed to the pluralistic structure of our health care system but would offer one-time savings through incomes policies aimed at providers.

Mandatory Reinsurance

A mandatory reinsurance program would require each insurer to purchase insurance against unexpected increases in risk. This would serve to shift risk to a more desirable (that is, broader) basis. A small employer group would be protected from large premium increases if one of its members suffered a high-cost episode. If reinsurance were purely voluntary, plans experiencing favorable selection would not perceive the need for reinsurance and their enrollees would be kept out of the reinsurance pool. This option does not address the problem of access for persons who are unable to purchase health insurance.

Mandatory Community Rating

Mandatory or universal community rating represents another method of creating larger risk pools; this approach treats the entire health plan membership as a risk pool, rather than establishing separate employer-related groups. If all health plans are community-rated, then every consumer gains the benefit of joining a much larger risk group than would have been available under his/her group-specific experience-rated plan. In a health benefit program with only community-rated (CR) plans, adverse selection within the group to any one plan is spread across the plan's entire membership. For the affected health plan, the likelihood of adverse selection in every group is much lower than in any single group—some groups will have favorable selection, some adverse selection, and others no selection. Community rating reduces plan sensitivity to selection effects in any one employer group. Thus, a world of CR plans may be able to function effectively and efficiently without concern for selectivity effects.

Operating experience-rated and community-rated plans side by side within the same health benefit program presents significant difficulties, however. In employer groups with below average risk, experience-rated (ER) plans can easily underprice community-rated plans. In groups with employees who have above-average risk, experience-rated plans can survive only by skimming or offering fewer benefits. In the long run, market forces inside a health benefit program drive low-risk persons into ER plans and high-risk persons into CR plans, imposing de facto experience rating. Thus, community rating has to be mandated to provide stable and efficient risk sharing.

Open Season Lottery

Random assignment of employees to health plans would prevent risk selection; distribution of risk among plans would be equalized by definition, varying only by chance. This, of course, defeats the principles of the competitive market because inefficient plans would be guaranteed stable market shares.

Community Representation

If every insurer enrolls a large, representative cross-section of the community, health status selection effects are likely to be very small and risks are likely to be approximately equal. Each insurer would have a sufficiently large and diverse enrollee group to achieve stable and equal risk. This represents one view of the desired long-run equilibrium in a competitive health insurance market. Under a multi-option, experience-rated health benefit program, however, risk pools can become very small, especially in smaller firms, with a concomitantly high likelihood of adverse selection; community representation would only be achieved by chance.

Extended Enrollment Periods

Private health insurance has fixed terms for enrollment contracts, typically a year. The longer the enrollment period, the greater the degree to which enrollees provide their own risk sharing. Health care utilization is typically clustered so that with shorter risk periods, some persons will be very heavy users and most will be low or non-users. Over longer periods, the probability of continuous good health and non-use drops (Goodman et al., 1991). In the logical extreme, risk sharing over an individual's lifespan is achieved via individual health accounts that would be built up during healthy periods and drawn down to care for illness. Mandating longer enrollment periods, say, two to five years, would work to dampen selection effects as the outlier cases regress towards the mean over time.

Risk-Adjusted Premium Contributions

In private group and governmental health insurance programs, consumers do not pay the full premium. Rather, the premium is split into a consumer contribution and an employer or governmental contribution. The consumer contribution is the out-of-pocket price that influences the demand for health insurance and choice of health plan, as well as the proportion of risk shifted to the enrollee population. The employer/government contribution represents a redistribution of risk to the workforce or taxpayers, respectively. If we posit a total budget for health care that is available to an employer-related group based on fringe benefit entitlements or to a target population based on legislative appropriations, the formula for allocating this budget to the entitled persons can be a means for redistributing risk.

Specifically, risk adjustment is a mechanism for employers and government health financing programs to adjust their contributions under multi-option health benefit programs to compensate for the relative risks of the enrollees across the available plans. In this context, "risk" is defined as the expected value of the distribution of per capita costs of efficiently provided preventive, diagnostic, and therapeutic health care services delivered to a defined group of enrollees for a specific future period (Hornbrook and Goodman, 1991). Health plans that happened to enroll a sicker, that is, riskier, mix of persons, would receive a greater share of the health benefit budget or, alternatively, relief from the adverse selection by an infusion of lower-risk enrollees. Because this is a relative adjustment, any revenue or enrollment increase for one health plan or individual is automatically accompanied by reductions to other plans or individuals. Risk adjustment is not necessarily a means to increase the total budget for health care, only to reallocate a defined budget.

"Risk adjustment" involves three steps: first, decomposing total risk into its logical components; second, assigning each component to the appropriate actor; and third, modifying payments to health plans or premium contributions from enrollees to compensate for risk. The first two steps are embodied in the model used to assess risk.

Two factors not under plans' control are included in risk-assessment models—enrollee permanent health status and use propensity characteristics (Hornbrook and Goodman, 1991). Methods and models for classifying risk are discussed in Parts II and III of this volume (Hornbrook and Goodman, 1991; Hayes, 1991; Hornbrook, Goodman, and Bennett, 1991; Hornbrook, Goodman, Bennett, and Greenlick, 1991). Consumers should face the risk that derives from their own (in)efficiencies in interacting with the medical care system, all other things being the same. Similarly, providers should face the risk that derives from their own cost-influencing behaviors, holding output and other factors constant. Health plans should face the risk from (in)efficiencies in their own operations and, conversely, should not face the risk from those factors controllable by another actor. These postulates establish criteria for the variables to be included in a risk-assessment model. Provider and health plan characteristics should not be included. If an insurer handles claims inefficiently, its financial liability is greater, but that should not be passed on to the employer and the employee. This inefficiency should result in higher premiums, which serve as signals both to individuals to choose a different, more efficient plan and to the plan to improve. Risk adjustment removes the risk from health plans when it is beyond their control and transfers it to a more appropriate set of actors. The component of risk that derives from stochastic illness factors should be assigned to the entire enrolled population equally. The larger the risk population, the more efficient is risk spreading because the marginal cost of any individual's illness episode is spread over more (presumably healthy) individuals.

Under this approach, a firm's entire workforce serves as a risk pool, rather than forcing a complete separation of risk for each sub-group selecting a particular health plan. Similarly, under governmental risk-contracting programs, adjustment of government payments to health plans to reflect risk differentials among their beneficiaries redistributes risk to a much larger and more appropriate group—taxpayers. Without such adjustments, risk contractors may be forced to subsidize enrollees under public programs from their private memberships if risk selection is adverse to the plan, or may receive excess payments if risk selection is favorable. Risk adjustment maintains choice among competing plans, but enlists employers and governments to create a more efficient mechanism for risk sharing. With proper risk-adjustment models, employers and governments can serve as pro-competitive forces in the health insurance market.

Risk adjustment cannot be applied in a universal fashion nor is there a single correct method of implementing a risk-adjustment scheme. In the remainder of this paper, we examine the various approaches to adjusting risk and how they interact with the different types of health benefit programs.

WHAT IS ADJUSTED?

The logical possibilities for the focus of risk adjustment are three-fold: total premium, consumer's contribution, or the employer's/government's contribution. Each variable presents a different interpretation for risk adjustment and these differences are policy-relevant.

While the process suggested in this paper looks at risk in terms of all actors, only the portion attributable to the employee should be included in the adjustment of employer contributions. This differs from Enthoven (1989), who simply adjusts for the total risk independent of health plan efficiency, which increases the likelihood of moral hazard from some health plans.

Total Premium

Risk adjustment of the health plan's total premium represents direct price control. Plans would find their revenues established via the risk-adjustment mechanism. If they could not survive financially, they would have to leave the market. This would represent a system in which a per capita health budget is allocated by means of a prospective case-mix-adjusted payment system, similar to the Medicare Prospective Payment System, except that instead of using a Diagnosis-Related Group (DRG) as the unit of payment, a population risk class serves as the unit of payment. Alternatively, this type of risk adjustment could take the form of a mandatory all-payer national health system in which consumers were issued risk-adjusted vouchers that health plans have to accept as payment in full when an individual elects to enroll during an open season. This is, in essence, a version of national health insurance, an option which was presented earlier. Sicker persons would have higher valued vouchers which would make them as attractive to health plans as lower cost (and lower revenue) healthy persons.

Employee's Contribution

A second possibility is to adjust the employee's contribution according to the individual's risk. Sicker persons would pay a higher premium than healthier persons. This is experience rating carried to the individual level and would obviate the need for health insurance because risk pools would be narrowed to the extent possible by our risk-assessment models.

Employer's Contribution

The third possibility is to adjust employers' or governmental contributions. This has two sub-options, defined according to whether health plan premiums are fixed or enrollee out-of-pocket contributions are fixed. When health plan premiums are fixed, contribution policy affects the relative prices faced by consumers, thereby influencing plan choice: a higher risk health plan would be assigned a larger risk-adjusted contribution that would offset the enrollee's contribution, reducing the effective relative out-of-pocket price for the plan and inducing persons to switch from other, more expensive health plans. With fixed enrollee contributions, a higher risk health plan would receive more revenue to compensate for the risk differential.

In this paper, we focus on the two options for contributions policy—shifting dollars or shifting enrollees. In the next section, we identify the major structural components of multi-option health benefit programs. Then we will show how the structure of a benefit program can interact with the risk-adjustment policy, creating additional complexities.

DIMENSIONS OF MULTI-OPTION HEALTH BENEFIT PROGRAMS

Employees and beneficiaries in dual- and multiple-choice health programs face a complex array of variables in making their choices. Defined by the employer, the government, and the competing health plans, these factors include the risk profile of each plan, the type of rating system, the contribution formula, who is covered, the number of plans, type of plans, the payer's role, and the benefit structures. If these elements functioned independently, the problem would be difficult enough, but consumers must also cope with complex interactions among these characteristics. We focus on nine salient dimensions of multi-option health benefits programs. Some of these factors relate to the immediate attributes of the options. Others relate to structural factors of the market that indirectly affect choice options and their dimensions.

Number of Health Plans Offered

The first critical dimension is whether more than one plan is offered. Risk adjustment is only necessary when more than one plan is offered. Moreover, all plans participating in a health benefit program must be included in a risk-adjustment scheme to achieve the desired effects.

Who is Covered

The contribution formula may cover an employee only, or it may include spouse and children as well as other dependents. All persons included in an employer's risk pool should be included in a risk-adjustment scheme; the same applies for public health-financing programs.

Benefit Structures

The nature and level of benefits in multiple-choice health programs are usually not identical. The selection bias literature has shown that risk is correlated with benefits—plans with more extensive benefits tend to attract persons who expect to use those benefits (Short and Taylor, 1989). If benefits are uniform across plans, with only a difference in administrative structure (that is, HMO versus indemnity), then this will not be a factor. If one plan offers drugs while another does not, this will influence the outcome of a risk-adjustment algorithm. The range of potential benefit differences includes copayments, total deductibles, requirements for second opinions prior to surgery, and others. Tailored, comprehensive benefits can, therefore, significantly influence the choices made by population subgroups, which, in turn, influence risk profiles. Equal premiums do not necessarily reflect the same bundle of services to different individuals. The minimum benefit package defines the least common denominator in a risk-adjustment scheme. Participating plans should have a mandated standard benefit package and this package should be the object of risk adjustment. Risk should not appear higher strictly because an individual possesses better coverage.

Types of Managed-Care Arrangements

Choice among different managed-care arrangements is different from the choice between two similar plans (that is, two indemnities). Traditional indemnity plans are interchangeable; they all provide coverage for the same set of providers (albeit a preferred provider organization (PPO) may impose some price discrimination among providers). Enrollment and disenrollment in prepaid group practices, on the other hand, require that patients switch providers. This makes it more difficult for less healthy individuals to switch into and out of these plans. PPOs provide another level of complexity by allowing a choice of providers with a higher copayment. Provider choice and plan exclusions are two examples of factors that increase information costs to employees. In a later section, this will be discussed in terms of transition costs.

As the choices multiply to include multiple indemnity plans, PPOs, IPAs, prepaid group practices, and other forms of managed and unmanaged care, the choice for consumers becomes more complex. The cost of gathering and understanding the information on each plan increases, thus increasing the cost of switching. Some plans cover the same physicians (as might be the case in a sparsely populated area), but switching may entail switching physicians and possibly hospitals.

Employer's Role

Employers have an incentive to protect a self-funded plan. The employer becomes the underwriter, with a strong incentive to engage in practices detrimental to other plans. Conversely, without a self-funded plan, the employer is, theoretically, a neutral broker. However, if managers are members of indemnity plans, their self-interest is enhanced if they protect the indemnity plan. This also applies to Medicare. The Health Care Financing Administration (HCFA) is concerned that voluntary choice by beneficiaries not leave the non-risk option with the highest risks because payment to risk contractors is based on observed costs in the fee-for-service plan (the Average Adjusted Per Capita Cost (AAPCC)) (Hornbrook, Bennett, and Greenlick, 1989). Selection bias results in inaccurate payments to Medicare risk contractors.

Rating Structure

Two principal rating structures are pertinent here: experience rating and community rating. Experience rating refers to the determination of a specific rate for a defined group of employees, usually those from a single company who elect a given health plan. Often this is little more than the previous year's claims costs adjusted for some projection for inflation; more complex rating models may account for expected changes in the demographic composition of a group. Groups with more expensive experience receive higher rates; groups with lower historical expense receive lower rates. Community rating may be contrasted with experience rating in that the rate is set for a defined geographic area. An individual company does not receive a rate specific to the firm. The mix of rating methods in a particular market significantly influences competition, including the prices and benefits of the various plans.

In mixed systems with both community and experience rating, the experience-rated plans can "skim" by offering lower prices to groups with a relatively lower risk while the community-rated plan must offer a premium for an "average" risk to all consumers. This reduces the price competitiveness of the community-rated plans, leaving them with a higher risk pool of companies and members, especially because these plans will have a price advantage in companies and employees with high-cost risk pools. Ultimately, as the mean rate of the community-rated pools increase, they are no longer competitive with experience-rated plans. Blue Cross plans have switched from community rating to experience rating. Similarly, perceiving pressure from employers, most HMOs have modified community rating to include community rating by class (CRC) and adjusted community rating (ACR), both of which adjust the rate charged to reflect different age, gender, and company-specific utilization criteria. Skimming is expected to be less of a problem in markets characterized entirely by large community-rated plans.

Experience-rated plans may also vary their rates in response to employer contribution formulas by raising the rates for plans which are fully employer paid, and using this additional revenue to cross-subsidize lower rates for other groups. Such distortion is enabled by the market power induced by removing the out-of-pocket price to employees. That is, by not negotiating true experience rates, the employer pays too much for health coverage.

Employer/Employee Contribution Formulas

The out-of-pocket premium faced by employees is influenced by the employer contribution formula. The usual options are either a percentage of each health plan's rate, or a fixed dollar amount per employee or enrollee. The percentage contribution can, of course, include 100%; this option obviates risk adjustment (because the employer pays whatever premium is negotiated with each health plan). The contribution formula represents a potential confounding factor in the structure of relative out-of-pocket prices facing consumers. A uniform dollar contribution means that each consumer faces the full absolute differences in premiums among the various plans. A uniform percentage contribution means that the relative structure of the premiums is maintained but absolute differences are shared between the employer and the employee. Varying contributions alter the relative structure of prices. For example, some employers contribute more to higher-priced plans and less to lower-priced plans so that the price differences to the employees are narrowed considerably.

Size of Risk Pool

The absolute size of a risk pool is a technical factor influencing the competitiveness of health plans. When the number of enrollees in a plan falls below a certain threshold, the risk profile of the plan becomes more volatile. A very high-cost disease episode has the potential to significantly influence a group's overall risk profile. Ideally, a risk-assessment model will be sufficiently refined to avoid this outlier problem, but the plan's rating methodology may not have such sophistication. To protect against this eventuality, small health plans can purchase reinsurance.

Comparative Risk Profiles of Plans

Each plan, when rates are offered, has a particular risk profile. For experience-rated plans, the rate reflects the profile of the enrolled subset of an employer's total risk pool. As employees switch health plans, selection effects may affect the premiums of the plans. In some cases, adverse selection in an individual plan can result in other competitive problems. An HMO, for example, may experience access problems if a large number of high-using persons join; this will likely make membership less attractive which serves to reinforce adverse selection—only the sickest persons receive good access. Risk and benefits are also correlated and plans may alter their benefits in an attempt to attract (or repel) a particular population. Although it would be useful for some purposes to mandate homogeneous benefits and uniform risks, the reality is that only when the risk is sufficiently different to threaten the survival of an efficient health plan is an adjustment of the risk desirable.

TYPES OF HEALTH BENEFIT PROGRAMS

The impetus for risk adjustment may originate with a socially-responsible employer concerned about the health and economic well-being of employees. This section examines three approaches to providing health benefits to employees—exclusive triple options, self-funded plans, and dual/multiple choice. These examples represent different employer roles in providing health benefits. We must emphasize that anything other than strict neutrality among plans on the part of an employer will confound efforts to adjust risk. An employer entering into risk adjustment without the aim of leveling the playing field among all competing plans will not improve efficiency in the health care market and may cause further deterioration in market performance. Employers interested only in assisting an established indemnity or self-funded plan will probably not be amenable to accurate adjustment of health plan contributions to reflect the permanent health status of enrollees. Two of the systems discussed below, the Federal Employees' Health Benefits Program (FEHBP) and self-funded plans, have been studied extensively in recent years—the FEHBP because of rising costs, and self-funded plans because of their increasing prevalence in the market.

Exclusive Triple Option Plans

One strategy being pursued by health benefit managers is to contract with a single insurer to assume the risk of all employees and offer multiple health care arrangements: free choice of physician (traditional indemnity plan), discounts for selected providers (PPO), and restricted choice of physician (HMO). Exclusive triple options (ETO) are growing in popularity after initial failures due to administrative difficulties (Kenkel, 1988). The entire workforce of a firm forms the risk pool. By negotiating the entire health benefit program with a single insurer, employers can reduce the administrative and support staff devoted to managing employees' fringe benefits.

When a single insurer assumes all the risk, risk adjustment is not necessary. The insurer reinsures selectivity in one option with converse effects on another option—within a single employer group, when an employee chooses one option, he/she is not enrolled in the other options and the selection effects are automatically self-cancelling in the combined risk pool.

An ETO is protected against selectivity by the experience-rating model. The insurer accepts any risk from a potential adverse selection represented by the entire employer group. The latter occurs only from a failure of the risk-rating model—an omitted variable that accounts for the selection effects of the firm's particular set of employees. Such a failure of the rating model, that is, selection bias, is the only concern of an ETO.[3]

Non-exclusive triple option plans within multiple-option programs should be treated as a single insurer for purposes of risk adjustment—the three options should be combined in comparing the risks to other health plans. This becomes equivalent to the dual/multiple choice program discussed below.

Self-Funded Health Plans

Self-funding of health insurance offers numerous advantages to employers. The most important are avoidance of state insurance regulations, including premium taxes, reserve requirements, and mandated benefits. The latter provision means that the plans can avoid coverage for mental health, chiropractors, alcohol and drug abuse treatment, among other services. Self-funded plans should enjoy a considerable cost advantage over regulated insurers. Employers can gain additional savings if they are able to "skim" low-risk employees into a self-funded plan and "dump" high-risk employees into a commmunity-rated plan (which redistributes part of the risk to other employers).

Employers deciding to discontinue a self-funded plan face a one-time loss because of incurred, but unpaid claims. This may cause employers to attempt to save plans even if they are losing money (in the sense that the employer's administrative cost for the self-funded plan is higher than that for a competing health plan).

Under ordinary health insurance arrangements, the employer is neutral among the plans: the employer's role is to negotiate the best deal from each. Membership by senior management in a particular health plan may color the negotiations, but an efficient employer remains a neutral broker, seeking the best value from each plan.

Under a self-funded plan, the success or failure of an insurance plan is reflected as a profit or loss: the employer is no longer neutral. If employers engage in risk adjustment for the sole purpose of unfairly supporting their self-funded plans within multiple option health benefit programs, risk adjustment will become an untenable choice. This is not a minor problem. In 1984, 80% of firms with more than 5,000 employees offered a self-insured health insurance option. This proportion declines as firms get smaller (McDonnell et al., 1986). Because larger firms are more likely to self-insure, this means that self-funded plans are the fastest growing segment of the health insurance market.

The primary mission of a "predatory" self-funded plan is to skim the low-risk employees, move high-risk employees into other plans, and reduce contributions to other health plans in order to subsidize the self-funded plan. Self-funded plans are already subsidized by escaping premium taxes and mandated benefits. The predatory self-funded plan will participate in a risk-adjustment scheme only when it goes in the plan's favor. Because socially efficient risk adjustment requires cooperation from employers, it will not work in conjunction with this type of plan.

A socially responsible self-funded plan, on the other hand, will support a risk-adjustment scheme on principle. Such a self-funded plan will compete with other health plans on the basis of efficiency rather than skimming.

Dual/Multiple Choice

The simplest health plan choice scenario involves a choice between two plans. This usually involves an HMO and an indemnity insurer, so that individuals have a clear choice of practice mode. The choice may be complicated by different benefit structures between the plans. Multiple option programs are more prevalent in large employers because a subset of the total pool of potential enrollees is still a viable risk pool. In a small firm, the workforce is almost certain to be nonrandom and difficult to underwrite. From the insurer's point of view, a small pool creates a stronger possibility of adverse selection. Federally qualified HMOs, generally, will not enter a market as the sole insurer, preferring dual or multiple choice situations to situations that would force individuals into closed-panel provider coverage. Risk adjustment is likely to work better in large firms that offer multiple experience-rated health plans and that behave as neutral brokers with respect to health plan choice.

APPLICATION OF RISK-ADJUSTMENT PRINCIPLES

For purposes of exposition of the principles of risk adjustment and its implications, let us specify eight different scenarios defined by three factors—risk, premiums, and employer contributions—under dual/multiple option health plans. Let us assume that the risk distribution among the various health plans is either equal or unequal within the company (or beneficiary group for a public health insurance program). Further assume that differences in premiums are either perfectly correlated with the risk differences (which we will term "risk-adjusted" or experience-rated) or highly uncorrelated (which we will term "non-risk-adjusted" or community-rated). Notice that an ambiguous case can exist where one plan's rates are correlated and the other's are not. Finally, let us assume that the differences in employer contributions among the health plans are either perfectly correlated with risk or uncorrelated. Our goal is to explore the implications of these various scenarios for the functioning of health insurance markets and health benefit plans.

Equal Risks, Risk-Adjusted Premiums, Risk-Adjusted Contributions

In this first scenario, health plans are assumed to have equal risk. We further assume that premiums and employer contributions are equal across plans, so that by definition they are risk-adjusted. Consumers face prices that give appropriate signals regarding health plan choice. Each plan would have equal attractiveness to individuals at any level of risk. Even without special efforts to risk-adjust premiums or contributions, no intervention is necessary in this market. For this reason, equalizing risk among health plans is desirable because it reduces the need for governmental intervention.

If we relax the assumption of identical premiums, a risk-adjustment scheme is required to assure that benefit and efficiency effects do not confound risk differences. Thus, with equal risks, employer contributions will be equal and premiums will vary only with differences in benefit and efficiency levels. Consumers will face out-of-pocket premiums reflecting the actuarial costs of the variations in benefits plus health plan "internal slack," without any additional contributions from employers to subsidize benefits above a standard level.

To show how risk adjustment could work from a dynamic perspective, assume a dual option with equal risks and equal benefits but unequal efficiency. Employer contributions will be equal between the the two plans and employee out-of-pocket expenses will be higher for the inefficient plan. This will provide incentives for persons to switch out of the inefficient plan into the efficient plan (we assume that low-risk persons have lower switching costs and will switch faster than high-risk persons). Risk will rise for the inefficient plan, but, in the next year, employer contributions will increase to reflect this risk and will drop for the other plan to reflect the lower risk; therefore, stayers and new enrollees in the inefficient plan will not bear the full brunt of an increase in risk, although the efficiency difference may remain unless the health plan takes action to reduce costs. The higher out-of-pocket price for the favorably-selected plan will induce some persons at the margin to switch to the adversely-selected plan. Thus, risk adjustment can act as a stabilizing influence on market dynamics.

In the case of a community-rated plan, the latter scenario is ambiguous. A CR plan may have higher- or lower-risk members in other groups, so the community rate varies for reasons other than efficiency. If the rate is higher, members may still receive inappropriate signals despite the risk adjustment, which assumes that differences in premiums stem entirely from differences in efficiency.

Unequal Risks, Risk-Adjusted Premiums, Risk-Adjusted Contributions

Now let us relax the assumption of equal risks, but assume that any difference in risk is perfectly correlated with premiums and employer contributions. In this scenario, employers pick up the full difference deriving from risk, leaving enrollees to face equal out-of-pocket premiums for equal coverage. Again, individual choices are not distorted by pricing patterns and high-risk persons are equally attractive to all health plans. Out-of-pocket premium payments will vary only with differences in the benefits and operating efficiency of health plans.

Equal Risks, Non-Risk-Adjusted Premiums, Risk-Adjusted Contributions

Under this scenario, health plans have equal risks and equal employer contributions, but premiums do not reflect risk in the given group, that is, some plans are community-rated. This creates distortion because the community-rated plans will appear more or less attractive depending on whether the subsidy is towards or away from a particular employer (group). If workers in a particular firm have significantly lower risk than a community-rated plan, that health plan will appear much more expensive than experience-rated plans. The community-rated plan will tend to be selected by only the highest risk persons in the firm, and the employer will gain the advantage of shifting some of the health benefit costs to other employers. Similarly, if the community-rated pool is favorable to the workforce, much larger numbers of employees will select this plan, shifting a greater portion of health benefit costs to other employers. Note that consumers will face out-of-pocket premium differences equal to the level of cost-shifting, net of any differences in benefits and efficiencies.

Unequal Risks, Non-Risk-Adjusted Premiums, Risk-Adjusted Contributions

This scenario is identical to the previous scenario, except that employer contributions will vary with the level of risk across the health plans.

Equal Risks, Risk-Adjusted Premiums, Non-Risk-Adjusted Contributions

Here employers set up distortions in the relative prices faced by consumers. With equal risk and equal premiums, consumers should face equal out-of-pocket payments. When employers establish different contributions that are uncorrelated or inversely correlated with risk, consumers will disproportionately select the plan with the higher contribution. Only persons with very high risk, if anyone, will select the lower contribution plan. This is equivalent to a tax on the enrollees of the unfavorably treated health plans.

Unequal Risks, Risk-Adjusted Premiums, Non-Risk-Adjusted Contributions

This scenario is equivalent to the previous one with the exception that perverse employers can create even greater differences in out-of-pocket payments for enrollees by contributing less to high-risk, high-premium health plans.

Equal Risks, Non-Risk-Adjusted Premiums, Non-Risk-Adjusted Contributions

Health plans with equal risks in a particular group but with a mixture of community- and experience- rating practices will give misleading signals to consumers. Community-rated plans may use their risk-sharing pools to finance higher benefits, greater managerial slack, or adverse selection in a particular group.

Unequal Risks, Non-Risk Adjusted Premiums, Non-Risk-Adjusted Contributions

The final scenario is current reality. Health plans have unequal risks, benefits, and efficiency; some health plans are experience-rated and others are community rated; employers have arbitrary or perverse contribution formulas; and consumers are totally unable to interpret the relative price differences they face among the health plans.

COMPENSATING FOR RISK VERSUS EQUALIZING RISK

When implemented correctly, risk-adjusting employer contributions will compensate health plans for adverse selection effects, either by redistributing dollars among health plans according to an efficient relative pricing scheme or by redistributing enrollees so as to equalize risks. In this section, we explore the principles and mechanics of these two options.

Risk Compensation Option

We begin with each health plan submitting its benefit, rate, and risk-assessment data to an employer. Benefits and premiums are negotiated and cannot be altered after settlement is reached. Employees know the out-of-pocket premium contributions prior to selecting a health plan. The employer computes the risk structure of each plan's current enrollment based on last year's experience. Following the principle of equal contribution for equal risk, employees face price variation for efficiency and benefit variations. The employer sets the per capita health benefit budget and allows the risk-adjustment process to allocate this budget to each health plan as $C_i/C_j = R_i/R_j$, where C_i is the employer's contribution to Plan *i* and R_i is the relative risk coefficient for Plan *i*. (This is known as the ratio method; two other risk-adjustment formulas are described in Bowen and Slavin (1991)). Payroll deductions are promulgated for each plan based on the relative premium differences after risk has been factored out.

Four principles of risk adjustment guide this approach: (1) health plans enrolling relatively higher risk workers within a group should receive higher payments per capita, all other things being the same; (2) relatively inefficient health plans should have higher out-of-pocket premium contributions from employees; (3) health plans with richer benefits should have higher out-of-pocket premium contributions from employees, unless these costs are offset by higher efficiency levels; and (4) risk adjustment should be made at the level of individual enrollees to avoid unintended cross-subsidies based on subscriber unit size and composition.

This scenario assumes that only a small portion of the membership of each health plan will turnover in any given year. At the margin, if new enrollees have substantially different risk than leavers, the risk-adjusted contributions will be biased. Hence, contributions are always one year behind. Risk adjustment will always face potential bias because of this one-year lag. If the risk selection effects move in both directions in succeeding years, the net financial impact may be negligible to affected health plans. If, however, the selection effects move consistently in one direction over several years, the health plans will suffer significant financial problems or gain substantial windfalls, depending on the direction of the selection effect.

The risk weights are not likely to exactly reflect the health plan's own cost structure, but they should provide acceptable revenue. If the health plan cannot survive on the revenue differential, one could argue that it probably deserves to fail. Under this scenario, health plans could continue to operate indefinitely with adverse or favorable selection. With the revenue set correctly, health plans, employers, enrollees, and the government would be satisfied with the way the market functions. This policy perspective would enable health plans to specialize in meeting the needs of different risk groups. While this has little relevance to indemnity plans (because bills are homogeneous entities), HMOs and PPOs may find this to be a natural evolution in a competitive market. Smaller HMOs may find it difficult to achieve efficiency in all areas of medicine, surgery, and health promotion. Health plan specialization may give access to economies of scale in a particular clinical field.

Hypothetical examples of two different implementations of risk adjustment in a firm with three health plan options are presented in Table 1 to illustrate the operation of the risk-compensation option. The scenarios developed below are concerned with the influence of changes on two actors: employees and health plans. A third actor, the employer, chooses the type and magnitude of the change. The variable of interest is the relative risk among the health plans. Employers must decide among a variety of tools to redistribute the relative risk. Any method reduces to one of two choices: either health plans will be directly compensated for differences in risk or employees will receive incentives to change plans. We have not explored which approach would be preferred by health plans, although one might presume that they would prefer not to have their average revenues modified by an employer, other things being the same. The other option assumes price and benefit sensitivity among employees. We assume that the three health plans have different premiums, risks, and enrollment shares. The employer is assumed to provide a fixed contribution across the three plans. Plan A has the highest risk, the highest enrollment share and the lowest premium. Plan C has average risk, 30% enrollment share, and a premium in-between its two competitors. Plan B has the lowest risk, the highest premium, and a 20% enrollment share. From this baseline, we impose two different risk-adjustment schemes representing budget neutrality to an employer or not.

The first scenario, where health plan revenues are altered in accordance with relative risks, is shown in Table 1 (scenario II.A): Plan A, with the highest risk, receives an increase of $30 per person per month, while payments to Plan B are reduced by $30 per person per month, and payments to Plan C are unchanged because risk is similar to the overall workforce. In this scenario, enrollee out-of-pocket payments are unchanged, which assumes that they appropriately reflect the relative benefits and efficiency of the three plans; that

Table 1. Hypothetical Risk-Adjustment Scenarios

	Plan A	Plan B	Plan C
I. Before Risk Adjustment			
Monthly Premium	$200	$250	$225
Relative Risk*	1.2	.8	1.0
Enrollment share	.50	.20	.30
Employer contribution	150	150	150
Employee contribution	50	100	75
II. After Risk Adjustment			
A. Risk Compensation: Health Plan Faces Entire Residual After Risk Adjustment, Not Budget Neutral			
Health Plan Monthly Revenue	$230.00	$220.00	$225.00
Employer Contribution**	180.00	120.00	150.00
Employee Contribution	50.00	100.00	75.00
Health Plan Gain (Loss)	30.00	(30.00)	-0-
B. Risk Compensation: Budget Neutral to Employer			
Health Plan Monthly Revenue	219.81	$213.21	216.51
Employer Contribution	169.81	113.21	141.51
Employee Contribution	50.00	100.00	75.00
Health Plan Gain (Loss)	19.81	(36.79)	(8.49)
C. Risk Equalization: Employee Faces Entire Residual After Risk Adjustment, Not Budget Neutral			
Healthy Plan Monthly Revenue	$200.00	$250.00	$225.00
Employer Contribution**	180.00	120.00	150.00
Employee Contribution	20.00	130.00	75.00
D. Risk Equalization: Budget Neutral to Employer			
Health Plan Monthly Revenue	$200.00	$250.00	$225.00
Employer Contribution:	169.81	113.21	141.51
Employee Contribution	30.19	136.79	83.49

Notes: *Relative risk is based on current health plan enrollments from this firm just prior to open season.
**Total employer outlay increases by 6% over non-risk-adjusted scheme because enrollment proportions interact with relative risks.

is, Plan B has the highest level of supplemental benefits and/or inefficiency of the three plans, followed by Plan C. Note that this scheme serves to narrow the premium differences from a range of $50 to a range of $10.

If we desire budget neutrality for the employer (scenario II.B), more revenue must be redistributed from Plans B and C in order to finance the risk contribution to Plan A, which is not as high as under the non-budget-neutral scenario. Neither the employer nor the health plan should be allowed to alter contributions or premiums after enrollment patterns are established in these latter two scenarios. This would only serve to defeat the risk-adjustment scheme.

This scheme places health plans on a one-year lag cycle. An adversely selected plan must wait until the next contracting cycle to obtain relief in the form of higher payments or enrollment incentives. If enrollment switching is significant, current payments would not reflect the current enrollments.

Risk-Equalization Option

Another option is for consumers to absorb the full effects of the risk-adjustment scheme. In this case, the health plan premiums are fixed and health plan revenues are not directly affected by the risk mix of enrollment. Once all the rates and benefits are negotiated and fixed, the employer collects the risk data on all the current health plan members and computes the risk coefficient for each health plan. Contributions are set proportional to risk, as before. Persons enrolling in high-risk plans will receive greater employer contributions, regardless of their own individual risk status, thereby reducing their payroll deductions. This lowers the effective out-of-pocket price of the adversely selected plan to all employees and raises the out-of-pocket price of the favorably selected plan. This creates incentives for individuals to switch from the low-risk plan to the high-risk plan, at the margin; if this process continues, risks are expected to converge and create a stable basis of competition.

This is predicated on a model of health plan choice in which price plays a dominant role. While this is certainly the assumption underlying economic models of consumer behavior, empirical studies of health plan choice indicate that factors other than price enter into the decision about whether or not to switch health plans (Neipp and Zeckhauser, 1985). Thus, risk differences may persist for some time and price differences may have to be quite large to induce significant shifting.

Returning to our hypothetical example, Plan C, with average risk, is unaffected under this scenario (II.C). However, Plan A incurs a drop in employee contribution from $50 per month to $20 dollars per month while Plan B faces an equal increase. This would be expected to induce some enrollees to shift from Plan B, the low-risk plan, to Plan A, which has now become even more rate favorable, or Plan C. If enrollees do not switch, this plan is not budget neutral, so a small increase in total health plan budget by the employer is required.

If we assume that aggregate employer health benefit outlays are fixed (budget neutrality, scenario II.D), then enrollees in Plan C face some increase in out-of-pocket payments to help finance the risk adjustment to Plan A, and Plan B enrollees must pay even more, while Plan A enrollees do not receive as high a subsidy as under a non-budget neutral plan. The net effect is still to provide incentives for employees to move into Plan A from Plans B and C.

Note that in this scenario, it is possible for payroll deductions to be negative—employees who choose one plan may have such serious risk selection that they will receive cash in addition to a full health plan membership. In reality, when this occurs, either benefits are raised or employers keep the subsidy.

If consumers actually do switch as desired, the employer's total health plan outlays will be considerably increased because more persons will be enrolling in the more highly subsidized plan. If the employer readjusts the contribution scheme at this point, the contract with the employees is broken because they made their enrollment decisions on the basis of fixed premiums for at least the duration of the enrollment period, usually a year. If employers insist on readjusting contributions after enrollments are known, then a different risk-adjustment scheme is required (or else no risk adjustment at all).

The main complicating factor besides transition costs and employer neutrality involves shifts in benefits by insurers in response to risk adjustment. It has been suggested that one reason that HMOs fail to save employers health care costs is that they pass their efficiency benefits to employees in the form of richer benefits (Jones, 1990). Plans receiving more or less contributions from employers can change the benefits offered to employees to remain at roughly the same competitive position. It might be necessary, therefore, to restrict plans' choice of benefits before the determination of the employee contribution.

HEALTH PLAN CHOICE

If our goal is to equalize risk among health plans, which has important benefits because it obviates the need for risk adjustment, then we have to understand the determinants of choice of health plan. An individual's decision to join a particular health plan is usually not driven solely by price. Rather, choice incorporates a variety of non-price factors, including benefits, current health state, available providers, prior experiences with competing health plans, expected future utilization, and a variety of other factors not controllable by the health plan. As such, attempts to characterize the health plan choice as simply a function of relative plan price will almost certainly prove unsatisfactory. Moreover, removal of risk differentials from consumers' contributions toward health plan premiums may not induce consumers to switch to the most efficient plan. Even among plans with seemingly identical benefits, the cost of switching may be substantial if the information required to understand the differences between plans is too costly to obtain and comprehend (Enthoven, 1989).

High-risk and low-risk individuals are expected to have differential price sensitivity. High-risk individuals are expected to be more likely to remain with a particular health plan through significant price changes. This assumption has never been directly tested. Rather, experience in two areas indicates differences in price sensitivity. The cost-premium spiral notion is based on the fact that, when relative price increases, the relative risk of a plan increases. This happens as the low-risk individuals leave. The best example of this is the experience of the high-option plans in the Federal Employee Health Benefits Program (FEHBP) (Price and Mays, 1985; Price, Mays, and Trapnell, 1983; Schuttinga, Falik, and Steinwald, 1985). Second, switcher studies seem to show that those able to switch health plans have lower utilization in the year prior to a change in health plans (Eggers and Prihoda, 1982). Evidence concerning regression to the mean, however, would tend to mitigate both effects.

At least two non-monetary costs are incurred in switching health plans: information costs to understand the plans and transition costs involved in switching. The greater the number of alternatives or the greater the difference in benefits, the higher the relative information costs of a switch. This does not mean that an employee is forced to consider every alternative. The typical choice process may involve narrowing the alternatives to a small subset.

Transition costs refer to the costs involved in changing systems. Will the member need to switch physicians, lose coverage for a pre-existing condition, or face some other non-price barrier to switching? An individual in poor health, with established physician relationships, would incur greater transition costs than an individual in good health without such relationships. Thus, although the price to the two employees might be the same, the total cost of switching may be significantly different.[4] These factors indicate that more than price should be involved in risk adjustment if equalizing risk is the goal. To further complicate the situation, different individuals will be influenced by different combinations of variables. Risk adjustment must compensate for the opportunity cost of switching plans rather than just the pure difference in risk. The former is a much more difficult concept to operationalize.

COMMUNITY RATING AND RISK ADJUSTMENT

Risk adjustment tacitly assumes that the risk within a particular group's enrollees is reflected in the premium; an adversely selected plan has higher rates, for example. This is the essence of an experience-rated plan. In a community-rated plan, however, risk is spread across the entire enrollment of the health plan so that the risk for a specific group is not accurately reflected in the premium; the premium reflects the community's risk. If a community-rated health plan happens to be adversely selected in one employer, that risk is effectively spread across all other groups in the health plan's membership by the community rate, and is not restricted to the group's premium.

Assume a situation with one or more experience-rated plans and one community-rated plan. The community-rated plan is adversely selected within an employer, so its risk is higher than average.[5] The remaining plans are either favorably selected or neutral. In order to equalize risk, the employer adopts a risk-adjustment scheme and reduces the out-of-pocket premium contribution for employees for the community-rated plan. This has the effect of providing a double incentive for plan switching because the rate for the community-rated plan is already low relative to the actual risk within this employer group. Then, enrollees' out-of-pocket contributions are further reduced by the employer's risk adjustment. This effect is symmetric; employees choosing a favorably selected plan in a given group would face higher community-rated premiums relative to experience rating and a risk-adjustment scheme would raise employee contributions yet again. Thus, the effect is likely to be to accelerate the movement of enrollees back and forth to equalize risks among the plans.

On the other hand, if a risk-adjustment scheme reallocates employer contributions to compensate the adversely selected community-rated health plan directly, the plan is able to collect twice for this risk; once through spreading the risk among all groups and once from the employer. If a community-rated plan is favorably selected in a given group, risk adjustment of health plan revenues will reduce payments and require the plan to raise the community rate because it is not receiving the full rate for the enrollees in this group.

Therefore, if one health plan in a multi-option health benefit program is community rated, then risk adjustment should take the form of modifying employee contributions to mutually reinforce the incentive effects. If health plan revenues are risk-adjusted, community-rated plans should be disqualified from the scheme so that employers are not confused about possible risk shifting and double payments.

CONTEMPORANEOUS RISK-ADJUSTMENT PROCEDURES

Each consumer should face a risk- and benefit-adjusted price for each health plan when making a selection. Under the scenarios previously discussed, the risk-adjustment process lags one year (or more, depending on data availability). The acceptability of the lag depends on the relative stability of health plan enrollments, so turnover is likely to have only marginal effects on the risk coefficients. In this case, it is the health plan that is the target of risk adjustment. An alternative is to focus on the individual as the target.

This option requires that each consumer carry a risk coefficient with him/her and plug it into the rate-setting formula for each health plan in order to compute the out-of-pocket price. The employer could issue risk-rated health plan vouchers with stated face values so that higher-risk persons would be able to compute their net contribution toward the full premium of each plan. One advantage of this option is that the employer's total health budget would be known before choices were made. The employer would administer the risk-assessment scheme, collecting the data required to classify workers and their dependents. After risk levels were established, the employer would set the total health benefit budget and issue risk-adjusted vouchers to each worker. Participating health plans would have to accept the vouchers as full or partial payment for the mandated benefit package, but employees would have to pay for supplemental benefits plus any copayment for the minimum benefit package. Supplementary benefit pricing would need to be regulated to prohibit cross-subsidies from these benefits to the minimum benefits, although one could argue that competition among health plans would keep cross-subsidization to a minimum.

CONCLUSIONS AND POLICY IMPLICATIONS

Dual- or multiple-option plans, so long as the employer (or government) acts as a neutral broker, should present a relatively straightforward application of risk adjustment. Some complexity arises when one of the plans is a prepaid group practice because switching to or from such a plan imposes higher transition costs. With two or more experience-rated indemnity plans, the differences are likely to involve only benefits rather than providers. This situation can be complicated by the option of a self-funded plan to the extent that the employer foregoes neutrality as a broker. Without neutrality, a suitable risk-adjustment strategy cannot be developed.

The increasing cost of health care has provoked significant interest in the cost and structure of the world's largest multi-option health benefits program—FEHBP. Many commentators have proposed reforms to FEHBP that would realize potential savings or greater efficiency (Enthoven, 1989; Welch, 1989; Jones, 1989; Towers, Perrin, Forster, and Crosby, Inc. (TPF&C), 1990). FEHBP offers more than 400 different health plan choices to federal employees throughout the country (TPF&C, 1990); in any given area, employees have a choice among more than 20 plans (Francis, 1986). This gives health plans tremendous flexibility to influence their risk profile through variations in benefits, provider choices, or other factors that influence medical care and health plan choice. Unlike typical private sector employers, FEHBP offers several different indemnity and service benefit plans, which, because they have not emphasized selective contracts with providers (PPOs), are highly inefficient. The FEHBP contribution formula is based on two plans in a "death spiral," further removing incentives for efficient health plan choice. These factors have resulted in adverse selection in the program, leading to an inflation rate nearly double that in the rest of the health economy (Enthoven, 1989).

As the number of options in a health benefit program increases, the average size of each risk pool shrinks. This leads to greater variance in risk for each insurer. Voluntary choice among differentiated health insurance plans may create differences in risk structures when sicker persons tend to choose one particular health plan. Such health selectivity creates strong incentives for insurers to compete on the basis of risk skimming rather than efficiency in underwriting and claims processing. Competition is undermined because high-cost insurers cannot find enough efficiencies to compensate for adverse selection. Moreover, asymmetric information prevents correct rate setting under experience rating because consumers know more about their future health status than insurers, giving rise to selection bias. The market fails when insurers are driven from it through no fault of their own which, in turn, forces their members to switch to other health plans. The costs of switching from a closed-panel HMO plan can be relatively high because the members must find a new set of health care providers (while the HMO physicians are unlikely to stop practicing medicine, they may not be able to convert to fee-for-service practice in a seamless fashion).

Health plan choice is a very complex subject, and policy initiatives in this area become entangled in these complexities. In this section, we attempt to highlight needed policy reforms in private and public health insurance markets.

First, standardized mandatory minimum benefits reduce the complexities of sorting out risk, efficiency, and benefit variations (Lundy, 1990). Without limitations on the types of benefit packages that insurers can offer, risk-based rivalry provides incentives for insurers to develop low-cost, low-coverage options, forcing consumers to choose among inadequate health insurance coverage options. A minimum national standard for adequate health care coverage should be established to assure uniform access for all persons. This will ameliorate some of the distortions in the market.

Second, risk adjustment of employer contributions should be mandated for large employers to avoid continued distortions in the health insurance market. If risk adjustment is voluntary, an employer with a favorably selected self-insured plan has no incentive to participate in a risk-adjustment scheme, including collecting data for risk assessment. This would preclude reallocating contributions to compensate for risk differences and would, in essence, tax the high-risk persons who select traditional health plans to pay for the health care of low-risk persons in the self-insured plan. Risk adjustment only makes sense for employers of sufficient size for the law of large numbers to take effect; virtually no benefit is obtained from spreading risk over a small workforce.

The scenario where risk adjustment is most appropriate is multiple experience-rated plans. Risk adjustment is already operative for Medicare, although the risk-assessment model needs much improvement. Medicaid risk contracts are not typically risk-adjusted, relying only on negotiation to establish correct relative contributions between risk- and non-risk clients.

Third, if at least one health plan in a multi-option health benefit program is truly community-rated (we exclude adjusted commmunity rating here), then risk adjustment should take the form of modifying employee contributions to mutually reinforce the incentive effects. In other situations, however, risk adjustment and community rating probably should not coexist in the same health benefit program. If health plan revenues are risk-adjusted, community rating will give rise to confusion on the part of employers regarding possible risk shifting and will confound interpretation of premium differences among health plans. For community-rated health plans, employers cannot determine whether high premiums, after risk adjustment, reflect internal operating inefficiency, higher benefits, or risk shifting from other employers. Employers wish to avoid paying for the latter and want their employees to pay for both former elements. This means that HMOs must abandon any pretense of community rating for large employers (but not for small groups). With risk adjustment, the employer should serve as the final risk pool, so that there is no cross-subsidization to or from other employers.

Fourth, community rating is preferred for small employers so as to minimize the chances of adverse selection. All insurers should be required to establish a community-rated product for employers with fewer than 500 workers. Small groups and individuals would then be pooled and face group rates.

Fifth, benefits should not be adjusted after premiums have been submitted in a risk-adjustment scheme. This is equivalent to letting health plans escape from the scheme.

Sixth, self-funded plans should be required to meet the same requirements that other types of health plans must meet. If employers wish to lower their health benefit costs, they should reduce the overall per capita contribution, not set up mechanisms to shift the risk onto other employers via hidden cross-subsidies.

Seventh, exclusive triple options should be carefully regulated. Large employers really have no need for this option because it confers too much market power to a single health plan and offers only quasi-choice to employees. This product increases the cost of plan switching (because all employees must switch at once), thereby conferring the health plan with a degree of market power. ETOs offer administrative simplicity to employers but impose a hidden cost on employees in the long run. ETO advocates claim that they offer a full range of types of health plans for employees, but no matter which option the employee selects, the ETO collects the premium, so there is no incentive effect of potential enrollment loss.

When most health insurance plans were a sole offering to a group of employees, health plan failure largely resulted from their own inefficiencies. Consumer choice of health plans has increased the likelihood of failure for reasons beyond plans' control. Market failure in health insurance markets can be observed as systematic exclusion of consumers from the market, survival of inefficient health plans, arbitrary restrictions on health plan choice, and failure of adversely selected health plans. Risk adjustment of employer contributions and elimination of preferential treatment for self-funded health plans can reduce the chances of market failure.

ACKNOWLEDGMENTS

This research was supported by a grant from Kaiser Foundation Health Plan, Inc. The views expressed in this paper are those of the authors, and no official endorsement by Kaiser Foundation Health Plan is intended or should be inferred. This paper evolved from a series of meetings of the Technical Subcommittee of the Kaiser Permanente Risk Adjustment Task Force, including the Workshop on Risk Adjustment of Employer Contributions, sponsored by the Kaiser Permanente Center for Health Research, Otter Rock, Oregon, July 16, 1990. We are grateful to Arlene Ash, Nelda McCall, Bill Thomas, Richard Scheffler, and Pete Welch for their comments and suggestions on this paper. We are also grateful to Margaret R. Sucec for providing technical editorial assistance.

NOTES

1. We assume that persons have adequate incomes if they are required to pay premiums to participate in a risk pool and that persons are not forced to self-insure by lack of income. Persons who are not able to afford a health insurance policy covering the basic minimum services that meet community standards of access to health care should receive a subsidy to purchase health insurance. Under the model posited above, poor persons would receive an income-related risk-adjusted voucher to purchase health insurance. This would enable disadvantaged populations to participate in the private health insurance market at a level deemed desirable for all persons regardless of income.

2. The functional equivalent of a random lottery may be achieved if each health plan enrolls a representative cross-section of the community and practices community rating.

3.One issue for an ETO is the consumer contribution structure. Should the ETO encourage employees to choose the relatively more efficient plan? Who should receive the benefits if one option is more efficient than another? The question can be framed in terms of whether the choice should be a point-of-service choice—PPO, HMO, or free choice of any other provider—where the employee does not choose a single health plan at open enrollment, or whether the employee should designate only one plan for a specified enrollment period. The former option has significant negative ramifications for traditional HMOs that operate within defined prospective budgets and do not accept fee-for-service business.

4. As defined by Neipp and Zeckhauser (1985), the lower an individual's health status and the higher his/her satisfaction with the current plan, the higher the transition cost and the lower the probability of switching plans. Switching between plans which requires a change in physician

entails greater transition costs than switching between indemnity plans, which do not require such a change. The effectiveness of risk adjustment can be attenuated if patients will not join an HMO or other particular type of health plan. A particular HMO might not represent an option to some employees because of the geographic location of its clinics or hospitals. Thus, an established organization with fixed facilities and a particular reputation may be unacceptable to a large percentage of potential switchers. Different benefits, such as a change to a formulary-based pharmacy with fixed facilities, may increase transition costs. An individual with prepaid drug coverage now facing a less expensive plan without drug coverage may incorrectly calculate the benefit of the drug plan. Thus, although the benefits may be actuarially equivalent, for an individual using the benefit, they impose a direct cost. In effect, this raises both the information cost of finding out about the new plan and the transition cost of switching plans.

5. This discussion assumes that the direction of selection within an employer mirrors the direction of selection within the entire health plan. Thus, if we assume a plan is adversely selected, we are assuming that the risk relative to other health plans used by that employer and relative to other groups using the health plan are higher than average. This latter assumption may be incorrect. In a healthy group, those in the adversely selected plan may be healthier than the remainder, on average, in that plan. A similar problem can happen with favorable selection.

REFERENCES

Abraham, K.S. (1986). *Distributing Risk.* New Haven: Yale University Press.

Borch, K. (1990). *The Economics of Insurance.* New York: Elsevier Science Publishing Company, Inc.

Bowen, B. and E. Slavin (1991). "Adjusting Contributions to Address Selection Bias: Three Models for Employers." In M. Hornbrook (Ed.), *Advances in Health Economics and Health Services Research: Vol. 12. Risk-Based Contributions to Private Health Insurance* (pp. 77-96). Greenwich, CT: JAI Press.

Eggers, P. and R. Prihoda (1982). "Pre-Enrollment Reimbursement Patterns of Medicare Beneficiaries Enrolled in 'At-Risk' HMOs." *Health Care Financing Review* 4:55-73.

Enthoven, A.C. (1989). "Effective Management of Competition in the FEHBP." *Health Affairs* 8:33-50.

Evans, R.G. (1983). "Incomplete Vertical Integration in the Health Care Industry: Pseudomarkets and Pseudopolicies." *The Annals of the American Academy of Political and Social Science* 468:60-87.

Feldstein, P.J. (1988). *Health Care Economics.* Third Edition. New York: John Wiley and Sons.

Francis, W. (1986). *Checkbook's Guide to Health Insurance Plans for Federal Employees: 1987 Edition.* Washington, DC: Center for the Study of Services.

Goodman, M.J., D.W. Roblin, M.C. Hornbrook, and J.P. Mulloly (1991). "Persistence of Health Care Expense in an Insured Working Population." In M. Hornbrook (Ed.), *Advances in Health Economics and Health Services Research: Vol. 12. Risk-Based Contributions to Private Health Insurance* (pp. 149-173). Greenwich, CT: JAI Press.

Hayes, S. (1991). "Demographic Risk Factors Derived from an HMO." In M. Hornbrook (Ed.), *Advances in Health Economics and Health Services Research: Vol. 12. Risk-Based Contributors to Private Health Insurance* (pp. 177-196). Greenwich, CT: JAI Press.

Hornbrook, M.C., M.D. Bennett, and M.R. Greenlick (1989). "Adjusting the AAPCC for Selectivity and Selection Bias Under Medicare Risk Contracts." In R. M. Scheffler and L. F. Rossiter (Eds.), *Advances in Health Economics and Health Services Research,* (Vol. 10, pp. 111-149). Greenwich, CT: JAI Press.

Hornbrook, M.C. and M.J. Goodman (1991). "Health Plan Case Mix: Definition, Measurement, and Use." In M. Hornbrook (Ed.), *Advances in Health Economics and Health Services*

Research: Vol. 12. Risk-Based Contributions to Private Health Insurance (pp. 111-148). Greenwich, CT: JAI Press.

Hornbrook, M.C., M.J. Goodman, and M.D. Bennett (1991). "Assessing Health Plan Case Mix in Employed Populations: Ambulatory Morbidity and Prescribed Drug Models." In M. Hornbrook (Ed.), *Advances in Health Economics and Health Services Research: Vol. 12. Risk-Based Contributions to Private Health Insurance* (pp. 197-232). Greenwich, CT: JAI Press.

Hornbrook, M.C., M.J. Goodman, M.D. Bennett, and M.R. Greenlick (1991). "Assessing Health Plan Case Mix in Employed Populations: Self-reported Health Status Models. In M. Hornbrook (Ed.), *Advances in Health Economics and Health Services Research: Vol. 12. Risk-Based Contributions to Private Health Insurance* (pp. 233-272). Greenwich, CT: JAI Press.

Jones, S.B. (1989). "Can Multiple Choice be Managed to Constrain Health Care Costs?" *Health Affairs* 8:51-59.

Jones, S.B. (1990). "Multiple Choice Health Insurance: The Lessons and Challenge to Private Insurers." *Inquiry* 27:161-166.

Kenkel, P.J. (1988). "Triple-Option Plans Thrive." *Modern Health Care* 18:26-33.

Luft, H.S., J.B. Trauner, and S.C. Maerki (1985). "Adverse Selection in a Large Multi-option Health Benefits Program: A Case Study of the California Public Employees' Retirement System." In R. M. Scheffler and L. F. Rossiter (Eds.), *Advances in Health Economics and Health Services Research* (Vol. 6, pp. 197-230). Greenwich, CT: JAI Press.

Lundy, J. (1990). "Design of Health Plan Benefits for the Nonelderly," In Pepper Commission, *A Call for Action,* Supplement to the Final Report of the U.S. Bipartisan Commission on Comprehensive Health Care (pp. 57-66). Washington, DC: U.S. Government Printing Office.

McDonnell, P., A. Guttenberg, L. Greenberg, and R.H. Arnett, III (1986). "Self-insured Health Plans." *Health Care Financing Review* 8:1-16.

Neipp, J. and R. Zeckhauser (1985). "Persistence in the Choice of Health Plans." In R. M. Scheffler and L. F. Rossiter (Eds.), *Advances in Health Economics and Health Services Research* (Vol. 6, pp. 47-72). Greenwich, CT: JAI Press.

Pepper Commission (1990). *A Call for Action.* Final Report of the U.S. Bipartisan Commission on Comprehensive Health Care. Washington, DC: U.S. Government Printing Office.

Price, J.R., J.W. Mays, and G.R. Trapnell (1983). "Stability in the Federal Employees Health Benefits Program." *Journal of Health Economics* 2:207-224.

Price, J.R. and J.W. Mays (1985). "Biased Selection in the Federal Employees Health Benefits Program." *Inquiry* 22:67-77.

Schuttinga, J.A., M. Falik, and B. Steinwald (1985). "Health Plan Selection in the Federal Employees Health Benefits Program." *Journal of Health Politics, Policy and Law* 10:119-139.

Short, P.F. and A.K. Taylor (1989). "Premiums, Benefits, and Employee Choice of Health Insurance Options." *Journal of Health Economics* 8:293-311.

Siu, A.L., F.A. Sonnenberg, W.G. Manning, G.A. Goldberg, E.S. Bloomfield, J.P. Newhouse, and R.H. Brook (1986). "Inappropriate Use of Hospitals in a Randomized Trial of Health Insurance Plans." *New England Journal of Medicine* 315:1259-1266.

Towers, Perrin, Forster, and Crosby, Inc. (1988). "Study of the Federal Employees Health Benefits Program." Submitted to U.S. Office of Personnel Management, April 22. New York: TPF & Co., Inc.

Welch, W.P. (1989). "Restructuring the Federal Employees Health Benefits Program: The Private Sector Option." *Inquiry* 26:321-334.

Zeckhauser, R.J. (1970). "Medical Insurance: A Case Study of the Trade-off between Risk Spreading and Appropriate Incentives." *Journal of Economic Theory* 2:10-26.

ADJUSTING CONTRIBUTIONS TO ADDRESS SELECTION BIAS:

THREE MODELS FOR EMPLOYERS

Bruce Bowen and Elizabeth Slavin

INTRODUCTION

Over the past few decades, employers have faced increasing costs of health care coverage for their employees. As employers have examined the causes of this price escalation, they have focused on the issue of selection bias. Selection bias occurs when health risks or expected medical costs are distributed unevenly across health plans. With a disproportionate number of sick employees in one plan, that plan will likely raise its rates (assuming rates are based on risk), which will force healthy people out of the plan. In extreme circumstances, this situation can lead to what is called the "death spiral," where the adversely selected plan or the plan with sicker employees becomes no longer viable.

This situation is unfortunate not only for the health plan involved but also for the employer, who loses the ability to maintain choice in the health benefit offerings. Choice is eliminated because escalating rates make affected plans unaffordable to enrollees, and the prohibitive risk forces plans to drop out.

Advances in Health Economics and Health Services Research, Vol. 12, pages 77-96.
Copyright © 1991 by JAI Press Inc.
All rights of reproduction in any form reserved.
ISBN: 1-55938-241-4

In addition, the employer is affected by selection bias because of the financial implications of the changing risks which result from enrollees shifting to and from plans with differing efficiencies. Only when the rates of every health plan reflect their risks, when the benefits are the same, and when efficiencies are equal, will a death spiral not have an adverse financial effect on the employer. When the adversely selected plan raises its rates to reflect the higher risk, the other plans will lower their prices to reflect the lower risks of those enrolled in them. As long as the above conditions are met, the total health care expenditure for the employer will not change. Unfortunately, this situation does not reflect reality. Not only are benefits and efficiencies not uniform across plans, but also plans that attract healthier members may be less efficient, and consequently may not drop their rates to reflect the lower risk. If employees shift to a less efficient plan, the employer's total health carc expenditure will increase. But if employees move to a more efficient plan, the employer's costs may decrease. Employers have a profound interest in assuring that the number of enrollees in the most cost-effective plans is maximized. Thus, employers have a large stake in eliminating selection bias.

Employers have had various responses to the selection bias phenomenon. These include adopting uniform payroll deductions, reducing the number of plans offered, implementing exclusive replacement arrangements, and restricting enrollment. Adopting an exclusive arrangement with one organization for the provision of health benefits to employees eliminates the issue of selection bias since risks are pooled to a single underwriter. In addition, employers have turned to two related means of removing selection bias from their plans: risk assessment and risk adjustment. Risk assessment measures the magnitude of selection among different plans by calculating the relative risk of each plan. Risk adjustment, in turn, alters the employer's contribution on the basis of the risk assessment so that risk differences among plans are removed from the price the employees pay for the plan. In other words, employees' prices (payroll deductions for health benefits) reflect efficiencies of the system and benefit differences, but not the health of the other people in the plan.

An important point is that risk assessment and adjustment compensate only for rate differences that result from unevenly distributed risk. They do not eliminate other sources of price differences such as benefit design, inefficiencies in plans, or cost-shifting. It is certainly possible that benefit design influences the direction and magnitude of selection bias. For example, if an employer offers two plans, one which has extensive mental health benefits and another which does not, the plan offering the extensive benefits is likely to be adversely selected by those employees anticipating mental health expenses. Risk-adjusting the employer contribution does not solve this problem unless the employer picks up the entire cost of the mental health benefit.

This paper examines employers' motives for conducting risk adjustments of employer contributions. Then three models are presented for risk-adjusting employer contributions. These methods are: the *Ratio Method,* the *Absolute Difference Method*, and the *Everyone in Fee-For-Service* (*FFS*) *Method.* These three methods represent the fundamental types that employers and consultants use. The implications of each type of method for the employee, employer, and health plan, as well as other issues pertaining to risk-adjustment models, are described.

EMPLOYER MOTIVES FOR RISK ADJUSTMENT

Employers have varied reasons for adopting risk-adjustment contribution schemes. Some will adjust their contributions in order to preserve plan choice in their health benefit offerings. In extreme cases, the distribution of risk has become so distorted that the plan with the adverse selection—more often than not, the FFS plan—will cease to be viable unless some action is taken. Employers will then adjust their contributions to compensate for selection effects, which will lower the employee price of the adversely selected plan so that it is more attractive to employees. At the same time, the employer makes up the lost revenue by increasing the employees' price in the other offered plan. Though yet to be empirically tested in any scientific way, this process should reverse the death spiral if selection bias is the true cause of the problem. Other factors probably contribute to the death spiral as well, and will need to be addressed in order to eliminate the entire selection bias problem.

Often an employer will decide to undertake a risk adjustment purely for financial reasons. For example, employers may own the FFS plan—that is, be self-insured. In this situation, the losses in the FFS plan are implicit subsidies to the rate. Therefore, the employer has a short-term economic interest in preserving the plan.

On a more conceptual level, employers will assess risk because they believe in the theory of managed competition as originated by Alain Enthoven (1988). Managed competition advocates mechanisms that counter deficiencies in the health care market and facilitate cost-conscious choice among health plans in order to achieve equity and efficiency in the delivery of health care. Selection bias is one failure of the marketplace that can be managed through "risk rating" or risk-adjusting employer contributions. As part of this concept, the risk adjustment of employer contributions would be an ongoing process, not a solution to a one-time problem. The most important consequence of managed competition is the removal of risk differences from price so that health plans can compete more directly on efficiency.

RISK-ADJUSTMENT MODELS

In almost all cases, an accurate and unbiased risk assessment should precede a risk adjustment of employer contributions. After determining the quantitative value of the risk for each health plan through a risk assessment, employers can compensate for that risk by adjusting their contributions. However, employers have occasionally made arbitrary, data-free decisions about the level of risk in each plan and have changed their contributions according to their assumptions. The efficacy of any risk adjustment is related to the adequacy of the model underlying the risk assessment.

The key to any risk adjustment is that it adjusts the employer contribution according to the risk. We assume that the health plan rates charged to employers do not change in a risk adjustment of employer contributions. Although the relative contributions of the employee and employer change, the total amount paid to the health plan is the same. Also, the models of adjustment do not necessarily alter the employer's total health care expenditure. Independently, the employer can increase or decrease the total budget for health care while risk-adjusting the contributions.

Because of the timing in an employer risk-adjustment program, it is extremely difficult to guarantee budget neutrality for an employer. During the normal sequence of events, rates are submitted by health plans and a risk assessment is conducted before the employer contribution is set. After the contribution is determined (that is, after employees know how much they will have to pay for each alternative), employees are then asked to choose plans in an open enrollment period. If there is a different contribution for each health plan, it is impossible to predict precisely how many employees will choose each plan. Without that precise prediction, absolute budget neutrality cannot be achieved. When the employer contribution depends on the risk of each employee (or employee unit) rather than on the aggregated risk of the health plan, this problem will be overcome; absolute budget neutrality is possible. This individual type of adjustment method will be discussed in detail later in the paper.

Several other timing issues merit discussion. First, the risk assessment needs to be done before the employer contributions are set (and obviously before the open enrollment period). Therefore, the model used in the risk assessment must be capable of predicting health care risk for more than one time period into the future. It frequently must be able to predict next year's risk from last year's data. Sometimes that time frame can be narrowed. Second, in some of the risk-adjustment models, health plan rates need to be known before the employer contributions are set. However, all health plan rates must be determined before the open enrollment period.

The methods described in detail in the paper are subsets of three fundamental types of adjustments. One type, exemplified by the Ratio Method, does not utilize any of the offered health plan rates in the adjustment. Other methods, such as the Absolute Difference Method, use all of the health plan rates. Lastly, there are the "surcharge" adjustment methods, which are those most commonly used by employers and consultants. Demonstrated by the Everyone in FFS

Table 1. Variables Utilized in the Three Methods of Risk Adjustment

Ratio Method	*Mean Absolute Difference Method*	*Everyone in FFS Method*
• Relative risks of all health plans • Employer health care budget • Subscriber distribution	• Relative risks of all health plans • Employer health care budget • Subscriber distribution • All health plan rates	• Relative risks of all health plans • Employer health care budget • Subscriber distribution • FFS Plan rate

Table 2. Health Plan Information

	Single Step Relative Risk	*Standardized to Plan B Relative Risk*	*Single Step Rate*	*Number of Subscribers*	*Employer Contribution*
Plan A (FFS)	1.040	1.13	$160	200	$90
Plan B (HMO)	.921	1.00	$100	100	$90

Method, the "surcharge" methods use only the FFS rate in the adjustment. Although these are only three computational methods representing each class of adjustment methodology, many other logical derivatives follow from each kind of model.

Table 1 demonstrates the different variables that are necessary for each method. All of the methods require the three methods of information: the distribution of the enrollees in each plan, the average employer contribution for each enrollee, and the relative risks in each plan. The only difference among the methods is whether or not the health plan rates are needed.

In order to clearly depict the differences among the methods, the information in Table 2 will be applied to each method. The data in this example are drawn from the actual specifics of an employer who conducted a risk assessment and adjustment. In this employer group, there is a two-tier rate structure; the single step covers only one person—the subscriber—in the contract, and the family step includes two or more persons—the subscriber and dependent(s) in the contract. Although this example uses only two offered health plans, all of the methods can be applied to situations where many more plans are offered by the employer.

In Table 2, the relative risks show that the FFS plan, or Plan A, has a 4% higher risk than the average risk of the entire company; the HMO plan, or Plan B, has an 8% lower risk than the employer's average. The employer is contributing $90 per subscriber to each plan. Before any risk adjustment, given

Table 3. Variable Definitions

Contribution for Plan A	C_a
Mean Employer Contribution	C_m
Number of Subscribers in Plan A	N_a
Total Number of Subscribers in Company	N_t
Relative Risk for Plan A	R_a
Plan A Rate to Employer	W_a
Subscriber Price for Plan A	P_a

Note: Subscript letter indicates whether Plan A or Plan B.

the FFS rate of $160 and the HMO rate of $100, the employee out-of-pocket cost is $70 to FFS subscribers and $10 to HMO subscribers. In order to present the specific algorithms clearly, Table 3 defines the variables used in the models.

Ratio Method

The Ratio Method is based on an intuitive and simple concept; it sets the ratio of the employer contributions for any two plans equal to the ratio of those plans' relative risks. In other words, if enrollees in one plan are twice as sick as those in another plan, the employer contribution to the first plan would be twice as large as the contribution to the other plan. Assuming the information in Table 2, that Plan A has a relative risk of 1.04 and Plan B has a relative risk of .921, then the ratio of contributions should be 1.04 to .921.

Equations (1) and (2) represent the ratio and budget constraints, respectively. There are two unknowns (C_a and C_b) and two equations. The solution of this set of simultaneous equations is demonstrated below. If there were more than two health plans, there would be as many equations and unknowns. There would always be as many unique equations as unknowns, guaranteeing a solution.

$$\frac{R_a}{R_b} = \frac{C_a}{C_b} \tag{1}$$

$$(N_a * C_a) + (N_b * C_b) = (C_m * N_t) \tag{2}$$

To apply the Ratio Method, first calculate a risk ratio by dividing the relative risk of Plan A by the relative risk of Plan B. Then, rearrange Eq. (1) to solve for the contribution for Plan A.

$$\frac{C_a}{C_b} = \frac{1.04}{.921} = 1.129 = \text{Risk Ratio}$$
$$C_a = [(\text{Risk Ratio}) * (C_b)]$$
$$C_a = [1.129 * (C_b)] \quad (1.1)$$

Next, substitute Eq. (1.1) for the contribution for Plan A (C_a) into Eq. (2). Assume an average employer contribution of $90.

$$(N_a * C_b * 1.129) + (N_b * C_b) = (C_m * N_t)$$
$$(200) * (C_b) * 1.129 + (100) * (C_b) = \$90(300)$$
$$(200) * (1.129) * (C_b) + (100) * (C_b) = \$27{,}000$$
$$(225.8) * (C_b) + (100) * (C_b) = \$27{,}000$$
$$C_b * (325.8) = \$27{,}000$$
$$C_b = \$82.87$$
$$C_a = C_b * (1.129) = \$93.56$$

Manipulating the equations and using the employer's average contribution of $90, it is determined that the employer contributions are $93.56 for Plan A and $82.87 for Plan B. The ratio of the contributions, $93.56 to $82.87, is 1.129, the risk ratio.

One advantage of this method is that it does not use the rates charged by the plans in the calculation. It is better to set the contributions independent of the rates of the offered health plans. Inefficient plans that have high rates or those plans that arbitrarily raise their rates should not be rewarded with higher employer contributions. Another advantage is that the contributions can be set before the employer knows the rates for the health plans. A drawback to this method is that it does not allow determination of the absolute level of the employer's contribution if, say, the employer wanted to contribute 95% of the overall average expense for an average risk employee.

Absolute Difference Method

In contrast to the Ratio Method, which does not use any health plan rates, the Absolute Difference Method uses the rate of every offered health plan to determine the contribution. This method calculates iso-risk rates for all health plans at the average level of risk, and then maintains this absolute price difference between these risk rates in the out-of-pocket contributions faced by the employees. Like the other methods, this method enables the employer to set the dollar amount of the employees' contributions based on the budgetary considerations of the employer. If the adjusted price of a health plan is below the employer's contribution, the excess contribution can be distributed in various ways. The employer can keep the leftover or increase the contribution to other employees' rates, or pay it as cash to those choosing the low-risk plan. A fourth option is to allocate the excess dollars toward additional benefits for all employees.

In the Absolute Difference Method, the two constraints—the risk constraint (3) and the budget constraint—are expressed in the following two equations. The budget constraint equation is the same as in the Ratio Method (Eq. 2).

$$P_a - P_b = \frac{W_a}{R_a} - \frac{W_b}{R_b} \tag{3}$$

Equation (3) states that the difference in the average risk rates for the two plans should equal the difference in the prices that employees see. (The average risk rate for a plan is the health plan's rate to the employer divided by that health plan's risk: W_a/R_a.)

Given the identities

$$W_a = C_a + P_a \tag{4}$$

$$W_b = C_b + P_b \tag{5}$$

Equations (3)and (4) can be solved as a system of simultaneous equations. As with the Ratio Method, more health plans generate more equations to be solved, but there are no problems in principle.

The first step of the Absolute Difference Method is to determine the average risk rate for each health plan—that is, the amount each plan would charge if it had the entire employer group or the average risk. The next step is to calculate the absolute difference between the average risk rates of the health plans. The relative risk should be standardized so that the weighted average of the relative risks of all of the health plans in the employer group is 1.00. These are the same relative risks that were used in the Ratio Method computation.

$$P_a - P_b = \frac{\$160}{1.04} - \frac{\$100}{.921} \tag{3}$$

$$P_a - P_b = \$45.26 \tag{3.1}$$

From the identities Eqs. (4) and (5):

$$P_a = W_a - C_a = \$160 - C_a$$

$$P_b = W_b - C_b = \$100 - C_b$$

Substituting in (3.1):

$$(\$160 - C_a) - (\$100 - C_b) = \$45.26$$

$$\$60 - C_a + C_b = \$45.26$$

$$C_b = \$45.26 - \$60 + C_a = C_a - \$14.74$$

Substituting in (2):

$$(N_a) * (C_a) + (N_b) * (C_a - \$14.74) = (N_t) * (C_m)$$

$$(200) * (C_a) + (100) * (C_a) - \$1474 = (300) * (\$90)$$

$$(300) * (C_a) - \$1474 = \$27{,}000$$

$$C_a = \frac{\$27000 + \$1474}{300} = \$94.91$$

$$C_b = C_a - \$14.74$$

$$C_b = \$94.91 - \$14.74 = \$80.17$$

Using this adjustment method, the employer can set the absolute level of contribution to the available budget. But Health Plan A will always cost the employee $45.26 more than Health Plan B, regardless of the contribution level. For example, given a different average employer contribution, the employer could contribute $114.74 to Plan A and $100 to Plan B. This would result in an employee cost of $45.26 for Plan A and zero for Plan B. Or the employer could contribute $64.74 to Plan A and $50 to Plan B, with an employee cost of $95.26 for A and $50 for B. The critical issue is that Plan A should cost the employee $45.26 more than Plan B because that is the difference in the rates for those plans if they had average risk.

This method offers both advantages and disadvantages. While the Ratio Method alters the employer's contribution according to the relative risks, this method makes a further adjustment to the employer's contribution so that the employee out-of-pocket costs more directly reflect the differences in risk. In the spirit of managed competition, this method has more of an impact on the price to the employee—the person making the health plan choice. On the other hand, the health plan rates of all plans in the employer group are utilized in this method of adjustment. Since the rates include other factors besides risk, this method can overcompensate for risk by adjusting for these other components in the rate. This problem is demonstrated later in the paper when the methods are evaluated against theoretical criteria. Also, using the health plan rates in the method can be problematic because often the employer will not have access to each plan's rates prior to developing the risk-adjustment scheme. Lastly, no matter when the contribution scheme is applied, any plan that raises its rates is rewarded with a higher contribution.

Therefore, plans may have an incentive built in to the method to raise their rates.

Everyone in FFS Method

Probably the most widely used method for adjusting employer contributions is the "surcharge" method, which is exemplified by the "What if Everyone Were in the FFS" Method. This model sets the employee price for the FFS plan as if all employees (the entire risk pool) had chosen the FFS plan. The average contribution is then applied to that "average risk" price. The employer changes the employees' price in the other plans (the HMOs) to compensate for the FFS plan adjustment. Part of the popularity of this approach is that the employer can configure the playing field as though there were no HMOs. Although in the following example the FFS plan has the adverse selection, the method is indifferent to the direction of the risk selection. If the FFS plan has favorable selection, the employer contribution to the FFS plan will decrease relative to that of the other plan.

The first step in this method is to calculate the rate the FFS plan would charge if it had the average risk of the entire employer group. As shown in Eq. (6), this is the FFS rate divided by the relative risk of the FFS plan calculated using the entire employer group as the standard for the relative risk. (This is the same as the average risk rate discussed in connection with the Absolute Difference Method.)

$$\text{Average Risk Rate FFS} = \frac{\text{FFS Rate}}{\text{Relative Risk of FFS}} \tag{6}$$

After calculating the average risk rate, compute the difference between the actual FFS health plan rate and the average risk rate demonstrated in Eq. (7). The total amount of money needed to risk-adjust the contribution of the FFS plan is determined by multiplying the difference between the actual FFS rate and the average risk rate by the number of people in the FFS plan. Then, that amount is divided by the number of people in the non-FFS plan to calculate the amount the contribution is reduced for those members.

$$\text{Rate Difference} = (\text{Actual FFS Rate}) - (\text{Average Risk Rate FFS}) \tag{7}$$

$$\text{FFS Contribution} = C_m + \text{Rate Difference} \tag{8}$$

$$\text{Non-FFS Contribution} = C_m - \frac{\text{Rate Difference} * \text{Number in FFS}}{\text{Number in non-FFS}} \tag{9}$$

Using the same information in Table 2 and assuming that Plan A is the FFS plan and Plan B is the non-FFS plan:

$$\text{Average Risk Rate of Plan A} = \frac{W_a}{R_a} = \frac{\$160}{1.040} = \$154$$

$$\text{Rate Difference} = \$160 - \$154 = \$6$$

$$C_a = \$90 + \$6 = \$96$$

$$C_b = \$90 - \frac{\$6 * 200}{100} = \$90 - \$12 = \$78$$

The employer contribution to Health Plan A and Health Plan B is $96 and $78 respectively. The primary difference between this method and the other two is the emphasis on preserving the FFS plan. Also, this method uses the FFS plan rate to compute an appropriate contribution, which can be problematic (see disadvantages in Absolute Difference Method). Unlike the Absolute Difference Method, the Everyone in FFS Method does not use rate information for the other plan(s).

COMPARISON OF METHODS

Table 4 summarizes the results of the three methods. While the results of the example above show very little difference in the three models of risk adjustment, the similarity begins to diminish as the differences in relative risk among health plans increases. On average, the relative risks of plans vary by no more than 10-15% of the average risk of the employer group. For the purposes of this example, we change the relative risk of Plan A from 1.04 to 1.20 and that of Plan B from .921 to .60. This change produces the results shown in Table 5 with the different adjustment methods.

The differences among the methods are clearly more striking when the risk differential is larger. The HMO enrollees' price varies from $46 in the Ratio Method to $72 in the Absolute Difference Method and $63 in the Everyone in FFS Method. The Ratio Method only risk-adjusts the contribution; therefore it differs the least from no adjustment at all. Note that the risk of Plan A is twice that of Plan B and the contribution for Plan A ($108) is now twice that for Plan B ($54).

Method Comparison with Theoretical Criteria

Another way of comparing the adjustment methods is to look at how each method would risk-adjust the contribution in a hypothetical situation where we know a lot more information about the health plans than we could possibly know in a real situation. Table 6 represents the known information about Plan X and Plan Y. Plan X is an FFS plan.

Table 4. Results of Methods (Using Data in Table 2)

	Ratio Method	*Absolute Difference Method*	*Everyone in FFS*	*No Adjustment*
Contribution to FFS	$94	$95	$96	$90
Contribution to HMO	83	80	78	90
FFS Subscriber Price	66	65	64	70
HMO Subscriber Price	17	20	22	10

Table 5. Results of Methods Assuming Large Risk Differentials

	Ratio Method	*Absolute Difference Method*	*Everyone in FFS*	*No Adjustment*
Contribution to FFS	$108	$121	$117	$90
Contribution to HMO	54	28	37	90
FFS Subscriber Price	52	39	43	70
HMO Subscriber Price	46	72	63	10

Plan X and Plan Y both have the same base rate of $100. However, Plan X has correctly calculated that it enrolls a 30% higher-risk population than average and, in turn, has modified its rate to $130. Similarly, Plan Y has determined that it has 15% lower-risk enrollees and has modified its rate to be $85. Both Plans have added $5 worth of additional benefits, and Plan X is $20 more inefficient than Plan Y. In this example, the inefficiency in Plan X is a result of higher physician costs as well as a recent building campaign for a new hospital and medical offices. Although in the real world it would be unlikely that one could know all this information about these plans (especially the magnitude of each plan's inefficiency), this example illustrates how close each model is to the ideal adjustment.

Given the information in Table 6, the question is what prices should employees pay for the two health plans. The plans differ in only two respects: risk and efficiency. Plan X enrolls 30% higher-than-average risk and is $20 more inefficient. Plan Y has 15% below-average risk. Using the criteria set forth earlier, the ideal risk-adjustment method would remove the effects of risk from the price differences, but leave in the effect of inefficiency. Although employees should not have to pay more because the health plan they choose has sicker people in it, they should have to pay more if the health plan they choose is inefficient. Therefore, of the $65 price difference between the two plans, employees should pay the $20 caused by inefficiency, but not the $45 caused by risk.

Table 6. Hypothetical Example

	Plan X	*Plan Y*
Base Rate	$100	$100
Risk factor	1.30	.85
Number of subscribers	200	100
Rate modified by risk	$130	$85
Extra benefits	$5	$5
Inefficiency	$20	$0
Total rate to employers	$155	$90
Average employer contribution: $90		

As Table 7 demonstrates, none of these methods produces the expected $20 price difference. The Ratio Method comes the closest with a difference of $24.50 partly because the absolute value of the employer contribution is high. Both the Everyone in FFS and the Absolute Difference Methods suffer from including the cost of inefficiency in the amount they are risk-adjusting and, thus, are further from making an ideal adjustment of $20.

The inherent problem with the two methods that use any of the health plan rates is that it is nearly impossible to separate any rate into all of its parts as in the hypothetical example. The rate is in fact the sum of a variety of components (including benefits, efficiency, risk, and even profit) that are difficult to differentiate and quantify.

The Ratio Method does not give the inefficient plan an "extra" contribution as do the other two plans; however, it adjusts only the percentage of the cost paid by the employer and does not remove the full impact of risk.

Differences in Methods by Varying Risk

Figure 1 shows the difference between the FFS price that an employee would pay and the HMO price that the same employee would pay. (This price is the employee payroll deduction after the employer contribution.) The difference varies with the relative risk that the HMO faces. (Since this example is a closed system with only two plans, as the HMO's risk increases, the FFS plan's risk decreases and vice versa.) As the relative risk of the health plans deviates from 1.00, the three methods produce increasingly different results. For example, at a relative risk for the HMO of .90 (the relative risk of the FFS plan would be 1.0563), the Ratio Method would produce employee prices for the FFS plan that are $121 more than for the HMO, while the comparable number for the Absolute Difference Method is $91, and the Everyone in FFS Method is $86 more for the FFS plan.

Table 7. Employee Cost

	No Adjustment	*Ratio Method*	*Absolute Difference Method*	*Everyone in FFS Method*
Plan X	$65	$38.00	$30.57	$29.23
Plan Y	$0	$13.50	$17.22	$17.88
Difference in Cost	$65	$24.50	$13.55	$11.35

Although not illustrated in Figure 1, the Ratio Method would become increasingly different from the other two methods as the employer's contribution decreases from 100% of the average cost of the plans. The reason for this difference is that the Ratio Method is only risk-adjusting the part of the price paid by the employer.

The example illustrated in Figure 1 assumes an FFS rate of $500 and an HMO rate of $340. It also arbitrarily assumes that there are twice as many people in the FFS plan as in the HMO. The absolute value of the employer contribution is irrelevant in this case because we are looking at the difference only. When the relative risk of the two plans is 1.00, the difference in the prices is, in fact, the difference in the plan rates since all of the contribution methodologies yield equal dollar contributions for equal risk.

It can be seen from the slopes of the plots that the Everyone in FFS Method reacts more to changes in relative risk, while the Ratio Method reacts less. This would be true for any set of prices and contributions.

IMPLICATIONS OF THE METHODS

Implications for Employers

The method that is most appropriate for the employer is largely dependent on the employer's objectives and goals. Conflicting objectives often require the employer to make tradeoffs among the models. An employer whose primary concern is preserving the FFS plan or the self-insured plan will probably favor the Everyone in FFS Method. On the other hand, an employer might prefer to use an adjustment method that is very simple and requires minimal information. Models like the Ratio Method that do not require knowledge of the health plan rates would probably best meet these

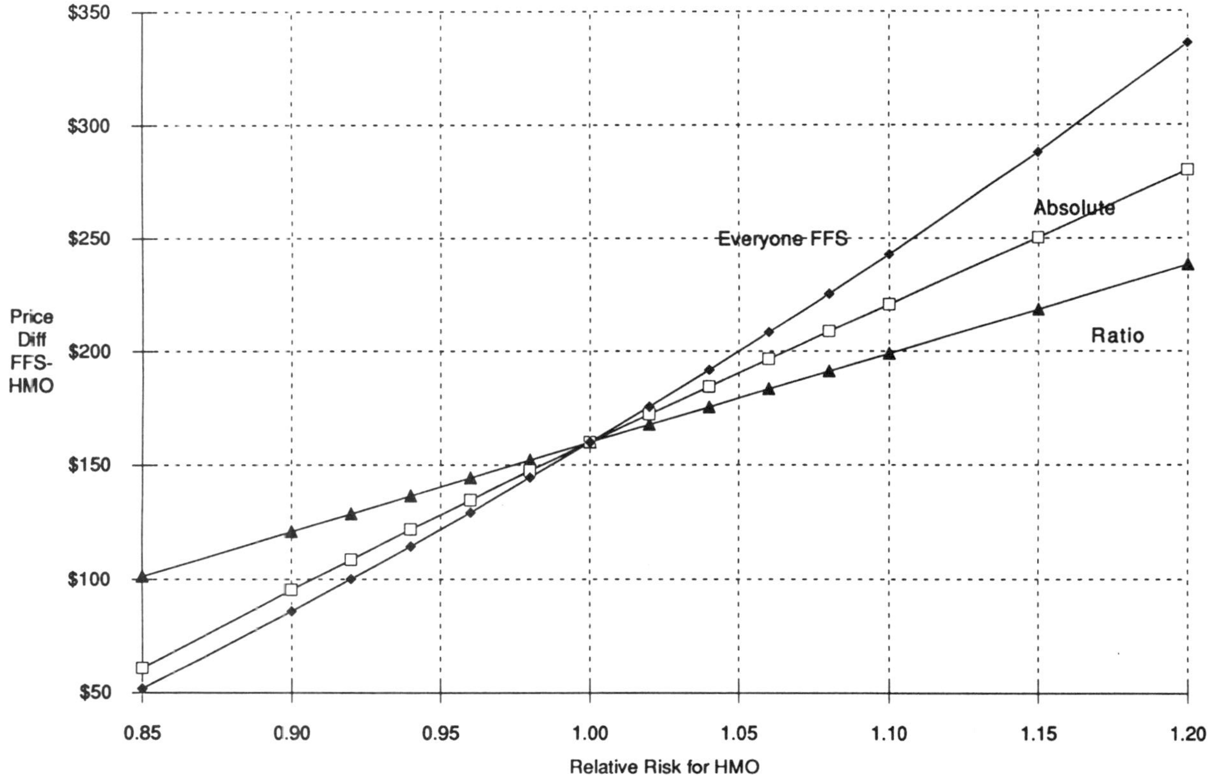

Figure 1. Price difference between HMO and FFS plans for different contribution methods varying relative risk.

objectives. Almost all employers want to maximize the number of enrollees in the most cost-effective plan. An employer who was very concerned about efficiency might choose the Absolute Difference Method because it most directly changes the employee price according to the relative risk of each plan. Yet, if the high-risk plan is also the most inefficient, this method will overcompensate for risk. Also, an employer might reject this method because it is so complicated and requires additional rate information from the health plans. The employer would like a model to be stable and easy to implement.

Implications for Health Plans

The implications for health plans are quite different from those for employers. In the short term, all health plans have an economic interest in maximizing employer contributions to their plan. Higher employer contributions mean lower employee prices and, therefore, higher membership for the plan. It follows that an FFS plan with unfavorable selection will favor the Everyone in FFS Method since it makes the greatest adjustment to the employer contribution. Likewise, a plan that has favorable selection will prefer the Ratio Method because it changes the employer contribution the least. When the risk differential among the plans is small, the amount of adjustment by the models is almost the same. In the longer term, health plans are more concerned with issues of accuracy, fairness, and stability in the models. Health plans should charge rates that reflect the risk of the people in the plan. If the adjustment to employer contributions dramatically changes from year to year, causing the risk mix to be substantially altered, health plans will need to be constantly changing their rates to compensate for the changing risk in their plan. Thus, to the health plans, it is important that the models not be volatile from year to year.

Implications for Employees

The amount of information provided to employees about their health benefits varies among employers. If employees know only the payroll deduction associated with each plan, and not the entire health plan rate, they may not need to know much about the risk-adjustment model. On the other hand, in a collective bargaining agreement, the union representative will receive full disclosure of the plan rates as well as the specific algorithm of the adjustment model. In this case, models like the Ratio Method, which are simpler to understand and use, may be preferred. In the short term, employees will want a wide array of plans to choose from. Real choice implies reasonable and affordable employee payroll deductions. When evaluating risk-adjustment models from the employee's perspective, it is important to consider the employee's relationship to a particular plan or doctor. Employees with close affiliations to a doctor or plan may not be sensitive to price change if it means switching to a plan that does not allow them to use their doctor. In other words, a risk adjustment of employer contributions may not counteract selection bias if the employees do not react to price changes.

OTHER ADJUSTMENT METHOD ISSUES

Rate Step Adjustments

Since employees pay different prices in different rate steps, and since health plans charge different rates, the risk assessment and risk adjustment of contributions should be done separately for each of the different rate steps. Steps, or rate tiers, are the family composition units used in rating (single, two-party, family, etc.). If assessments and adjustments are not conducted in separate steps, employers can easily confuse the family-type distribution with the health risk. Every step has a different risk associated with it. For example, larger families have a higher risk of incurring health expenses because of their size. This family size risk is very different from higher health risk. The best way to avoid this problem is to do separate analyses of and separate adjustments to the different rates in each step.

In some situations, it may be useful to examine the composite risk as well as the risk within each step. We have found some cases where a health plan has unfavorable selection on a composite basis and favorable selection in each of the rate steps (for example, see Tables 8 and 9).

Applying an actuarial risk-assessment model to the subscriber distribution in Table 8, we find in Table 9 that Health Plan B has a greater composite risk than does Plan A. In other words, it seems that Plan B has unfavorable selection. But when the adjustment is done separately for each step (single and

Table 8. Subscriber Distribution

		Age of Subscribers			
	STEP	*30-34*	*45-49*	*50-54*	*Total*
Plan A	Single	170	60	270	500
	Family	90	40	200	330
Plan B	Single	130	40	10	180
	Family	440	40	20	500

Table 9. Relative Risk

	Plan A	*Plan B*
Composite Risk	.9140	1.105
Single Step	1.038	.8949
Family Step	1.011	.9924

family), the results show that actually Plan A has unfavorable selection in each step. This difference is caused by a disproportionate number of large families in Plan B. The large size of the employee unit increases the risk or expected future cost, but the higher family rates compensate for this higher risk. Risk-adjustment models are designed to compensate for health risk, not for risk due to family size.

Individual versus Health Plan Adjustment

Thus far, we have made the assumption that any risk adjustment of contributions would be based at the health plan level. In other words, the employees' price for a health plan would change depending on the relative risk that the particular plan faced in the employer group. All employees in a rate step who choose a certain health plan would see the same price. Yet, it is possible to adjust at the individual level rather than at the health plan level. Virtually all of the risk-assessment models can determine the relative risk of individual employee units (preferably the risk of individuals/members). Thus, the employer would contribute a different amount for each individual according to that person's (or unit's) risk level. In order to use this method, health plans would need to provide risk class rates (termed Group Rating by Class).

While few employers are likely to adopt such a complex method of determining contributions, it does not pose problems in principle. This type of method is preferred because individual risk analysis and adjustment automatically account for size and composition of family units; rate-step approaches cannot capture the information on the content of a family unit. Also, risk-adjusting at an individual level eliminates the need to predict the number of people at each risk level who will choose each plan. Thus, individual adjustment provides a truly budget-neutral mechanism. In the perfect world, adjustment at the individual level and at a health plan level would have similar effects. However, the only major employer that we know of who has used this method, American Airlines, has abandoned it, in part because of this method's complexity.

CRITERIA TO EVALUATE METHODS

When evaluating a risk-adjustment method, there are some fundamental criteria to consider. First, the method should be based on a sound risk assessment. If the initial measurement of the magnitude of the selection bias is wrong, that is, the risk-assessment model is biased, the model's adjustment of the contributions is distorted. Second, the model should be a solution to the selection bias issue. The method should make the plan with the higher relative risk more attractive to enrollees by lowering the enrollee price for that plan. Furthermore, the model should be fundamentally fair. Just like risk-assessment models, the adjustment method should not have any built-in biases that benefit either of the health plans. This issue relates to the acceptability of the contribution scheme. Each of the three classes of players affected by the risk adjustment—the health plans, the employer, and the employees—must be reasonably satisfied with the proposed policy changes. Another criterion to judge the method is its practicality. A method that is extraordinarily complex and difficult to implement is less than ideal. Finally, the method should not be susceptible to gaming by any of the health plans. Plans that arbitrarily raise their rates should not be rewarded with higher contributions. An underlying consideration while evaluating any method is whether the method accomplishes the goals of the employer.

CONCLUSION

The three methods of adjustment described above all compensate for risk differentials by increasing contributions to plans with higher risk and decreasing contributions to plans with lower risk. The methods are more similar than different. As the relative risk differentials of the plans become larger, the differences in the methods become more pronounced. In general, the Everyone in FFS Method makes the greatest absolute adjustment in contribution, and the Ratio Method makes the smallest adjustment. Each method must be evaluated in terms of the objectives of the employer who will implement the model. Different goals will lead to different methods. Of the three models, it is not clear which is the best; none of the methods generates an objectively-defined "right" answer. Each method is subject to its own limitations.

Often many other factors contribute to the selection bias problem. There is no known empirical study that proves that a risk adjustment of employer contributions can, by itself, completely reverse a plan's death spiral. However, if done properly, risk assessment and adjustments are the tools that will mitigate if not solve the selection bias problem. Many employers have already adopted risk-adjusted contribution schemes; as the models become more sophisticated in the future, many more employers will follow.

ACKNOWLEDGMENTS

The views expressed in this paper are those of the authors, and no official endorsement by Kaiser Foundation Health Plan is intended or should be inferred. This paper evolved from a series of meetings of the Technical Subcommittee of the Kaiser Permanente Risk Adjustment Task Force, including the Workshop on Risk Adjustment of Employer Contributions, sponsored by the Kaiser Permanente Center for Health Research, Otter Rock, Oregon, July 16, 1990. We are grateful to Margaret R. Sucec for providing technical editorial assistance.

REFERENCES

Enthoven, A.. (1988). "Managed Competition of Alternative Delivery Systems." *Journal of Health Politics, Policy and Law* 3 (2):305-321.

RISK ADJUSTMENT OF EMPLOYER CONTRIBUTIONS:

HOW WELL WILL IT WORK?

Karl R. Iorio

INTRODUCTION

An employer who offers a multiple-choice health benefit program to employees faces the problem of how to best manage the program. The employer's goal is to minimize the cost of providing a certain level of employee health benefits. The economic problem then arises of determining the benefits that health plans offer and the prices that employees pay for the plans so as to achieve this goal. Properly set benefits and prices will encourage cost-conscious choices by employees and cost-efficient behavior by health plans.

Until recently, most employers have not actively involved themselves with the benefit/pricing problem; instead they have passively let health plans determine benefits and prices using traditional methods. This policy has not served employers well, as traditional pricing methods allow risk-selection effects to distort prices. Jones (1990) and Enthoven (1990) argue that risk-selection

Advances in Health Economics and Health Services Research, Vol. 12, pages 97-108.
Copyright © 1991 by JAI Press Inc.
All rights of reproduction in any form reserved.
ISBN: 1-55938-241-4

effects are seriously impeding employers' efforts to contain health care costs, and they urge employers to more actively manage their health benefit programs.

Risk adjustment of employer contributions based on demographic factors is a step towards active employer involvement in the health plan pricing problem. The main advantage of this approach is that it does not require health plans to change from their traditional pricing methods. The idea is to manipulate employer contributions to health plans to offset any price distortions that arise from risk selection. Group Rating by Class (GRC), as described by Enthoven (1988), is a more complete solution to the health plan pricing problem than risk adjustment. GRC requires health plans to change pricing methods.

Kaiser Permanente (KP) has developed a set of basic demographic cost factors for use in risk adjustment (Hayes, 1991). This paper offers a preliminary evaluation of the soundness of risk adjustment and GRC using demographic factors. We compare the KP factors with similar factors for fee-for-service indemnity insurers from Tillinghast (1990).

This evaluation leads to the following conclusions: There are two key requirements on cost factors for risk adjustment to work well for the employer, and these requirements are not satisfied by the demographic factors analyzed. Health plans will need to change to GRC, although the method probably needs modification to correct two selection effects. The first effect involves biased selection of health plans by families of different sizes. The second involves switching between health plans by employees in anticipation of their future medical needs. The best way to set benefits and prices to control this switching needs to be developed. This is an area for future theoretical and empirical research.

The remainder of the paper is organized as follows. In the next section, we develop the framework for our evaluation of pricing methods. In the following section, we evaluate risk adjustment and group rating by class using the KP and Tillinghast demographic risk factors. The last section contains our conclusions.

THE BENEFIT MANAGER'S PRICING PROBLEM

In this section, we give a model of the pricing problem of an employer's benefit manager that risk adjustment of employer contributions seeks to solve. We show how the employer's health care costs can be higher than necessary if the benefit manager passively lets health plans set prices using traditional rating methods. We then describe how to set prices using GRC and identify a key requirement for this method to work well for the employer. We next describe how risk adjustment of employer contributions combined with traditional rating methods can approximate GRC and identify an additional key

Table 1. Expected Costs by Health Plan

Employee Class	*Plan Costs*		*Plan H Cost Advantage*
	H	*F*	
Healthy	100	80	-20
Unhealthy	180	140	-40

requirement for this method. Through most of the paper, we only discuss the problem of setting health plan prices and not the setting of benefits. We touch on the setting of benefits at the end of the paper.

We assume an employer offers employees a choice between two health plans, Plan H and Plan F. Plan H is an HMO, while Plan F is a fee-for-service indemnity insurance plan. The model will illustrate the risk-selection problem that indemnity plans are often said to face, but it will also apply to more general situations.

There are two classes of employees, the healthy and the unhealthy. Table 1 gives the expected costs to the two health plans of insuring an employee in each class. These expected costs *exclude* costs covered by employees through coinsurance payments. Plan H has higher expected costs than Plan F for each class of employee. This is shown in the last column of the table, which gives the differences in costs between Plan H and Plan F. These differences are negative, so Plan H in this example has a cost disadvantage for each class of employees.

The differences in costs between the two plans could arise from differences in benefits, coinsurance payments, medical practice patterns, or productive efficiency. As long as employees are aware of the reasons for the differences, these reasons do not matter for the benefit manager's pricing problem. We will discuss this further below.

The Effects of Passive Benefit Management

The employer's health care costs can be higher than necessary if the employer passively allows health plans to set prices for employees using traditional rating methods based on cost (risk) averaging. With risk selection, Plan H can charge a lower price than Plan F despite Plan H's higher costs. Thus risk selection can give Plan H a positive price advantage despite a negative cost advantage, a discrepancy that will misdirect employees and raise the employer's costs.

To model the risk-selection problem that indemnity insurers are said to face, assume that unhealthy employees have a strong attachment to Plan F while healthy employees are mobile and indifferent between plans and only want to minimize their health insurance costs. We assume the employer in our model

Table 2. Price Effects of Risk Selection

Plan Rates		*Plan Contributions*				*Plan H Price Advantage*
		Employer		*Employee*		
H	*F*	*H*	*F*	*H*	*F*	
100	140	80	80	20	60	40

has enough employees to be fully experience-rated. For our purposes, experience rating means a health plan's rate equals the average (that is, expected) cost of the employees enrolled in the plan.[1] We only consider fully experience-rated employers because they pay the complete cost of their employees' health care, and we do not want to consider the subsidization among employers that occurs with other rating methods.

With experience rating, a plan is able to charge a relatively low rate if employees with relatively low expected costs select the plan. Suppose initially that healthy employees in the model all choose Plan H while unhealthy employees all choose Plan F. Then Plan H's rate will be equal to its expected cost for healthy employees, which from Table 1 is $100. Plan F's rate will equal its expected cost for unhealthy employees, which is $140. This gives Plan H a rate advantage of $40. Thus, selection of Plan H by healthy employees can give Plan H a rate advantage despite Plan H's overall cost disadvantage.

The price that employees pay for a health plan is usually not the plan's full rate; rather it is the employee's share of the contribution. If the benefits manager passively sets equal employer contributions for both health plans, then Plan H's rate advantage will translate into an equal price advantage for employees (see Table 2). The employer contribution for both plans is $80. The remaining employee contributions are $20 for Plan H and $60 for Plan F. Because the employer contribution is the same for both plans, Plan H's price advantage to employees is the same as its rate advantage, $40.

We assumed healthy employees chose Plan H to illustrate how risk selection can create an artificial price advantage. Plan H's price advantage now justifies that assumption: healthy employees in our example will indeed choose Plan H because it has the lower price. Despite Plan H's price advantage, unhealthy employees will choose Plan F because of their strong attachment to it.

The $40 discrepancy between Plan H's price and cost advantages sends a misleading economic signal to employees: Plan H appears less costly than it actually is. This raises the employer's costs. The employer could lower costs by $20 per healthy employee by moving those employees to Plan F while they continue to pay the Plan H employee contribution. The employees would be no worse off if the employer did this. Thus using the misleading prices in Table 2 raises the cost to the employer of providing a given level of employee satisfaction.

Table 3. Group Rating by Class

Employee Class	*Plan Rates*		*Plan Contributions*				*Plan H Price Advantage*
			Employer		*Employee*		
	H	*F*	*H*	*F*	*H*	*F*	
Healthy	100	80	60	60	40	20	-20
Unhealthy	180	140	80	80	100	60	-40

Active Benefit Management: Group Rating by Class

The benefit manager can minimize the employer's costs by setting prices for employees that accurately reflect the costs of their decisions. The conceptually simplest method for doing this is Group Rating by Class (GRC) (Enthoven, 1987) . Under the right conditions, GRC can be approximated by risk adjustment of employer contributions.

Under GRC, employees are divided into risk classes based on characteristics related to their health care costs. The benefit manager establishes a standardized set of risk classes and requires all participating health plans to quote a rate for each class. This enables comparison of rates across plans holding risk constant. The benefit manager fixes an employer contribution for each risk class independently of the health plans. The employee contribution for a plan is the difference between the plan rate and the employer contribution for the employee's risk class (see Table 3).

The last column in Table 3 shows the price (dis)advantages of Plan H for the different risk classes; these equal the cost advantages of Plan H shown in Table 1. Thus, the prices that employees pay reflect the costs to the employer, which is what we mean to accomplish with GRC.

When prices reflect costs, employees receive accurate economic signals and make sound choices. The employer's health care costs are kept to a minimum for a given level of employee satisfaction. In Table 3 the employer contribution for healthy employees is $60, as compared to $80 in Table 2. The employer contribution for unhealthy employees remains the same. Hence the employer spends less when prices are set accurately. Unhealthy employees choose Plan F and pay $60 as they did before. Healthy employees will now choose Plan F as it has a lower price and pay $20 as they did before.

The reasons for the differences in costs between health plans do not matter for the benefit manager's pricing problem as long as employees are aware of these reasons and as long as risk differences can be partitioned out. An alternative statement of a benefit manager's goal is to provide employees with maximum satisfaction for a given cost to the employer. Assuming employees have good information on health plans, the simplest way to maximize employee satisfaction is to let employees evaluate and choose health plans for themselves. To induce employees to make economically sound decisions (from the employer's point of view), they need to face the true costs to the employer of their decisions. Thus, the benefit manager should set prices for employees that accurately reflect the employer's costs and then let employees choose health plans for themselves.

Implicit in the above argument is the key assumption that the cost difference between health plans quoted for a risk class applies accurately and uniformly to each employee within the class. In our evaluation of pricing methods, we will find that the cost differences between health plans are probably distorted by selection effects within risk classes and thus are not accurate.

For health plans, GRC may seem similar to traditional Community Rating by Class (CRC), but there are important differences. Under CRC, health plans use a cost schedule to determine a single rate for an employer. Under GRC, health plans quote an entire rate schedule to an employer. Under CRC, the same cost schedule is used for every employer. Under GRC, different rate schedules may be quoted to different employers. The rate schedule for an employer can and should reflect that employer's cost experience so that the prices that employees pay reflect the employer's costs.

Though conceptually simple, GRC raises several issues. First, it requires a new rating method that is costly to implement. Federally qualified HMOs could not implement GRC without an amendment to the HMO Act. Second, GRC would increase employers' administrative costs, requiring them to keep track of employees' risk classes and prices. Third, GRC raises equity issues, as employers must decide how to set employer contributions by risk class. Enthoven (1988) provides a thorough discussion of these issues.

Risk Adjustment of Employer Contributions

GRC requires change and raises issues. An alternative requiring less change is to keep traditional methods of setting prices but to correct the prices for risk-selection effects by adjusting employer contributions. Risk adjustment of employer contributions can approximate GRC under the right conditions. The limitation of risk adjustment is that, as with traditional pricing methods, one set of health plan prices is used for different classes of employees.

Table 4 illustrates risk adjustment of employer contributions. Using experience rating, Plan H has a rate advantage over Plan F because of risk selection. If the employer makes equal contributions for the two plans, Plan H's rate advantage will translate into a price advantage. In Table 4, the risk-selection effect on prices is offset by setting a lower employer contribution for Plan H than for Plan F, raising the price for the employee of Plan H over

Table 4. Risk Adjustment of Employer Contributions

Plan Rates		Plan Contributions: Employer		Plan Contributions: Employee		Plan H Price Advantage
H	*F*	*H*	*F*	*H*	*F*	
100	110	30	70	70	40	-30

Plan F. Plan H now has a price disadvantage that reflects its average cost disadvantage in Table 1.

The calculation of the health plan rates in Table 4 requires explanation. Under experience rating, a health plan's rate depends on the expected costs of the employees who enroll in the plan. Thus projecting a plan's rate after risk adjustment requires projecting the plan's enrollment by risk class after risk adjustment. In Table 4, we assume that there are equal numbers of healthy and unhealthy employees and that they all enroll in Plan F after risk adjustment. Plan F's rate of $110 is thus the average of the expected costs from Table 1 of $80 for healthy employees and $140 for unhealthy employees.

We do not need to delve into exactly how employer contributions might be calculated, but the goal should be to approximate the prices of GRC. One way to determine employer contributions is to fix a desired total employer contribution for all employees and then set the employer contributions by plan so that the price difference between health plans equals the average cost difference between the plans, as in Table 4. There the price difference between the health plans is set at -$30, which is the average of the cost differences in Table 1 (and Table 3). The level of the employer contributions is set so that the average contribution is the same as in Table 3. Given that all employees will choose Plan F, the employer contribution will be $70 per employee.

However risk adjustment is done, two key requirements must be satisfied before it can work well for the employer. First, as with GRC, cost differences between health plans should be accurate, and thus uniform, for all employees *within* a risk class. Second, the cost differences between health plans should also be uniform across risk classes because all employees across the risk classes will face the same set of prices. In our evaluation of risk adjustment, we will find that the cost differences between health plans are significantly nonuniform both within and across risk classes.

We justified moving to GRC by showing that the employer's costs could be reduced without making any employee worse off. This will not automatically be so under either GRC or risk adjustment of employer contributions: some employees may be worse off unless the employer takes special steps to compensate them. In Table 4, healthy employees will choose Plan F because the $40 cost is less than Plan H. This is more than they paid in Table 2 before risk adjustment, so healthy employees are now worse off. Unhealthy employees are also paying $40 for Plan F, but this is less than before, so they are better off. The employer could use the gains of the unhealthy employees to offset the losses of the healthy ones via a transfer of $20 from the employees who were in Plan F to the employees who were in Plan H.

In general, the employer can ensure that neither it nor its employees are worse off after a change to GRC or risk adjustment if it gives each employee enough money to purchase the health plan they chose before the change. Although no employees will be worse off with this approach, some will be better off—those who switch plans. The employer will not be worse off providing prices after the change accurately reflect costs.

EVALUATION OF RISK ADJUSTMENT

The key requirements for risk adjustment of employer contributions to work well are that cost differences between health plans should be accurate and uniform both within and across risk classes. Here we will compare demographic cost factors developed by Kaiser Permanente (KP) with similar factors for indemnity insurers developed by Tillinghast. These cost factors do not meet risk adjustment's key requirements. Moreover, GRC using these cost factors would not be appropriate without modifications.

Comparison of Costs by Age Class

Table 5 compares expected costs by employee age class for families in KP and in Tillinghast's sample of indemnity insurers. The costs are for families of male employees with two or more dependents. With these cost factors, the age and sex of the employee are used as a proxy for the health status of the family. The costs are in dollars per month and include maternity costs.

The expected costs for KP were derived from the coefficients of the basic actuarial cost model given in Hayes (1991). The KP model uses a traditional three-step classification of families as having one, two, or three-plus members. We used the coefficients for step-three families. We aggregated these coefficients into the age categories used here and scaled them so that the resulting average costs roughly produce the rates that KP charged a particular large employer in 1990.

The expected costs for indemnity insurers were derived from demographic cost factors and average costs given in Tillinghast (1990). Tillinghast gives separate maternity and non-maternity factors by employee age for employees, spouses, and children. We weighted these factors by average costs and summed them to form expected costs for families of male employees by age.[2] The cost factors represent a combination of the claims experience of many large national

Table 5. Expected Costs by Health Plan
Families with Three or More Members

Employee Age	*Plan Costs*		*KP Cost Advantage*
	KP	*Indemnity*	
0-29	400	344	-56
30-39	344	394	50
40-49	327	436	109
50-59	369	503	134

indemnity insurers and of age-specific rates charged by those insurers (for example, for small groups rated by age). The costs are for standard indemnity coverage (typically, a $150-$200 deductible, 20% coinsurance rate, and $1,500 stop-loss limit).

The expected costs in Table 5 represent those of a sample employer considering risk adjustment. Because of their derivation, these costs are only illustrative. They are derived from actual data and appear to reflect typical KP and indemnity insurance rates, but they are not necessarily representative in any formal sense.

The salient feature of Table 5 is a marked difference between KP and the indemnity insurers in the pattern of costs by age. For KP, young families are the most costly, while for the indemnity insurers they are the least costly. Table 5 shows KP with a $56 cost disadvantage for younger families, but with a $134 cost advantage for older families.

We cannot say at present why KP and the indemnity insurers have such different patterns of costs by age because we do not have utilization data for the indemnity insurers. KP's high costs for young families are concentrated around maternity and child care. Table 6 gives Tillinghast-style cost factors for female spouses and children by health plan. The KP cost factors initially decline with employee age, while the indemnity insurer factors initially increase with age. Factors for male employees individually are not shown, but they are very similar for the two plans and increase with age.

Implications for Risk Adjustment

The nonuniform cost differences across age classes violate a key requirement for effective risk adjustment of employer contributions. Charging all families the same prices for health plans, as risk adjustment with these expected costs would do, would send the same economic signal about costs to both young and old families. This would not be appropriate because KP does not have a uniform cost advantage across families.

Table 6. Age Factors by Health Plan

Employee Age	*Female Spouse*		*Children*	
	KP	*Indemnity*	*KP*	*Indemnity*
0-29	1.00	1.00	1.00	1.00
30-39	.77	1.07	.79	1.22
40-49	.67	1.16	.66	1.27
50-59	.82	1.50	.54	.94

An alternative to risk adjustment of employer contributions is GRC. But whether GRC based on these expected costs is appropriate depends on the reasons for the different patterns of costs by age across health plans. There are several possible reasons for these differences. One may be differences in the way the plans share costs with families. For example, young families with indemnity insurance may pay a higher proportion of their total health care costs through deductibles and coinsurance payments than older families. This may lead to a steeper age profile of costs for indemnity insurers than for KP, where cost sharing with employees is not as significant a factor. Another reason for the different patterns may be differences in medical practice. For example, KP may provide more preventive care for children, such as routine physical examinations, and KP's low cost sharing may encourage this.

If these are the only reasons for the different patterns of costs between health plans, then GRC based on these costs is appropriate. As shown previously, differences in benefits, cost sharing, and medical practice do not affect the benefit manager's pricing problem as long as employees are aware of these differences.

Another key requirement for GRC, that the cost differences between health plans apply accurately to employees within risk classes, is probably not satisfied. The cost difference between KP and the indemnity insurers for young families may be inaccurate because of selection effects. KP may have higher costs of child care within the class of young families because it attracts young families with an above-average number of children and thus an above-average expected cost. KP's low cost-sharing may contribute to this effect. This problem can be corrected simply by eliminating the traditional three-step classification of families and substituting family size as a risk factor in GRC.

KP's high costs of maternity care for young families suggests a larger problem: the switching of plans by employees in anticipation of future medical needs. KP may attract young families expecting to use maternity services in the future, possibly because of KP's low cost sharing. This is another example where GRC would need modification because a cost difference between health plans is inaccurate due to a selection effect.

Switching between plans by employees requires the employer's attention to the setting and pricing of benefits. There is no value to the employer in having an employee switch health plans to take advantage of differences in benefits if the plans priced those benefits without knowledge of expected costs anticipated by the employee. Some switching is justifiable. Families, for example, may be attracted to KP's maternity services because of the quality of the services. The theory and practice of setting benefits and prices to best control unjustifiable switching behavior needs further development. Wrightson (1990) summarizes current knowledge on the switching behavior of employees.

CONCLUSIONS

This paper offers a preliminary evaluation of the soundness of two methods for setting health plan prices in a multiple-choice health benefit program. The methods are risk adjustment of employer contributions and group rating by class, both using basic demographic cost factors. We find that risk adjustment of employer contributions using basic demographic factors would not work well as a pricing method because the cost differences between health plans are significantly nonuniform across risk classes. To use group rating by class with these factors probably requires at least two modifications to the method. First, family size should be included as a risk class in place of the traditional three-step classification of families. Second, account must be taken of selection effects arising from switching between health plans by employees in anticipation of their future medical needs. Developing how to best set benefits and prices to control this selection is an area for future theoretical and empirical research.

ACKNOWLEDGMENT

I am grateful to Steve Hayes, who collaborated on the empirical work for this paper and discussed several versions of the paper with me. I thank Douglas Roblin for sharing empirical analysis of his. I thank Rena David, Michael Goodman, Mark Hornbrook, Andrew Karp, Pam Kotler, Bill Kramer, Shirley Langlois, and Marie Miller for very helpful comments on various drafts. I also thank participants of the Kaiser Permanente Conference on Risk Adjustment at Otter Crest and participants of workshops and a seminar sponsored by the Department of Medical Economics and Statistics of Kaiser Permanente, Northern California Region. The views expressed in this paper are mine and not those of Kaiser Permanente.

NOTES

1. Federally qualified HMOs cannot use experience rating under the HMO Act. They can use a form of prospective experience rating called adjusted community rating. See Wrightson (1990).

2. The factors are listed on page I-3 of Tillinghast (1990). The average costs used to weight the factors for employees and spouses were $1,480 for non-maternity and $133 for maternity. The average costs for children were $1,298 for non-maternity and $21 for maternity.

REFERENCES

Enthoven, A.C. (1988). *Theory and Practice of Managed Competition in Health Care Finance.* Professor Dr. F. DeVries Lectures in Economics, (Vol. 9). New York: Elsevier.

Enthoven, A.C. (1990). "Multiple Choice Health Insurance: The Lessons and Challenge to Employers." *Inquiry* 27(Winter):368-375.

Hayes, S. (1991). "Demographic Risk Factors Derived From HMO Data." In M. Hornbrook (Ed.), *Advances in Health Economics and Health Services Research: Vol. 12. Risk-Based Contributions to Private Health Insurance* (pp. 177-196). Greenwich, CT: JAI Press.

Jones, S.B. (1990). "Multiple Choice Health Insurance: The Lessons and Challenge to Private Insurers." Inquiry 27(Summer):161-166.

Tillinghast, Inc. (1990). *1990 Group Medical Insurance Rate Manual.* St. Louis: Tillinghast, Inc.

Wrightson, C.W. (1990). *HMO Rate Setting and Financial Strategy.* Ann Arbor, MI: Health Administration Press.

PART II

DEFINING AND MEASURING RISK

HEALTH PLAN CASE MIX:
DEFINITION, MEASUREMENT, AND USE

Mark C. Hornbrook and Michael J. Goodman

INTRODUCTION

Variations in annual per capita expense among health plans related to enrollee health status and propensity to use medical care can create barriers to access for consumers and inefficiency in health plan markets (Enthoven, 1989). Adversely selected plans, through no fault of their own, face difficult choices among: increasing premiums, which results in further adverse selection; reducing services and benefits, which has similar negative consequences; and spending financial reserves. Fear of a premium-cost spiral leads many health plans to compete by risk skimming, or, at the least, by excluding high-risk individuals or groups (Abraham, 1986). Such practices leave the sickest persons without health insurance or place them in high-risk plans. From a social perspective, this discriminates against lower income high-risk persons and fails to spread risk over the largest possible population base.

Advances in Health Economics and Health Services Research, Vol. 12, pages 111-148.
Copyright © 1991 by JAI Press Inc.
All rights of reproduction in any form reserved.
ISBN: 1-55938-241-4

As a result of recent changes in health care and the health insurance industries, the distribution of the burden of health care expenses is of increasing concern, both to the government and to employers. The Health Care Financing Administration (HCFA), under its risk contracts with health maintenance organizations (HMOs) for Medicare services, wishes to ensure that HMOs are not risk skimming, a practice that creates overpayments to HMOs (Langwell and Hadley, 1986). Employers seek to manipulate their contributions to employees' health care benefits as a means of controlling their exposure to the premium-cost spiral. HMOs, faced with more competitive markets, are moving away from traditional community rating of premiums to risk-adjusted rate-setting schemes. The common theme is minimizing exposure to risk, but myopic pursuit of risk avoidance serves only to increase the proportion of persons without adequate health insurance coverage.

If contributions to health plans—both HMOs and indemnity plans—could be adjusted to account for the fundamental dimensions of health plan output, namely, the permanent health status and use propensity of their enrollees, then the provision of health insurance through private markets could be expanded to reach many persons who would otherwise be denied health insurance coverage. From health plans' perspective, markets would become more stable; from society's perspective, more individuals would be protected from the cost of illness; and from employers' perspective, health plan rates would be more predictable. This requires the development of risk taxonomies or prospective risk-assessment models.

Prospective risk assessment—using information on permanent health status and behavioral and environmental health risk factors in a baseline period to predict efficient use of health services in a future period for a defined population—is complicated by a number of technical problems. Sources of health risk differ among populations in ways that are difficult to measure. Risk-assessment models must predict future diseases and health problems, as well as interactions among comorbidities and underlying health status. A young person with diabetes, for example, will require different treatment than an older diabetic patient with multiple chronic complications; both diabetics will have different health care use than persons with lung cancer. Actuarial models based on age and gender, while simple and easy to understand, exhibit high within-cell heterogeneity and, as a result, are easy for consumers and health plans to defeat.

Voluntary choice of health plan may lead to the enrollment of disproportionate shares of persons with higher- (or lower-) than-average expected expense in a particular health plan; how to quantify the direction and magnitude of such selectivity effects is the subject of this paper. The concepts of health plan output, risk, risk assessment, risk adjustment, selectivity, and selection bias are defined in the first section. A conceptual framework for risk classification is presented in the second section. Sources of risk are hypothesized next as the basis for selecting predictors. The fourth section describes eight different approaches to risk modelling. Criteria for evaluating alternative risk-assessment models are outlined next, followed by methods of validating and constructing prediction models. Applications of risk classifications to other areas of health care management are discussed in the next section. Finally, a number of technical problems in specifying and estimating risk-assessment models are discussed and some directions for future research on risk taxonomies are highlighted.

DEFINITION OF CONCEPTS

Health Plan Output

From the perspective of prepaid health plans, both health maintenance organizations and indemnity insurers, total output has three fundamental dimensions: volume, case mix, and quality. Volume of output is defined as the total number of enrollees in a specified period, that is, total person-months of eligibility. The level and variation of expected use patterns of health plan benefits among enrollees constitute the case mix of health plan output. Health plan case mix is termed "risk" to reflect the stochastic nature of each enrollee's future medical care needs. Different levels of risk represent different health plan outputs and a system of iso-risk groups comprises a classification of the multiple products of health plans. Risk-assessment models quantify the case mix of a defined population on a prospective basis. Quality of health plan output is, ultimately, defined as satisfactory outcomes to eligibility periods, holding risk constant. Structural and process measures of quality, such as treated disease episodes and use of preventive services, constitute intermediate outputs. In this paper, we focus on the conceptualization and measurement of only one of these three output dimensions—health plan case mix or risk.

Risk

"Risk" is defined as the expected value of the distribution of per capita costs of efficiently provided preventive, diagnostic, and therapeutic health care services delivered to a defined group of enrollees for a specific future period. Persons with similar expected values of annual per capita costs next year under an efficient medical care system are termed an "iso-risk grouping." In the insurance literature, the concept of risk usually applies to the variance of a distribution, reflecting the fact that exact predictions for individual members in a population are not possible nor desirable (Newhouse et al., 1989). For the purpose of this paper, however, we mean something different; the definition of risk contains five primitive concepts: (1) utilization; (2) future; (3) probability distribution; (4) efficiency; and (5) group.

Risk relates to real use of health care services. Inflation, differences in input prices, and pricing strategies which give rise to variation in nominal annual per capita medical care expenses, are not included in our concept of risk. Measuring use in dollar terms is useful because it provides a *numeraire* for aggregating dissimilar goods and services. Observed expenses, however, contain price differences and these relate to provider attributes rather than enrollee attributes. We do not want to confound the financial implications of living in areas with differing costs of living with those deriving from variations in the incidence and severity of disease. Our aim is to be able to distinguish moderately ill persons living in large cities from seriously ill persons living in rural areas. If we consider risk from a purely financial perspective, all factors influencing the size and frequency of health care use are melded into a single amorphous concept. Risk, as we are using it here, relates to the nature of health plan output and the resources required to produce that output, not to basic conditions of demand and supply in input and product markets that create price variations.

Risk is a forecast of future use of health care, not an explanation of contemporaneous expense. Forecasting, strictly speaking, requires only correlation between (any arbitrarily selected set of) predictors and future use; thus, an important validity criterion for an *ex ante* model is *ex post* performance—the prediction accuracy. Many reasons may account for poor predictions, some of which are beyond the scope of our concept of risk. Therefore, observed correlation between predictors and future use is not a sufficient validity criterion. Risk models should incorporate the causes of illnesses and injury as well as correlated antecedents. Both correlation and causation, from predictors to future use, are necessary and sufficient conditions for risk. The future time period must be well-defined in health plan contracts, usually a calendar year, although several reasons for truncating this period are recognized (for example, death, loss of employment, divorce).

Risk applies to a probability distribution. The expected value is the moment of the distribution pertinent to risk as we have defined it, but our ability to predict that moment is related to an understanding of the overall shape of the distribution. The fact that health plan enrollment groups are not randomly selected places a greater burden on risk models to account for the factors that give rise to the non-normal distribution of medical care use.

Risk applies to efficient use of medical care—the minimum services necessary to provide acceptable access and quality of care. Risk relates to the efficient cost of producing health care output of specified dimensions—who should have access to care (case mix) and what level of quality should be provided. Measures of risk should incorporate clinically pertinent attributes of patients that affect the satisfactory outcomes of their illness episodes. These include the dimensions of permanent health status related to the future incidence and severity of illness and injury in a population in the specified time period, as well as patients' habits in using (or not using) health services in response to these health problems.

Risk applies to a group, not an individual. We are not attempting to predict each individual's use of health care next year. Indeed, the latter would be antithetical to the efficiency element of risk because the prediction of each person's use would require identifying instances of over-use, under-use, poor quality of care, and access barriers. By pooling, individual differences are assumed to become randomly distributed and, via the law of large numbers, grouped attributes carry prediction potential. The other element of a group is that it is defined on an *ex ante* basis before medical care outcomes are known. This means that the membership of the group cannot be altered on an *ex post* basis after the patterns of use become known. Removal of outliers from a distribution to achieve a more "well-behaved" distribution and, consequently, higher prediction accuracy is not appropriate because they are an intrinsic, consistent feature of the distribution of medical expense.

Risk Assessment

"Risk assessment" or "risk classification" is the determination of the relative risks of subsets of persons within a defined population. For example, when a population is classified by gender, the expected annual use of health care for males can be expressed as a multiple of the expected value for females. A risk coefficient of 1 indicates equal risk in the two groups, while a coefficient less than 1 indicates that men are predicted to be less service-intensive than women.

Risk Adjustment

"Risk adjustment" is decomposing variation in health care utilization into its logical components, assigning each component to the appropriate actor, then modifying payments to health plans to compensate for risk deriving from exogenous (that is, not under the health plan's control) characteristics of enrollees (Hornbrook and Goodman, 1991). Expenses vary for several reasons, including variations in enrollee health status, health plan efficiency, providers' style of practice, and community expectations for medical care. Risk adjustment requires identifying these factors and quantifying their contribution to overall expenses. The responsibility for the costs of treating iatrogenic illness, for example, should be assigned to the providers who caused the illness, or else they receive a "free ride" for their inefficiencies.

Selectivity

"Selectivity" is defined by known systematic patterns of health plan enrollment that create differences in expected annual per capita use (that is, case mix) across health plans and that can be accounted for by factors known after the choice of plan has been made but before the start of the eligibility period (Hornbrook, Bennett, and Greenlick, 1989). Selectivity can be the result of conscious choice processes by consumers, providers, and health plan managers, or it can be the indirect result of other behaviors. Note that we are only concerned with selection effects that are correlated with risk. HMOs, by their nature, have well-defined geographic service areas; residence will discriminate among health plan enrollments in different cities, but this factor may or may not be related to small area variations in permanent health status.

Selection Bias

"Selection bias" is the residual difference in risk across health plans that cannot be accounted for by information available at the time of enrollment (Hornbrook, Bennett, and Greenlick, 1989). Bias arises whenever factors related to both health plan choice and risk are omitted from the risk-classification scheme. Neither selectivity nor enrollees need be viewed as "biased;" we do not "correct" enrollees or their choices. Bias results when risk taxonomies do not account for all of the correlation between risk and choice of health plan. Such model bias derives, at least partly, from asymmetric information—consumers (behave as if they) know more than the risk-adjustment model so that an omitted variable is correlated with risk. Also, we may not be modeling available information as well as possible. With a biased model, even experience rating will be defeated because the prior use coefficients will be incorrect and will not predict accurately for a membership with significant turnover. This is not to say that enrollees in different plans should have equal risk; we want to be able to measure whatever risk differentials may exist across health plans.

MORAL HAZARD AND SELECTION BIAS

Voluntary choice of health plan creates two sources of inefficiency: moral hazard, because risk pooling shelters each actor from the true social opportunity cost of their actions; and, selection bias, because health plan choice systematically discriminates among risk pools and delimits risk sharing (Hornbrook and Goodman, 1991).

Our goal in adjusting for variations in risk is to remove responsibility for expense from one set of actors when the cause of that expense is beyond their control, and transfer the responsibility (or at least part of it) to a more appropriate group. The purely random, exogenous component of expense variation should be spread among the entire risk pool. Measures of risk should not incorporate inefficiency on the part of consumers, providers, or insurers. By measuring exogenous risk, we can reduce incentives to avoid or evade risk by health insurers. By specifying unbiased models for risk assessment, we can improve the efficiency of health plan pricing by reducing under- and over-payments.

We start from the premise that total variation in annual per capita health care expense must be decomposed; expenses deriving from permanent attributes of enrollees that are not controllable by the individual in the short run are the target of risk adjustment.

SOURCES OF RISK

Permanent health status and propensity to use health services are postulated to be the only enrollee characteristics that should be incorporated in an (efficient) risk-assessment model. Our goal is to identify variables related to physical and mental health that predict efficient utilization of health care in the future. Acute transitory variations in health status are not likely to be relevant because, by definition, they do not persist long enough to affect future use of health services. Recurrence of acute diseases, however, may signal a persisting reduction in health status, or just an unfortunate random occurrence. While it is relatively straightforward to show that current treatment is related to an ongoing illness, interposing a time delay creates a number of theoretical and practical difficulties. In this section, we provide the theoretical rationale for permanent health status and use propensity as risk factors.

Permanent Health Status

One dimension of permanent health status is the existence of chronic conditions. Chronic disease refers to a permanent or ongoing condition that changes or reduces the functioning of body systems (Hornbrook, Hurtado, and Johnson, 1985). This is contrasted with acute disease, or a single episode, after which the patient returns to a health level unchanged from the pre-disease period. Chronic conditions increase expected expense both through the direct effect of treating the disease and the comorbid effects on other body systems which, in turn, require treatment. For example, in addition to the cost of monitoring and treating diabetes, a diabetic may have related cardiovascular problems that need treatment. Since chronic disease occurs, by definition, in both the baseline and subsequent periods, retrospective measurement of this risk component is possible. That is, health plans could receive a contemporaneous adjustment for newly discovered cases of chronic disease. This presumes that the diagnosis is neither preventable nor curable and its severity is relatively unchangeable by known treatments over the relevant time period (two to three years).

Residual effects of acute disease may result in increased use of medical services. An acute disease requiring surgery may require significant follow-up treatment. Similarly, a disease requiring prolonged convalescence may require physical therapy or other treatment. An individual who has had an episode of acute disease may be at increased risk for recurrence of that or related disease. Some diseases produce immunity from future episodes while others weaken the immune system so that future infection is more likely.

Individuals differ in their levels of immunity. Populations exposed to many viruses or bacteria may have initially higher levels of acute disease but, as their immune systems adapt to the new strains, become healthier. Generally, older persons have weaker immune systems than younger persons.

Individuals face different health risks from their environments. A teacher is exposed to a wide variety of relatively benign, infectious diseases in the school environment as different viral agents move through the school-age population. An individual working in a hospital is similarly more likely to be exposed to infectious agents. Individuals engaged in high-risk occupations may be more subject to traumatic accidents. Athletes, although generally healthier, may be subject to more traumatic injuries such as torn ligaments and fractures. Persons living in areas with high levels of contaminants in their water or air may have a higher incidence of cancer and respiratory conditions than persons who have clean air and water.

Aging is related to the deterioration of various body systems. The ability to resist a virus or recover from strenuous activity declines. Age is also correlated with degenerative diseases such as cataracts and arthritis.

Frequent contact with the medical care system engenders greater possibility of iatrogenesis—adverse consequences that would not occur except for the contact with the system. The most frequent example is adverse drug reactions. More prescriptions, with more contacts with the system, are likely to result in a higher probability of adverse drug reactions.

Finally, those who engage in unhealthy activities are at greater risk of higher expense. Smokers are likely to have more respiratory problems. Excessive consumption of drugs, such as alcohol or cocaine, or poor nutritional habits are likely to degrade general health status, leading to additional expense. Reductions in permanent health status relate to ongoing deficiencies in physiologic systems and homeostatic mechanisms, as well as current behaviors that increase the likelihood of contact with etiologic agents.

Use Propensity

Attitudes and knowledge lead to differences in the propensity to seek medical care. Someone who seeks a significant quantity of preventive services is different from someone who must be critically ill before seeking medical services, other things being the same.

Some individuals demand medical care at the first perception of a symptom, while others seek care only when their functional abilities have been severely impaired. Thus, a headache may signal a potential brain tumor to one individual and a minor annoyance of daily life to another. Use propensity contributes to the variation in expected medical care for a given distribution of illness in a population. From the perspective of a health plan, epidemiology and use propensity are difficult to sort out while still maintaining ease of access for enrollees; risk-adjustment models will likely include both factors until we have developed better techniques to control access.

Rossiter (1989) has suggested that individuals' propensity to consume medical care should be omitted from a risk-assessment model because it is controllable by providers. He contends, for example, that prior use reflects the providers' practice style and risk preferences rather than those of patients. Moreover, an efficient health care system would focus on pure health risk in determining access to health care and ignore individual habits and hypochondriasis; individuals are presumed to need medical care because they are actually sick, not simply because they are worried they might be sick. To stimulate health plans to develop more effective access triage, use propensity could be omitted from a risk-adjustment scheme.

A major drawback to omitting use propensity from a risk-assessment/adjustment scheme is that it is likely to raise barriers to access for a subset of the population. If health plans dump hypochondriacs, these persons would become medically uninsurable. Our goal is to improve the performance of competitive health insurance markets so that the overall costs of care will be lowered and access increased. Incorporating use propensity as a risk adjuster will help protect individuals who are, perhaps, overly concerned with their health, but who, if denied access, may manifest more severe mental and psychosomatic conditions requiring even more treatment.[1] Moreover, the possibility always exists that a seemingly well person really is sick. We start with the assumption that, until proven otherwise, early and appropriate access is more cost-effective than crisis management of illness and injury.

RISK-CLASSIFICATION SCHEMES

A number of different approaches to operationalizing health/propensity risk groups have been suggested. All are proxy measures with varying degrees of validity, reliability, and administrative feasibility. In this section, eight different approaches are highlighted. These approaches can be classified on two dimensions—source of data and general class of variables being measured—as summarized in Table 1. We will not discuss every logical possibility shown in the table; rather, we will focus on specific classes of risk predictors—demographics, inpatient morbidities, ambulatory morbidities, drug orders, prior use, major procedures, self-reported health status, and mortality. We expect that a fully developed risk-assessment model may turn out to be eclectic, capitalizing on useful predictors from each approach. Future research will also need to address the implications for validity, reliability, and the cost of collecting a given risk factor from various sources.

Demographics

The most straightforward approach is to employ the readily available demographic characteristics of enrollees. Sociodemographic factors are known to be correlated with future health status, as well as with attitudes and habits regarding use of the medical care system (McClure, 1984; Lubitz, 1987). Examples of these variables include age, gender, subscriber unit type and size (single person, subscriber plus dependent, subscriber plus two or more dependents), marital status, and education. Other factors that may prove useful are length of time in health plan, previous health plan enrollment behavior, social security disability status, employment status, occupation, and industry. These variables demonstrate a high degree of stability from year to year, increasing their reliability and ease of measurement. Some of these variables are typically available in employers' personnel systems.

Age and gender are useful proxy measures of health risk because they are correlated with social and epidemiologic risk factors—pregnancy and childbirth, developmental stage, deterioration of body systems, and ability to engage in strenuous athletic activities. Social structural factors are also indicators of risk—the protective effect of marriage on male health, the influence of education on preferences for use of medical care and for health promotion activities, and the shared exposure to infectious or traumatic etiologic agents in the family environment.

The principal drawback to these predictors is that they are not direct measures of health status, so the heterogeneity of expense within each demographic class is high. Pure demographic predictors can produce an accurate mean but their level of discrimination is poor—the prediction distribution is severely truncated. Additionally, separation among the risk classes will be poor.

Functional form is part of the specification of a risk-assessment model. Age can be entered as a linear variable, or in a number of transformed ways. As a linear factor, an assumption is made that the difference in expected annual

Table 1. Approaches to Classifying Health/Propensity Risks

Source of Risk Data	*Type of Risk Measure*
Individual	Demographics
	Self-reported health status
	Behavioral health risks
	Attitudes about illness and medicine
	Self-reported prior use
Medical records	Prior use
Provider information	Inpatient morbidities
Systems, and claims data	Outpatient morbidities
	Drug orders
	Prior medical and surgical procedures
	Mortality
Employer/Government	Demographics
	Mortality

expense is the same between a 4- and a 5-year-old child as between a 44- and 45-year-old adult. Examination of the distribution of medical expenses by age, however, reveals a U-shaped, rather than linear, function. When gender is treated as an additive factor, the expense difference for males and females is assumed to be the same for all age groups. This does not hold in reality; women use more health services in their child-bearing years than men, and less in old age.

The solution used in many studies is to define discrete age and gender categories, so that the functional form of the risk-assessment model is not restricted to be linear and additive. A large number of categories presents difficulties because, as the number of classes grows, each class becomes smaller, creating instability in the coefficients.

Demographic factors carry face validity and are relatively straightforward to collect, often contained in existing automated data systems related to employment and benefits. For these reasons, they are the first stage in the development of risk-assessment models.

Inpatient Morbidities

Under an age-sex adjusted model, all 55-year-old men are assumed to have the same risk; we know this to be false. More direct measures of health status are desirable. One approach is to use disease treated in a hospital during a baseline period as a risk predictor. Serious chronic diseases requiring hospital treatment, such as asthma, diabetes, cancer, chronic obstructive pulmonary disease, or congestive heart failure, are expected to persist over time and, thus, represent higher risk. Acute disease may recur or become chronic, so that persons with at least one episode of a disease are at higher risk than those with none. Serious acute diseases may have residual physiological and/or psychological effects that lead to additional expense long after an inpatient episode. The closer an inpatient stay to the start of the eligibility period, the more likely the tail of the illness episode will be included in the risk period. Iatrogenic effects of hospital stays may create higher expense relative to non-hospitalized persons. Hospitalization may be a general indicator of poor health—for example, frailty, compromised immunity, or injury proneness, especially for older persons (Ellis and Ash, 1988, 1989). Persons whose health has deteriorated to the point of requiring hospitalization may not, on average, be expected to recover to the same level of health as persons not hospitalized. Ellis and Ash have proposed that elevated risk status be granted to older persons as soon as they are discharged from the hospital for qualifying reasons (Ellis and Ash, 1989).

One factor working in the opposite direction to these effects is the clustering of use. To the extent that a hospital stay represented a successful cure or exhausted the efficacy of medical intervention, utilization in the succeeding period would be expected to be lower than average. This effect would mute the influence of the previous hypothesized effects.

Prospective payment, accreditation regulations, and automated billing systems mean that inpatient diagnostic data are available for nearly all patients. This approach has been suggested for the Medicare population in the work on Diagnostic Cost Groups (DCGs) (Ellis and Ash, 1988, 1989). Another approach is to ask individuals to list their diagnoses for any prior hospitalization in the past two years. This data will be much less detailed than inpatient discharge abstracts, but the DCGs' level of aggregation is so great that self-reported hospital morbidities may perform almost as well.

Three major weaknesses of the inpatient morbidity approach can be identified. First, a modest proportion of individuals are admitted to the hospital in any given year, so that the majority of a population is grouped in a non-hospitalized risk group differentiated by demographics only; this comprises more than 90% of the population (National Center for Health Statistics, 1990, Table 69). As an example of an inpatient morbidity scheme, the DCGs classify less than 10% of persons age 65-years and over (Ellis and Ash, 1988; Hornbrook, Bennett, and Greenlick, 1991a). In nonaged populations, the concentration of hospital admissions is even more pronounced, and the bulk of admissions is associated with obstetric activities.

Second, assessment of risk via this approach is sensitive to physician practice patterns. This is particularly relevant to assessing the relative risk of fee-for-service indemnity health plans versus HMOs, particularly prepaid group practice plans. A hospital-conserving style of practice would confound measurement of risk under this approach, causing HMO memberships to appear to be healthier than indemnity memberships, on average (Hornbrook and Berki, 1985). Ellis and Ash (1988, 1989) have attempted to address this problem by limiting the risk measures to non-discretionary diagnoses—those conditions hypothesized to be less sensitive to economic incentives and organizational arrangements in hospital use.

Another drawback of a diagnostic approach is the sheer complexity of disease taxonomy. *The International Classification of Diseases,* 9th Edition, *Clinical Modification* (ICD-9-CM) contains thousands of disease codes. This level of detail is not supported by the empirical work on expense prediction. Much more aggregative classification schemes are required. The basis for such aggregation is not obvious and more research is required. The DCGs represent a useful initial foray into this area. Comorbidities and severity variations pose considerable challenge to risk-adjustment research.

Outpatient Morbidities

The next logical step is to obtain information on diseases treated in the ambulatory setting. Treated outpatient morbidities are expected to predict expense for the same reasons specified for inpatient morbidities. They offer the potential to significantly reduce the problem of concentration observed in models using only inpatient morbidities, as well as the bias introduced by different styles of using the hospital. The ambulatory morbidity approach detects presence of a disease, whether treated in the inpatient or outpatient settings, which provides more accurate comparisons of risk between HMO and FFS health plans.

In addition to chronic disease (Howland et al. 1987), and acute disease with its residual effects, iatrogenic effects, recurrent episodes, and sentinel events, ambulatory morbidities can provide information on use of preventive care in the baseline period, which may provide direct protection from disease, as with an immunization, or it may indicate good health protective behavior. Similarly, ambulatory morbidity data can be used to indicate a propensity to seek treatment for relatively benign conditions (the worried well). Risk predictions from ambulatory morbidity variables may be improved by classifying patients according to their prognosis: stable, deteriorating, or improving.

In addition to diagnoses, the ambulatory morbidity approach may include measures of illness derived from clinical assessments (for example, blood pressure and temperature) and from laboratory analyses (for example, blood chemistries and urinalysis) (Newhouse et al., 1989). The advantage of these indicators as predictors of disease is that they are objective, do not rely on clinical judgment, and may detect pre-clinical disease. Some biochemical markers may serve as sentinel events of a number of diseases and, thus, may be efficient predictors of future medical care use. The primary deficiency of these types of measures is that they are not typically available in automated form for linkage to expense data.

Drug Orders

Diagnoses may be listed on patients' medical records but have little pertinence to overall intensity of resource use. Obesity and previous history of heart disease are two examples. Some indicator is needed of the amount of attention providers devote to each morbidity and, therefore, the likelihood that future treatment decisions will be influenced by each disease.

Prescribed drugs can provide information about clinical pertinence and severity of treated conditions (Hornbrook, Goodman, and Bennett, 1991). Diseases that receive no treatment or very low intensity treatment are hypothesized to have less effect on future use than diseases severe enough to require therapy. Drug use, when measured by therapeutic class or specific product, can also be used as a proxy measure of treated morbidities when diagnostic data are not available. (Analogously, procedures could be examined, instead of, or in addition to, diagnoses, as we will show below.) Dosage intensity may also be a rough proxy measure of disease severity. Finally, drugs may create iatrogenic disease, so that the greater the number of drugs an individual consumes, the more likely adverse effects are to occur.

Because many individuals do not have prepaid drug benefits, information on drug use is not readily available. With increased automation of pharmacy information systems, drug use data may become more feasible as a risk predictor. Another problem caused by the rather uneven provision of drug benefits is that groups with drug coverage may appear to be sicker than groups without coverage simply because lower out-of-pocket price increases the quantity demanded, other things the same.

Drawbacks to drug use data include the problem that drugs can be prescribed inappropriately, which incorporates inefficiency bias into the risk-adjustment process. Also, a risk-adjustment model based on drugs may contain incentives for health plans to rely more heavily on those drugs that most inflate future revenues.

Prior Use

Prior use predicts future expense for older populations more accurately than for working populations (Hornbrook, Bennett, and Greenlick, 1991b; Hornbrook, Goodman, and Bennett, 1991). Prior use reflects both appropriate and inappropriate components of risk. Persons with established habits of access to medical care enable better prediction of future expense. Persons with chronic conditions requiring continuing care and persons with severe acute conditions that have residual care requirements will be captured with prior use factors (Beebe, Lubitz, and Eggers, 1985; Lubitz, Beebe, and Riley, 1985; Gruenberg, Tompkins, and Porell, 1989). High levels of prior use may, as indicated previously, carry a iatrogenesis risk.

The weaknesses of prior use predictors are three-fold: first, they capitalize on provider prescribing habits, which may be independent of patient health status and which incorporate inefficient treatment patterns (Newhouse, 1986); second, in HMOs, where the insurer is the provider, prior use provides an incentive to increase the intensity of treatment in order to raise future payments; third, efficient health plans appear to have lower risks than inefficient plans. To address the problem of provider discretion, Anderson et al. (1986) and Ellis and Ash (1988, 1989) developed models that focus on non-discretionary prior use.

Major Procedures

Surgical and invasive diagnostic procedures are a form of prior use, but because they do not represent the entire constellation of use, they may alleviate some of the drawbacks of crude prior use. The risk hypothesis for a procedure classification system is that certain procedures may be performed only in response to specific clinical indications that are highly correlated with subsequent disease. For example, persons who are biopsied would be expected to have a higher probability of cancer than the persons who are not biopsied.

Another risk hypothesis is that certain procedures are in themselves risky, so that even without the presence of an underlying condition, persons receiving these procedures have a higher than expected level of use to care for adverse effects of the procedures.

Ash (1990) has examined use of inpatient procedures in refining the DCGs, but no work has been done on ambulatory procedures. Procedural data are widely available for both inpatient and ambulatory episodes. It remains for future research to determine how much predictive power such data add to inpatient and ambulatory morbidity risk-assessment models.

Self-reported Health Status

All of the previous morbidity and prior use models require an individual to come into contact with the medical care system in order to obtain the information required to assign a risk class. Thus, nonusers are still lumped into a demographically defined grouping with considerable heterogeneity. Social survey techniques offer a means of obtaining the data required to classify users and non-users (Thomas and Lichtenstein, 1986; Whitmore et al., 1989). Self-reported health status is hypothesized to serve as a valid and useful risk-adjustment factor because it measures underlying health status and propensity to use medical care. This makes three assumptions concerning individual respondents: first, that individuals can validly and reliably report their chronic illnesses, especially those that have been diagnosed; second, that they are aware of the relative severity and stability of each problem; and third, that they are aware of and will report prodromal conditions. Individuals can report functional and structural deficits that require ongoing medical intervention and support, such as maintenance of prostheses, implants, and transplants. Respondents are aware of their own attitudes regarding health care, and their health care utilization habits and propensities. Individuals can report on plans and expectations regarding future use of health care. In particular, they may be aware of prodromal conditions for which they have not yet sought care, which provides risk data unavailable from even the best clinical data systems.

Individual attitudes toward illness and health care utilization are complex and heterogeneous in most population groups and result from the interplay between expectation and experience. These attitudes are likely to be correlated with choice of health plan and rates of use. In managed care systems, providers may limit access in ways that change attitudes about appropriate response to illness. This may provide the desired effect of making consumers more efficient in their utilization decisions or it may induce them to switch to a new health plan. Switchers may then change their attitudes upon encountering the new plan or they may represent persons whose attitudes are more volatile than those staying with their same health plan. Attitudes reported in social surveys, like patterns of use, should be treated as system-specific and subject to change with changes in delivery system.

Self-reported health status surveys can also assess behavioral risk factors—for example, smoking, drinking, athletic activities, sexual practices—as well as psychological symptoms and conditions such as depression and anxiety. Given the basic problem of selection bias, that is, the correlation between risk and choice, surveying the persons who make the health plan selection decision would appear to offer potential advances in prediction performance of risk-assessment models.

Self-reported health status has drawbacks. First, individuals may not understand the implications of their health problems for future needs for medical care. For example, they may mistakenly assume a serious condition is benign, or they may perceive a self-limiting or easily cured condition to be very serious. Subjective judgment may, therefore, misread the true nature of conditions. Second, survey research always involves errors of measurement because of differences in respondents' interpretations of items, social response bias, and failure of recall. Third, if self-reported health status is perceived as leading to an economic benefit or penalty via the premium structure or plan choice, individuals have an incentive to "game" the system. Fourth, if health status surveys are administered by personal interviews, the interviewers should not be associated with the health plan because they have a direct interest in gaming the risk-assessment model.

Self-reported health surveys can assess prior use, current illnesses (or diagnoses), and health history. Individuals are able to recall fewer details of prior use than are available in medical records and claims data systems (Harlow and Linet, 1989). The exact dates of a prior hospital episode are often recalled erroneously, as are the number of physician office visits. Individuals can report on their own current health problems, but these may have only broad congruence with how medical providers view them; for example, "breathing problems" may be reported for asthma, COPD, or congestive heart failure. A condition may be reported by its functional impact rather than its diagnosis.

Self-reported health status is administratively feasible because individuals can be surveyed via mail or telephone procedures in a reasonably cost-efficient fashion to obtain pertinent risk information. Obtaining information on children and cognitively impaired adults requires that suitable procedures be developed to identify surrogate respondents, for example, parents and caregivers.

Mortality

For an aged population, Manton and Tolley (1988) have proposed cost-weighted mortality rates as a risk model. This approach is based on the fact that a large portion of Medicare expenses are consumed by terminal illness episodes. Manton suggests that cause-specific death rates, weighted by the average cost of caring for the terminal episode of the given disease, can be used to predict risk for a defined demographic group. The basic hypothesis is that the ecological process that created the observed death experience for a given cohort is likely to persist within the one- to two-year prediction period. Thus, while the individuals who die contribute nothing to future expense, persons aging into a demographic cell next year can be expected to have the same death (and expense) experience as the previous cohort.

For nonaged populations, deaths are much less frequent events relative to an aged population. This model is likely to experience considerable instability unless very large groups are used. More importantly, this model presents severe challenges to acceptability because it appears to contain incentives for health plans to increase mortality rates in pursuit of higher revenues next year. Many observers are concerned that this model would lead to significant rationing of services to critically and terminally ill persons.

Eclectic Models

None of the above approaches has to be used in isolation. Different sets of risk factors may capture different components of risk. Inpatient morbidities, ambulatory morbidities, self-reported health status, and demographics may be combined to improve prediction power. In eclectic models using many different types of predictors, multicollinearity will become an increasingly large problem as several variables measure the same underlying dimension.

PERFORMANCE CRITERIA FOR RISK-ASSESSMENT MODELS

How do we know whether a particular risk-assessment model is useful? We define five theoretical criteria for judging among risk-assessment models: validity, bias, stability, administrative feasibility, and political acceptability. These criteria represent both qualitative and quantitative dimensions of performance.

Validity

Validity is a measure's ability to measure what it is supposed to measure. How appropriate are the inferences made from the measures used (Ghiselli, Campbell, and Zedeck, 1981)? A risk-assessment model should accurately predict future medical care expense based on the health status and use propensity characteristics of enrollees. The coefficients assessing the relative risk of disease, frailty, and injury should reflect the most efficient patterns of care. They should not be distorted by access problems, poor quality of care, unnecessarily elaborate care, or unproductive providers and health plans. Risk coefficients represent shadow prices, or opportunity costs of treating one group of enrollees relative to a standard comparison group (such as the overall average cost for the population). Thus, validity derives from the types of variables included as predictors and the nature of the data set employed to compute the risk coefficients.

A risk-assessment model predicting the risk for individuals in different health plans should incorporate only enrollee characteristics; it should exclude insurer and provider characteristics under the control of the health plan. If risk adjustment is used to set premiums prospectively, predictors must be based on information available prior to the start of the risk period.

Incorporating any information on enrollee characteristics obtained after the eligibility date may move the payment system toward cost reimbursement by confounding risk with the quality of care provided during the first phase of the enrollment period while enrollee characteristics are being assessed. For example, if health status is assessed via a survey administered to all enrollees during their first quarter of eligibility, any health problem arising from lack of access to or poor quality of care during that period may be converted into higher risk, which, in turn, garners higher payment.

To be valid, retrospective risk measures should focus on permanent health status factors that are not likely to have been created or modified by post-enrollment utilization patterns. For example, one might argue that a health plan should receive an adjustment for the number of AIDS cases diagnosed among the enrollees during the current year. This would provide an incentive to perform outreach and HIV screening tests for groups at risk for AIDS and would remove some of the incentive to select against HIV risk groups in marketing and enrollment efforts. The argument is two-fold: first, we assume the incidence of AIDS is not affected by health plan actions; and second, plans should not be forced to underwrite the costs of treating new cases of AIDS for the remainder of a rate-setting period until these cases can be counted in a risk-adjustment model. In sum, retrospective risk assessment can be useful if specified carefully.

Bias

The policy goal for risk adjustment is to establish the correct relative payment for a defined group of enrollees. To predict perfectly for each individual is neither necessary nor sufficient for risk adjustment. Even with perfect prediction, we would have to identify which components represented health status and use propensity factors and ignore the rest. Perfect prediction of observed expenses means that all inefficiencies and problems in access and quality of care have been incorporated into the model. From our previous validity criterion, risk adjustment should account for only health and use propensity risk, weighted by the relative costs of diagnosis and treatment by an efficient provider.

Bias, or accuracy, in a model relates to its ability to meet the overall prediction goal. For large randomly selected populations, a simple demographic model with age and gender factors can predict fairly accurately. Indeed, the overall mean for the population may work just as well as any risk-assessment model. Large sample sizes, however, reduce the effects of random variation only; they may intensify the problem with systematic error.

While successful prediction of all subgroups in a population guarantees successful prediction of the overall mean, the converse is not true. Models with very heterogeneous risk classes, as with demographic classes, offer a substantial opportunity for selection bias to operate within risk groups. This represents the essential challenge to modeling correlated risk and choice. A risk-assessment model should be able to predict the mean for any subgroup of that population, no matter if it is drawn systematically or randomly. Indeed, the best model cannot be defeated by any systematic selection process created on an *ex ante* basis. (Anyone can defeat a model on an *ex post* basis because the random errors are known.)

Instead of focusing solely on the overall mean prediction error, we should also focus on the predictions for defined subgroups to assess the bias inherent in a model. The best models will be able to predict accurately across sick and well, old and young, male and female, or any other collection of *ex ante* enrollee attributes. Ideally, the included attributes will also provide unbiased prediction for the attributes not included (because they are either highly correlated or totally uncorrelated). Any omitted risk factors should be uncorrelated with choice of health plan. These omitted factors may still be correlated with choice in some other time or place outside of the immediate data set.

Stability

Risk-assessment models should be reliable, in the sense of performing consistently over time and place. Models can be accurate, on average, but have considerable instability in their prediction performance. The same model applied to similar populations or to the same population at a different time should yield similar predictions. The same individual appearing in different data sets should be predicted to have similar expenses.

A model can be stable but inaccurate. The choice between bias and stability is a normative judgment. Ideally, one would like to have a consistently accurate prediction model. HMOs may prefer to give up some degree of accuracy for stability because they can manage more effectively in a stable environment, even if slightly underpaid.

Administrative Feasibility and Political Acceptability

The above standards reflect criteria related only to prediction performance. Equally important are questions of feasibility—is the assessment technically possible with finite, defined resources—and political acceptability—do the relevant actors agree that a model performs as advertised? Although not easily measured, ease of implementation is critical to the determination of performance. When data on risk factors are not likely to be available or are burdensome or expensive to collect, a model is difficult to implement. Parsimony is desirable. Given otherwise equal performance, a model with fewer data requirements is preferred.

More generally, we need to examine the marginal contribution, across a range of criteria, of various predictors. This would be equivalent to a stepwise regression program that shows the marginal contribution of each additional variable to explained variation.

Directly related to implementability is acceptability to the users. If employers, employees, the Health Care Financing Administration (HCFA), Medicare beneficiaries, and health plans do not accept a model, significant political opposition to its use in a risk-adjustment scheme will emerge; if implemented anyway, compliance is likely to be low.

Risk-Class Criteria

The criteria above relate to the performance of the overall model. Abraham (1986) suggests four additional criteria for the evaluation of risk-assessment classes: separation, reliability, incentive value, and homogeneity.

Separation is the degree to which different risk groups have different expected losses. In traditional insurance, this is related to the fact that different groups are charged different premiums. Conceptually, if two classes have different expected expense, the overlap of the tails of the loss distributions should be minimized. This reduces the chances of classification error and increases accuracy.

Reliability refers to the possibility of errors in assignment, that is, the ability to avoid misclassification based on administrative, measurement, or other error.

Incentives relate to the meaningfulness of the risk differentials to the health plans. Pursuit of prediction precision beyond the perceptual thresholds of health plan managers is wasteful. Risk assessment should not rely heavily on variables that can be readily manipulated by a health plan; this creates incentives to manipulate the measures to alter relative payments.

Finally, from a social perspective, Abraham (1986) suggests that the risk of loss should be reasonably homogeneous within classes. That is, the risk of loss should be similar for each member of a class so that unacceptable within-class implicit price discrimination does not arise.

VALIDATION PROCEDURES

The validity of risk-assessment models relates to how well they predict for samples other than the ones used in their derivation, and especially for systematically constructed samples. Alternative models should be compared on their overall prediction error, the goodness-of-fit of their prediction distributions to actual expense distributions, the amount of variance explained, and level of internal bias.

Cross-validation

The choice of empirical validation strategy is dependent on two factors: sample size and computing resources. Large samples can be randomly split in half. A model is generated on the first half and validated on the reserved half. As long as the original sample is large and the split is randomly generated, this method maximizes the size of both samples and should produce an unbiased model. One problem, however, is overfitting; the estimated model will capitalize on random variation correlated with the included predictors.

This will manifest as prediction error when the model is applied to the validation data set. To obtain a better estimate of overfit effects, the model should be validated on multiple independent samples.

A benefit of the split-sample approach is that it maximizes the size of both data sets while maintaining control of all other factors (for example, data availability, measurement error). Split samples can be created on a systematic basis to assess how well a model is able to respond to selectivity effects. Note that random splits are desired for model construction in order to preserve as much information in the data as possible (but still withhold an independent set for validation).

Monte Carlo methods rely on a splitting procedure as well. Models are generated over many (theoretically, infinitely many) random samples of defined size drawn from the entire population with replacement (the so-called "bootstrap" technique) (Efron and Gong, 1983). The smaller the size of the selection sample, the greater the independence among the models but the greater the variance of the risk coefficients. The parameter estimates from the collective set of models generated are unbiased for the population used. This approach is usually used when the total number of observations is so small that separation into two independent data sets would make estimation extremely unstable.

The jackknife technique deletes one observation at random and estimates risk coefficients on the remaining observations (Efron and Gong, 1983). This can be repeated *n-1* times, where *n* is the number of observations. This creates *n-1* estimates of the risk coefficients. The mean, median, mode, or some other measure of central tendency could be used to "average" these observations on risk weights to create a single risk-assessment model. This technique works best for small samples where deletion of one observation may have a relatively large effect. In large samples, one observation will have little effect on the coefficient estimates, so computing resources are wasted.

Large samples with large numbers of variables may run into memory capacity constraints in some statistical analysis software libraries and computers. This may require considerable ingenuity in developing a validation strategy. The preferred method, however, is to find a larger computer to run the analysis.

Models developed on large but systematically selected data, such as from fee-for-service enrollees, do not provide information on the validity of the model in omitted populations (for example, HMO members). Any model ought to be validated on as many independent data sets as possible. This means that validation should not cease with publication of the model.

Empirical Measures of Model Performance

Four measures of the prediction performance of risk-assessment models are outlined here. These measures are used to guide the search for improved models.

Overall Prediction Error

Prediction error is computed as the arithmetic average of the difference between predicted and actual expense for a group. This can be expressed as a percentage of the overall mean to provide a measure of the accuracy of the risk-assessment model. Models ought to predict accurately, say, 2 or 3% error or less, for any a priori selected population group; it should not be possible to defeat a model by systematic a priori selection of individuals, for example, women between the ages of 20 and 44. Note that correct prediction for a single individual is not our goal; risk sharing involves a random distribution of a relatively rare event. Hence, accuracy in prediction refers to group means not individual values. Prediction models are usually estimated on an individual level because accurate prediction for individuals is sufficient to achieve accurate group predictions and because no information is lost to aggregation. While group prediction models can be more accurate (because the variance of the mean is smaller than the variance of individual observations), any basis for aggregation (for example, family unit, age/gender groups) may mask sources of selection bias.

Goodness-of-Fit

A point estimate of prediction error does not show whether the prediction model generated a series of relatively accurate predictions or the arithmetic sum of the errors is low because of self-canceling effects. The standard deviation of the prediction error and a measure of the goodness-of-fit of the distribution of predicted values to the distribution of observed values are useful. One such goodness-of-fit measure is the R^2 of the regression of actual on predicted expenses in the validation data set. These measures show how well the predicted values conform to the shape of the realized distribution of expenses.

Proportion of Variance Explained

Models are evaluated on the proportion of variance explained in the derivation data set, even with the possibility of over-fitting. Correctly specified models (containing only variables consistent with our theory of risk assessment) should account for a statistically significant portion of the variance in expense. Newhouse suggests that the maximum explainable percentage of the variance (R^2) in annual health care expense is about 14.5% (Newhouse, 1982; Newhouse et al., 1989). The essential reasons for this are that many health care events are truly random and the measures themselves, both expenditures and predictors, contain random error. This represents the maximum feasible performance of a prediction model and is equivalent to the proportion of the variance in expense that is explained by an individual's stable or nearly stable characteristics, such as age and sex.

This can be viewed heuristically as a pooled cross-sectional, time-series regression of expenses on dummy variables for each person in the sample:

$$E_{i,t} = b_0 + b_1P_1 + b_2P_2 + \ldots + b_iP_i + e_{i,t} \quad (1)$$

where $E_{i,t}$ is total annual expenses for person *i* in year *t,* P_i is 1 if person 1 and 0 otherwise. This equation partitions expense variation into that between persons and that within persons over time; the coefficients capture between-person variance, leaving within-person variance as the unexplained residual, $e_{i,t}$. Thus, if each individual can be assumed to have an underlying time-invariant permanent health status, this is the best that prediction models can do because acute, short-term transitory fluctuations in health status will be random.

Elevated blood pressure is a risk factor for stroke, for example. If a population is split into two groups with respect to blood pressure—above a critical threshold and below that level—the high pressure group will be predicted to have higher expenses than average because of a higher incidence of strokes. But not everyone will suffer a stroke during the expense period, and those who do will have strokes of varying severity. The cost of caring for these events will be spread across all persons with high blood pressure. Randomness is introduced because we cannot predict when a stroke will occur and who will suffer it. Also, some persons will be misclassified into each group because of errors in pressure measurement.

As medical science advances, risk factors for strokes become more well-defined and blood pressure techniques become more reliable. New drugs are introduced to control hypertension, which creates a much more predictable course. Variation introduced by a lack of compliance with medication regimens indicates the need to incorporate behavioral risk factors into our models.

A prediction model that performs perfectly—100 percent of the variance explained—is not desirable for two reasons. First, we can be reasonably certain that any observed distribution of health care expense will include some waste from provider and insurer inefficiency. This should not be shifted to the risk pool if it is feasible to separate it from other sources of variation. Second, perfect prediction is equivalent to cost reimbursement—payment for any level of expense is guaranteed.

Internal Cross Subsidization

For risk to be shared, some portion of expense variation must be left unexplained. At our current state of development, unexplained variance is likely to represent over 90% of the total variance. This unexplained variation may also represent the effects of omitted risk factors that give rise to bias. Thus, a final step in the validation process is to analyze the prediction errors for undesired patterns of cross-subsidy, such as by age or gender. If older women are consistently under-predicted relative to younger males, then a model contains internal bias. A good risk-assessment model should standardize for risk differences between men and women, blacks and whites, urban and rural residents, young and old, and so forth, so that only random prediction error remains. Beebe (1988) illustrates how a series of deliberately biased subsamples can be used to evaluate prediction models. In other papers in this volume, cross-subsidization for policy relevant subgroups is examined directly within a given data set. These techniques are analytically equivalent. The issue of assessing the direction and magnitude of selection bias becomes important in the context of replacing an existing risk assessment model—the new model should at the least correct for the bias contained in the old model and should not contain its own equally serious bias.

TECHNICAL ISSUES

Several technical issues related to specification, estimation, level of measurement, and weighting procedures for risk-assessment models merit special emphasis here.

Definition of the Dependent Variable

Risk can be defined as a single global variable—total expected medical care expense—or it can be decomposed, such as into expected ambulatory expense and expected hospital expense. This is equivalent to an analysis of the total distribution versus analysis of subsets of the distribution. In regression, this translates into single-equation versus multiple-equation approaches. A single-equation model to predict total expense for the *i-th individual in year t* may be represented as follows:

$$\text{Total expense}_{t,i} = a + bR_{1,t-1,i} + cR_{2,t-1,i} + \ldots + e_{t-1,i} \qquad (2)$$

where $R_{j,t-1,i}$ is a risk factor in year *t-1* for the *i-th* individual. This is a linear regression approach to risk assessment using the individual as the unit of analysis. The coefficients on the predictors represent the marginal contribution of enrollee characteristics, such as age, to expected per capita expense.

Multiple-equation models start with predicting use versus no use; then, for users, the coefficients of an equation to predict ambulatory expense are estimated. The third stage is to predict hospitalization (yes or no); the final stage is to predict hospital expenses for persons who were hospitalized. Various types of multi-part models have been estimated by Luft et al. (1989).

Estimation of prediction models has proceeded in several ways, including ordinary least squares, logistic regression, and tree-structured classification approaches. The first two approaches are most appropriate when the underlying relationships are assumed to be homogeneous. That is, if the effect of having a particular disease on next year's expense is the same over all classes, controlling for other factors in the model, then linear regression is the appropriate technique. If, however, the effect differs—heterogeneity—then an appropriate tool is regressions with interaction effects and tree-structured analysis. The two approaches can be combined by using the tree approach to generate a set of mutually exclusive and exhaustive risk classes, and then using stepwise regression to generate separate models for each class (major branching). If the tree generates small terminal groups, the models produced may be unstable.

Adjusting for Benefit Differences

Comparison of risk among health plans requires adjustments to correct for differences in benefit levels to avoid confounding the effects of variation in enrollee health status (that is, differences in risk) with differences in levels of coverage. The services constituting "medical care" should be clearly and consistently defined over time and place, and coverage should be held constant so as to remove the effects of these factors on expense. Physicians' services and hospital care are typically included in a comprehensive health insurance policy, but chiropractic services and cosmetic surgery may be excluded. Coverage factors that may confound risk assessment are copayment levels, coverage for prescription drugs and other ancillary services, exclusion of certain services (for example, chiropractic, cosmetic surgery), and other forms of cost sharing.

This problem can be addressed, in part, by restricting the data base for risk-assessment modeling to persons with similar benefit levels. However, this reduces the potential generalizability of the models, since other populations may not have similar benefits, and the price elasticities of various medical services may induce different utilization patterns. The full treatment of this problem requires modeling the correlation between risk and benefits as well as that between risk and choice. Much more work is required to develop statistical approaches to standardizing benefits.

Derivation of Risk-Assessment Models

Three analytic approaches are available for constructing risk-assessment models—conceptual, empirical, and hybrid. The conceptual approach involves a pure a priori specification of the model on the basis of theory. This would include a specification of the weights assigned to the various risk classes.

Empirical techniques involve various statistical variance partitioning algorithms that search for the most powerful predictor structure for a given data set. These techniques include stepwise regression, automatic interaction detector (AID) (Sonquist and Morgan, 1964), computer-aided regression trees (CART) (Breiman et al., 1984), chi-square automatic interaction detector (CHAID) (Kass, 1980), and so on. The hallmark of these techniques is that they require the user only to offer a list of potential predictors. The computer algorithm takes over specification of the prediction model.

The usual model-building technique adopts a mixture of both approaches. Even linear regression with a set of a priori predictor variables computes the relative risk weights from empirical data. Hybrid approaches are characterized by the use of a priori information to interpret and modify empirical risk-prediction models. Pruning regression trees to conform to theoretical expectations and mixing linear regression inside of a tree structure are other hybrid approaches. An a priori approach enhances interpretation. Empirical techniques may capitalize on chance variation, defining risk classes that appear to share no common characteristic other than similar expense in a given data set.

Selecting Predictor Variables

The number of possible alternative specifications for risk-assessment models, even with limited data sets, is so large as to be overwhelming; it is not possible to test every conceivable version. Hence, the question always arises whether the "next version," after one decides to stop developing alternative specifications, is the one that will significantly improve prediction power. In model development, numerous specifications are tested, including different variables and functional forms. Each model is assessed by the empirical performance measures described previously. Guidelines to an efficient search strategy are needed, however, so as to avoid useless churning through inadequate models and to gain some assurance that the search process is not suboptimizing.

The most important guideline is to include only variables that meet the theoretical criteria for inclusion in a risk-assessment model—measures of permanent health status and use propensity. Careful explication of this theoretical framework will target the search process and allow prediction hypotheses to be tested empirically.

The performance of models at the estimation stage can provide useful proxy rules for model-building. Specifically, the overall proportion of variance explained and the direction, magnitude, and standard error of risk coefficients can guide the specification process. Among the set of variables that meet a priori theoretical criteria for inclusion, those variables explaining higher proportions of the variation in future expense are preferred because the prediction distribution will have a larger variance.

In examining an individual variable for inclusion, the direction, magnitude, and standard error of the coefficient can provide useful information. Plausible coefficients are preferred to implausible ones; the sign on a coefficient should be in the expected direction. If it is not, the variable may be picking up the effect of another unmeasured factor, which should, ideally, be measured directly, or the variable may be capitalizing on chance, so its performance will not be validated in an independent data set.

A variable with a small (standardized for units of measurement) coefficient will not add much to prediction; variables with large coefficients are preferred, other things being the same, because they contribute more variation to the prediction distribution.

Coefficients with small standard errors are preferred because they confirm the risk hypothesis and contribute to variation in the prediction distribution much more consistently and stably than statistically insignificant coefficients. A large standard error indicates substantial variability in the association between a predictor and future expense; hence, it will be a less efficient predictor than a statistically significant predictor. The level of significance is less critical for prediction models, so the 10% level may prove useful.

To summarize, useful rules of thumb for model search at the estimation stage are, first, maximize R^2 using appropriate variables; second, identify statistically significant predictors; and, third, identify predictors with large coefficients among the insignificant predictors.

Discrete versus Continuous Risk Measures

A linear regression risk-assessment model may provide a continuous, linear measure of risk, as contrasted with a set of mutually exclusive and exhaustive demographic classes in a discrete approach to risk assessment. The discrete approach is traditionally associated with actuarial predictions of expected expense. Interaction effects are left completely to empirical specification. Interactive regression models, on the other hand, require considerably more conceptual development because of the large number of potential functional forms for the prediction relationship. A simple discrete model is attractive because most users find it easy to understand, while a six-part nonlinear regression model using non-normality assumptions may be totally incomprehensible to many users. More complex models usually require more data, which, in turn, imposes higher implementation costs. Often improvements in accuracy require more resources, but decreasing returns to model sophistication may be realized. Research should identify the accuracy-cost tradeoff in selecting among alternative risk-assessment models.

Expense Risk versus Revenue Risk

The most important determinant of risk for a health plan is enrollment composition. Expense risk derives from the sum of all eligibility periods for enrollees in a particular health plan during a specified calendar period. Eligibility periods vary, just as health status varies. One month of eligibility for a very sick person will likely represent more expense than twelve months of eligibility for a healthy person. Both enrollment and disenrollment can affect selection bias, if leavers are different from stayers and joiners over the course of a year. Estimation techniques should account for the varying periods of exposure for both risk factors and expense. In a prior use model, for example, persons with twelve months of eligibility in the base period will have a greater opportunity to incur use than persons with only three months of eligibility.

Partial year periods of eligibility create another source of risk to the health plan. Typically, health plans collect a monthly premium to cover risk exposure for that period, even though a contract may specify an annual period of performance. If an enrollee dies or loses standing with a group (such as changing jobs or divorcing a subscriber), premium payments stop. These partial periods of eligibility cannot be ignored because these individuals do not contribute a full year's revenue to meet their expenses. Special analytic techniques are required to handle this problem.

One approach to dealing with varying eligibility periods is to model these periods explicitly. This would require a two-part risk-assessment model—the first equation would predict the average length of risk exposure for a group (that is, the total revenue), and the second equation would predict the average level of expense for the group, given the average eligibility period. This procedure would require specifying and measuring the determinants of voluntary and involuntary termination.

Ellis and Ash (1988) use an eligibility weighting procedure that permits collapsing the above two-part model into a single equation. First, the dependent variable, total annual expense, is reweighted to an annual rate of expenditure. Thus, total expense for a person with only six months of eligibility in the observation year is multiplied by a factor of 2, as if this rate of utilization continued for the full year. Then, in the regression of weighted total expense on predictors, the observation is weighted by a factor of one-half to reflect that the individual was present in the risk pool only for half of the year. The net effect of this procedure is to incorporate both enrollment and termination risk into the risk coefficients; that is, it assumes that the same factors that predict expense risk also predict revenue risk. To the extent that disease censors eligibility periods, this assumption presents no problems. The only drawback to this eligibility weighting procedure is that medical care utilization tends to be clustered (nonuse periods underestimate total use, and use periods overestimate total use), so that extrapolation to an annual rate inflates the variance in annual per capita expense. Moreover, utilization by terminees may be prematurely reduced (or increased) as persons anticipate switching health plans.

Elderly persons are much more likely to terminate health plan membership because of death, which is likely to be accompanied by a cluster of use for the terminal illness. Working persons are much more likely to terminate for reasons of change in jobs or voluntary plan switching. These reasons are more likely to be associated with anticipatory reductions in use of medical care services. Also, persons who are ill are less likely to change employment or relocate to a new city. Eligibility weighting may or may not be useful or necessary for nonaged populations.

Sources of Risk Weights

Selection bias itself can present significant obstacles to the derivation of risk-assessment models. When health plan choice is correlated with risk, the observed experience of any single health plan produces biased relative risk weights. A similar bias results when benefits differ and risk is correlated with benefits; a sample drawn from one plan will not represent another plan with different benefits. At the extreme, risk may be correlated with health plan efficiency; persons with a particular risk-profile may be likely to select an efficient plan, for example. The expense patterns in these cases are influenced by the omitted factor(s) that helped to create the enrolled group.

Ideally, we should have comparable data from members of all health plans to estimate an unbiased risk-assessment model. This is often not feasible because HMOs do not have the same operating requirements as indemnity insurers and fee-for-service providers: HMO data usually reflect costs to the plan, while fee-for-service data reflect charges to patients and insurers. Observed expenses will be confounded by differences across health plans in pricing practices, input costs, cost-accounting methods, and providers' productivity.[2] In addition to these feasibility problems, system-specific data pose serious conceptual problems. Different delivery systems may have different relative costs for persons of different health status. This would mean that a well-defined concept of the efficient relative cost structure of persons in different health status situations does not exist—one system is more efficient for some health problems and another system treats other health problems in a more efficient manner. This presents difficult choices in selecting the sources of risk weights.

In an efficiently operating market, choice and overall per capita expense would be expected to be correlated—consumers should disenroll from inefficient health plans and switch to lower-cost plans. We must attempt to separate the effects of health status and use propensity on inter-plan expense variation from efficiency effects. A good risk-assessment model would account for all selectivity effects—the correlation between risk and choice. The research goal is to develop a risk-adjustment model that accounts for all of the relationship between choice and risk among the options in a multi-option health benefit program.

Risk predictors must account for all the variability in expense due to differences in risk; this is likely to be very little of the total variability in expense. Selection bias is likely to be a problem in risk-assessment models derived from a single type of practice arrangement—the risk coefficients will reflect the practice patterns of that arrangement, be it HMO or FFS. To improve our ability to adjust for risk, we should develop larger data sets covering a variety of practice arrangements and develop better risk-assessment models. Data from different practice arrangements, however, bring other problems. Data sets characterized by wide variations in the scope of benefits, high deductibles and copayments, access barriers, and divergent organizational structures, will carry a greater likelihood of confounding by benefit, access, and efficiency factors. Selecting the source of risk weights will require tradeoffs between benefit/organizational heterogeneity and single system selection bias.

Regression to the Mean

The distribution of annual per capita expenses for a typical population is highly skewed—most persons have little or no use and a few persons have very high expenses. Examination of use patterns over time reveals, however, that outliers in any given year regress towards the mean in the next year (Goodman et al., 1991). Very expensive persons are not outliers in the previous or the next year, and persons with no expense in one year have mean expenses above zero for both previous and ensuing years. This means that some very healthy persons are likely to become sick and some very ill persons are likely to recover. Outliers are random occurrences and, as such, difficult to predict; we do know that any distribution is likely to have them. A good prediction model will generate a prediction distribution that accounts for this high expense tail. Ordinary least squares regression, which is based on the assumption of a normal distribution, accounts for the tail by spreading its effects over the other parameters in the model. The prediction distribution does not look exactly like the realized distribution. Of course, we do not require an exact match, only similar means. We raise the issue only to highlight that estimating techniques based on non-normal distributive assumptions may have useful applications for risk assessment.

Some persons are persistently healthy over time and others are persistently ill over time. Consequently, individuals do not literally regress to the mean. An autoregressive model (Welch, 1985; Newhouse et al., 1989) may prove to be a useful specification when multiple years of risk data are available. Risk in any one year may have a distributed lag effect over a number of years into the future.

Risk-Adjustment Procedures

Risk adjustment cannot proceed without an acceptable and valid risk-assessment model. On the other hand, an adequate risk-assessment model is only one part of implementing a risk-adjustment procedure. Consider, for example, an employer who pays all the premiums for all health plans offered to employees. Risk adjustment in this case would require adjusting the entire premium, which is tantamount to price regulation if the scheme is mandated by government or employer fiat. If risk adjustment is voluntary, risk-assessment models may provide additional information to guide premium negotiations with employers. Ideally, risk adjustment of employers' contributions to private health plans and governmental contributions to public health plans should increase revenue to adversely affected plans so that they can continue to operate without raising out-of-pocket premiums to enrollees, or provide incentives for enrollees to switch health plans so as to equalize risks. If risk adjustments are set high enough, enrollee contributions could be lowered in the high-cost plan, so as to attract low-risk individuals from low-cost plans (whose enrollee contributions have been raised). In this manner, both payer and enrollee can contribute to the equalization of risk in the long run (Hornbrook and Goodman, 1991).

USES OF RISK ASSESSMENT

Risk-assessment models have utility wherever standardization for baseline health status and use propensity are required. Resource allocation decisions in managing health care require forecasts of future service demand. Understanding patterns of service use and care outcomes requires information on individuals' health status prior to their entry into the system. This section highlights some alternative uses of risk-assessment models.

Risk Adjustment of Health Plan Premium Contributions

An unbiased risk model would enable, in the case of private group insurance, adjustment of employer premium contributions to redistribute the risk across all employees of a firm, instead of letting employees' choices partition risk to each health plan. Risk-adjusted payments to health plans would make them indifferent to selection effects, and they could compete on the basis of price and quality of service rather than risk skimming. Without adjustment, persons who unknowingly select higher-risk plans will carry a disproportionate share of the financial and health burden of illness and injury in a population. Risk taxonomies tailored to aged populations could be used to adjust for selectivity between risk contracts and fee-for-service providers in Medicare.

Primary Care Panel Size

The assignment of patients to a single provider for the management of primary medical care has become an important issue for organizing and delivering services inside ambulatory medical offices in HMOs. Patients are increasingly interested in being linked to an individual physician to coordinate all their health care. Patients tied to a particular provider may be less likely to change health plans. Physicians are better able to manage care if they are familiar with an individual patient.

Panel size is a critical factor in determining the total volume and mix of output produced by primary care providers in HMOs. Health plan managers face incentives to increase the volume of output per provider to control total health plan costs, while salaried providers face incentives to decrease the volume so as to obtain the preferred quality of care and work life. Some patients are relatively healthy and place little demand on the HMO; a panel comprised mostly of this type of patient could be much larger than one composed of chronically ill patients and still represent the same total volume of work for the primary care provider. Equity in workloads across HMO physicians is a critical determinant of professional satisfaction. If workloads are observed to vary in arbitrary and unreasonable ways, providers become alienated from the HMO and productivity is reduced as the highly motivated providers seek ways to evade heavy appointment schedules.

Permanent health status is one factor that ought to be taken into account in setting panel sizes. The other factor is the patient's propensity to seek care. Patients who expect to use the medical care system to evaluate every minor symptom demand greater access than those who wait until their symptoms significantly limit their functional abilities. The most important conceptual factors that should enter a primary care panel risk-adjustment model—health status and propensity to use services—are precisely the factors that a risk-assessment model should measure.

Resource Allocation

The efficient operation of clinics and hospitals at all levels demands an accurate allocation of system resources. A clinic operating, for example, in an area primarily populated by young families faces significantly different resource demands than one operating in an area populated by retirees.

With differing dependent variables to reflect the specific output of clinics or hospitals, risk-assessment tools could provide information useful for budgeting and other management decisions. Current systems are based largely on simple measures such as age-adjusted days, clinic visits, or similar measures. More accurate forecasts—and recognition of which activities are largely random as opposed to predictable—would offer significant advantages to managers. As efficient iso-resource groups, risk classifications can be used to construct area budgets in HMOs. Simple per capita budgeting may lead to inequities if health status varies across the service areas of an HMO.

HMO employee, clinic, and system productivity could also be measured more accurately with risk-assessment models to adjust for differential composition of memberships in particular geographic areas. Systems that measure output unadjusted for differences in expected utilization are likely to understate the work of some individuals and overstate that of others. Using dependent variables related to units of work, risk-assessment models based on health status and use propensity could be easily expanded for use in hospital or clinic productivity systems.

Quality Assurance Applications

Quality assurance examines patient outcomes to judge which cases exceed practice norms. The development of these norms could be significantly expanded using the risk-assessment modeling techniques. Specifically, models comparing outcomes across different treatments, providers, or clinics should adjust for the underlying health status of patients. This includes outcomes such as death, post-surgical infection rates, readmission to the hospital within seven days, and changes in functional health status. Modest outcomes in very risky patients are recognized for their true value; good outcomes in low-risk patients can be appropriately discounted.

Other Uses

Risk-assessment models represent an important addition to management techniques. The examples above only briefly hint at the potential applications for risk-assessment tools. Applications in medical economics (risk-adjusted utilization reports), financial management (risk-adjusted budget variances), and marketing research (risk assessment of different market segments) are yet additional examples.

IMPLICATIONS FOR RESEARCH

We began this methodological essay with the contention that a validated risk-adjustment scheme could be used to improve the overall efficiency of health insurance markets. The two major conceptual dimensions of risk that should not be loaded strictly on health plans are enrollees' permanent health status and their propensity to use medical care. These factors attach to the epidemiologic and cultural backgrounds of enrollees and are largely exogenous to health plans in the short run. Direct measures of permanent health status are preferred to distant proxy measures.

More research is needed on the development and testing of risk-assessment models. This research should include examinations of the predictors of health plan choice, length of eligibility period, decision to seek care, and level of use. A menu of validated risk-assessment models with known characteristics should be developed so that informed decisions about tradeoffs among accuracy, stability, and administrative feasibility can be made.

For health plans that do not skim risk, the health status of new enrollees is clearly exogenous. The issue becomes more complex for long-term members, however; their health status in any given year may be related to quantity and quality of care received in previous years. To improve social efficiency, payments to health plans should reflect plans' contributions to members' health, rather than, strictly, the treatment of inherited risks. The static risk-adjustment models discussed in this paper recognize resource needs for currently healthy persons who are engaging in unhealthy behaviors only by the treatment required for disease when it finally strikes, which may be far in the future. The resources needed to offer lifestyle interventions to prevent the onset of disease in some future time period are not included. An outcomes-based payment system might provide payment to health plans for improving the health status of their members, which could emphasize long-term lifestyle interventions that lower the incidence of heart disease, cancer, and stroke. Dynamic risk assessment focuses on transitions from one health state to another, rather than on the absolute severity of illness; permanent health status includes avoidance of infectious diseases (via immunizations), avoidance of cancer (via reduced exposure to carcinogens), and avoidance of strokes (via reduced blood pressure and serum cholesterol). Such models could provide incentives for health plans to improve access to care and preventive services by allocating resources on the basis of their relative efficacy. Such incentives could serve to reinforce other efforts to monitor and enforce outcome-based standards for access to and quality of care.

ACKNOWLEDGMENTS

This research was supported by a grant from Kaiser Foundation Health Plan, Inc. and by Cooperative Agreement No. 18-C-98804-1/04 from the Health Care Financing Administration. The views expressed in this paper are those of the authors, and no official endorsement by either Kaiser Foundation Health Plan or Health Care Financing Administration is intended or should be inferred. An earlier version of this paper was presented at the Workshop on Risk Adjustment of Employer Contributions, sponsored by the Kaiser Permanente Center for Health Research, Otter Rock, Oregon, July 16,

1990. We would like to acknowledge helpful comments on earlier versions of this paper from Arlene Ash, Marjorie Bennett, Jim Lubitz, Nelda McCall, Richard Scheffler, Jerry Riley, Bill Thomas, and Pete Welch. Finally, we would like to thank our technical editor, Margaret R. Sucec, for helping us improve the clarity of our presentation.

NOTE

1. Persons with higher use propensity, controlling for physical health status, could be viewed as having emotional health problems such that they require unusual levels of support and reassurance to treat their anxieties. Even if viewed as habits learned in inefficient health care systems, health plans require additional resources to develop new member orientation programs to teach desired behaviors. In either case, an argument can be made for incorporating use propensity as a risk factor rather than treating it as an inefficiency.

REFERENCES

Abraham, K.S. (1986). *Distributing Risk.* New Haven, CT: Yale University Press.

Ash, A. (1990). Personal Communication.

Anderson, G., J. Cantor, E. Steinberg, and J. Holloway (1986). "Capitation Pricing: Adjusting for Prior Utilization and Physician Discretion." *Health Care Financing Review* 8:27-34.

Beebe, J.C. (1988). "Medicare Reimbursement and Regression to the Mean." *Health Care Financing Review* 9:9-22.

Beebe, J., J. Lubitz, and P. Eggers (1985). "Using Prior Utilization to Determine Payments for Medicare Enrollees in Health Maintenance Organizations." *Health Care Financing Review* 6:27-38.

Breiman, L., J.H. Friedman, R.A. Olshen, and C.J. Stone (1984). *Classification and Regression Trees.* Pacific Grove, CA: Wadsworth and Brooks/Cole Advanced Books and Software.

Efron, B. and G. Gong (1983). "A Leisurely Look at the Bootstrap, the Jackknife, and Cross-Validation." *The American Statistician* 1:36-48.

Ellis, R.P. and A. Ash (1988). *Refining the Diagnostic Cost Group Model: A Proposed Modification to the AAPCC for HMO Reimbursement.* Final Report, Grant No. 18-C-98526/1-03, Baltimore, MD: Health Care Financing Administration.

Ellis, R.P. and A. Ash (1989). *The Continuous-Update Diagnostic Cost Group Model.* Final Report, Grant No. 18-C-98526/1-03, Baltimore, MD: Health Care Financing Administration.

Enthoven, A.C. (1989). *Theory and Practice of Managed Competition in Health Care Finance.* Professor Dr. F. de Vries Lectures in Economics, Vol. 9. New York: Elsevier Science Publishing.

Feldman, R., M. Finch, and B. Dowd (1989). "The Role of Health Practices in HMO Selection Bias: A Confirmatory Study." *Inquiry* 26:381-387.

Feldstein, P.J. (1988). *Health Care Economics,* 3rd ed. New York: John Wiley and Sons.

Ghiselli, E.E., J.P. Campbell, and S. Zedeck (1981). *Measurement Theory for the Behavioral Sciences.* San Francisco: W.H. Freeman and Company.

Goodman, M.J., D.W. Roblin, M.C. Hornbrook, and J.P. Mullooly (1991). "Persistence of Health Care Expense in an Insured Working Population." In M. Hornbrook (Ed.), *Advances in Health Economics and Health Services Research: Vol. 12, Risk-Based Contributions to Private Health Insurance* (pp. 149-173). Greenwich, CT: JAI Press.

Gruenberg L., C. Tompkins, and F. Porell (1989). "The Health Status and Utilization Patterns of the Elderly: Implications for Setting Medicare Payments to HMOs." In R. M. Scheffler and L. F. Rossiter (Eds.), *Advances in Health Economics and Health Services Research,* (Vol 10, pp. 41-73). Greenwich, CT: JAI Press Inc.

Harlow, S.D. and M.S. Linet (1989). "Agreement between Questionnaire Data and Medical Records." *American Journal of Epidemiology* 129:233-248.

Hornbrook, M.C., M.D. Bennett, and M.R. Greenlick (1989). "Adjusting the AAPCC for Selectivity and Selection Bias Under Medicare Risk Contracts." In R. M. Scheffler and L. F. Rossiter (Eds.), *Advances in Health Economics and Health Services Research,* (Vol. 10, pp. 111-149). Greenwich, CT : JAI Press, pp. 111-149.

Hornbrook, M.C., M.D. Bennett, and M.R. Greenlick (1991a). "Adjusting for Health Status under Medicare Risk Contracts Using Prior Inpatient Morbidities: The Diagnostic Cost Groups." Final Report, Cooperative Agreement No. 18-C-98804-01/04. Baltimore, MD: Health Care Financing Administration.

Hornbrook, M.C., M.D. Bennett, and M.R. Greenlick (1991b). "Prior Use Risk-Adjustors for the AAPCC Based on an HMO's Experience." Final Report, Cooperative Agreement No. 18-C-98804-1/04. Baltimore, MD: Health Care Financing Administration.

Hornbrook, M.C. and S.E. Berki (1985). "Practice Mode and Payment Method: Effects on Use, Costs, Quality and Access." *Medical Care* 23:484-511.

Hornbrook, M.C. and M.J. Goodman (1991). "Adjusting Health Benefit Contributions to Reflect Risk." In M. Hornbrook (Ed.), *Advances in Health Economics and Health Services Research: Vol. 12, Risk-Based Contributions to Private Health Insurance* (pp. 41-76). Greenwich, CT: JAI Press.

Hornbrook, M.C., M.J. Goodman, and M.D. Bennett (1991). "Assessing Health Plan Case Mix in Employed Populations: Ambulatory Morbidity and Prescribed Drug Models." In M. Hornbrook (Ed.), *Advances in Health Economics and Health Services Research: Vol. 12, Risk-Based Contributions to Private Health Insurance* (pp. 197-232). Greenwich, CT: JAI Press.

Hornbrook, M.C., A.V. Hurtado, and R.E. Johnson (1985). "Health Care Episodes: Definition, Measurement and Use." *Medical Care Review* 42:163-218.

Howland, J., J. Stokes III, S.C. Crane, and A.J. Belanger (1987). "Adjusting Capitation using Chronic Disease Risk Factors: A Preliminary Study." *Health Care Financing Review* 9:15-23.

International Classification of Diseases, 9th Revision, Clinical Modification. Ann Arbor, MI: Commission on Professional and Hospital Activities, 1978.

Kass, G.V. (1980). "An Exploratory Technique for Investigating Large Quantities of Categorical Data." *Applied Statistics* 29:119-127.

Langwell, K.M. and J.P. Hadley (1986). "Capitation and the Medicare Program: History, Issues, and Evidence." *Health Care Financing Review* (Annual Supplement):9-20.

Lubitz, J. (1987). "Health Status Adjustments for Medicare Capitation." *Inquiry* 24:362-375.

Lubitz, J., J. Beebe, and G. Riley (1985). "Improving the Medicare HMO Payment Formula to Deal with Biased Selection." In R. M. Scheffler and L. F. Rossiter (Eds.), *Advances in Health Economics and Health Services Research,* (Vol 6, pp. 101-122). Greenwich, CT: JAI Press Inc.

Luft, H.S., J.C. Robinson, L.B. Gardner, and E.M. Morrison (1989). *A Method for Risk-Adjusting Employer Contributions to Competing Health Insurance Plans Using Variables in Personnel Files.* San Francisco, CA: University of California, Institute for Health Policy Studies.

Manton, K. and H.D. Tolley (1988). "Assessing Health Care Costs in the Elderly." *Transactions of the Society of Actuaries* 36:71-90.

McClure, W. (1984). "On the Research Status of Risk-adjusted Capitation Rates." *Inquiry* 21:205-213.

National Center for Health Statistics (NCHS) (1990). *Health United States 1990.* DHHS Publ. No. (PHS) 90-1232. Hyattsville, MD: Public Health Service.

Newhouse, J.P. (1982). "Is Competition the Answer?" *Journal of Health Economics* 1:109-115.

Newhouse, J.P. (1986). "Rate Adjusters for Medicare under Capitation." *Health Care Financing Review* (Annual Supplement):45-56.

Newhouse, J.P., W.E. Manning, E.B. Keeler, and E.B. Sloss (1989). "Adjusting Capitation Rates using Objective Health Measures and Prior Utilization." *Health Care Financing Review* 10:41-54.

Rossiter, L.R. (1989). Personal Communication.

Sonquist, J.A. and J.N. Morgan (1964). *The Detection of Interaction Effects: A Report on a Computer Program for the Selection of Optional Combinations of Explanatory Variables.* Survey Research Center Monograph No. 35. Ann Arbor, MI: The University of Michigan Institute for Social Research, Survey Research Center.

Thomas, J.W. and R. Lichtenstein (1986). "Functional Health Measure for Adjusting Health Maintenance Organization Capitation Rates." *Health Care Financing Review* 7:85-95.

Welch, W.P. (1985). "Medicare Capitation Payments to HMOs in Light of Regression toward the Mean in Health Care Costs." In R. M. Scheffler and L. F. Rossiter (Eds.), *Advances in Health Economics and Health Services Research* (Vol. 6, pp. 75-96). Greenwich, CT: JAI Press.

Whitmore, R.W., J.E. Paul, D.A. Gibbs, and J.C. Beebe (1989). "Using Health Indicators in Calculating the AAPCC." In R. M. Scheffler and L. F. Rossiter (Eds.), *Advances in Health Economics and Health Services Research* (Vol. 10, pp. 75-109). Greenwich, CT: JAI Press.

Wrightson, C.W., Jr. (1990). *HMO Rate Setting and Financial Strategy.* Ann Arbor, MI: Health Administration Press.

Zeckhauser, R.J. (1970). "Medical Insurance: A Case Study of the Trade-off between Risk Spreading and Appropriate Incentives." *Journal of Economic Theory* 2:10-26.

PERSISTENCE OF HEALTH CARE EXPENSE IN AN INSURED WORKING POPULATION

Michael J. Goodman, Douglas W. Roblin,
Mark C. Hornbrook, and John P. Mullooly

INTRODUCTION

Much of the literature on selectivity and selection bias in health plan enrollment consists of "switcher" studies (Eggers and Prihoda, 1982; Buchanan and Cretin, 1986; Anderson, 1991). These studies compare service use in a year prior to changing health plans with use by individuals who do not change plans. Typically, "switchers" have lower use than "stayers" in the period leading up to the switch (Buchanan and Cretin, 1986). Some employers take this to mean that the health plans with the highest intake of switchers are enjoying favorable selection (Anderson, 1991).

Switcher studies usually contain two assumptions that are important for this paper. First, these studies assume that individual and group patterns of health care use tend to be consistent over time—high utilizers

Advances in Health Economics and Health Services Research, Vol. 12, pages 149-173.
Copyright © 1991 by JAI Press Inc.
All rights of reproduction in any form reserved.
ISBN: 1-55938-241-4

remain high utilizers and low utilizers remain low utilizers. Second, switchers are assumed to be a random sample of the health plan population. The first assumption may be valid for individuals with chronic conditions that require ongoing care, but many health problems are characterized by clustered, episodic care. Hence, high users in one period may not have any use in the next period, and nonusers in a prior period may experience an episode of care in the next period. The second assumption ignores the systematic determinants of voluntary health plan choice.

In nonaged employed populations, health care utilization has a large random component (Hornbrook, Goodman, and Bennett, 1991). Unlike health care expense for older persons, for whom a higher incidence of chronic illness makes annual per capita expense more predictable, nonaged health care expense is less predictable because it results from a combination of acute conditions, injuries, and obstetric/neonatal conditions. Thus, high or low use last year does not necessarily portend similar expense this year or in subsequent years.

The random element in use patterns has important policy implications. First, health care insurers' traditional rating methodologies employ information on prior use to predict future risk. This assumes that a sick individual will continue to be sick next year. Among large enough groups, this is not a problem because all that is required is that someone have a similar illness experience, even if not the same individual, in the future time period. In smaller groups, however, this assumption may not be valid because of higher levels of sampling variation. Second, as mentioned above, studies of adverse selection (to detect failure of rating methods) often rely on the health care utilization of persons who change health plans—switcher studies. If prior use is unrepresentative of actual future utilization and if switchers are in fact different from stayers, these studies are seriously flawed as measures of selection bias. Because these studies are often represented to employers as valid methods of measuring (and then correcting for) adverse selection, the underlying assumption of persistence of patterns of health care use should be explored.

This study focuses on whether patterns of health care use in nonaged populations persist over time. Does a high utilizer tend to continue to be a high utilizer? We employ the concept of "persistence of use" to denote a precise meaning. This phenomenon has often been labeled as "regression to the mean" in other literature. These two concepts refer to two different phenomena and can appear independently or together in a given population. Persistence of use is defined as the degree to which use levels by individuals or subgroups in a given year are similar to use levels in prior and future years. Regression to the mean is defined as the degree to which the outliers in a given distribution of use (or expense) tend to move toward the mean (or median) of the distribution in future years (and prior years). Regression to the mean derives from the random element in the distribution—extreme observations are created by chance events and the probability of recurrence for a particular individual of those events decreases markedly over time (by the product of the probabilities of a specified high or low level of use). We cannot predict who will be in the tails of a distribution, but once an individual appears in a tail, we can predict what is likely to happen in future periods—nonusers are likely to have at least some use and high users are likely to have lower use. If, however, the tails of a distribution are produced by nonrandom systematic factors, then the observed use distribution is actually the sum of multiple distributions. Our problem becomes that of identifying the various separate distributions and classifying each individual into the correct distribution. This is the essential task of risk assessment (Hornbrook and Goodman, 1991b).

In sum, persistence of use is the tendency of an individual to stay in a given distribution, as defined by their permanent health status, for example, and regression to the mean relates to the effect of random occurrences that generate a distribution around its expected value. Every individual is subject to both persistence and regression effects in this conceptualization.

Models to assess risk, as defined by Hornbrook and Goodman (1991a, 1991b), should, ideally, incorporate both persistence and regression effects. While use persistence is obviously an appropriate focus of risk adjustment, the speed of regression towards the mean may vary systematically across distributions. Moreover, regression may be asymmetric within the same risk class—nonusers may regress at different speeds than high users.

PREVIOUS RESEARCH

The main thrust of this paper is to explore ways of defining and measuring the persistence of nonaged health care expense. We use a simple demographic model to classify iso-risk groups. The published literature, mostly from older populations, has generally examined longitudinal use patterns from the perspective of persistence. A few studies, however, have assessed the temporal changes in terms of regression to the mean. This literature stems from the early work by Densen et al. (1959), who found that a small proportion of a health plan population were consistently high or low users. This work has been followed by other longitudinal analyses of high- or low-using subsets. Roos and Shapiro (1981) and Roos, Shapiro, and Tate (1990), using data on older persons from Manitoba, Canada, found a similar concentration of use among a small proportion of older persons.

Freeborn et al. (1990) found that persons over age 64 who were consistently high users tended to be older and report more chronic medical conditions, such as arthritis, high blood pressure, and heart conditions. McCall and Wai (1983), in a five-year study of Colorado Medicare aged beneficiaries using several different dependent variables such as medical office visits and Part A covered expense, found persistent use patterns among high utilizers. They may have precluded finding regression to the mean by using only four categories in the descriptive analysis because movement within large categories may mask a change in utilization patterns.

Anderson and Knickman (1984), using a shorter time period (1974-77), compared high utilizers in the Medicare population (expense over $10,000) to others. They found that mean expense remained above the population mean in each year for the initial high users.

Beebe (1988), using a population eligible for Medicare in 1974-75, studied utilization over the period 1974 to 1980. This study divided the population into eight initial expense strata. He found regression toward the mean in all groups, but over the study period the population mean was never reached by high utilizers. Consistent with other work (Hornbrook, Goodman, and Bennett, 1991a), Beebe found that those without chronic disease were characterized by randomly occurring acute episodes, but no long-term expense. Populations without significant chronic disease would, therefore, be likely to be characterized by less persistence of use.

We believe that a methodological gap exists between modeling of health care expense in the younger population compared to older persons. The higher incidence of chronic disease, and the associated higher use rates, creates more homogeneity in health care expense patterns for aged persons compared to younger persons. Other work leads us to hypothesize that the lower the degree of chronic illness in a population, the greater the degree of randomness in the overall risk distribution. Techniques developed for older persons may not always be appropriate for the more heterogeneous employed populations and their dependents.

Analyses of nonaged employed populations have been performed by benefit consultants, actuaries, and other consulting organizations on a proprietary basis (Anderson, 1991). These studies are suspect because they are neither widely disseminated nor subject to the scrutiny of blinded peer review. Benefit managers have the opportunity to review these studies. Even objective, methodologically sophisticated managers may be unable to evaluate the methodology and conclusions of these studies. Biased managers, searching for a way to save a self-funded plan or attempting to constrain spiraling health care costs in a favored plan, are likely to be even less critical of work that confirms their expectations.

Buchanan and Cretin (1986) have shown that utilization of switchers differs from that of non-switchers. Nevertheless, it is common to find the relative risk of future expense among different health plans measured by the use patterns of the small group of switchers (Anderson, 1991). Those interested in testing this assumption have looked beyond the year prior to switching and the first year after switching to see if, over time, use by switchers resembles use by non-switchers in the population. Since the number of stayers is larger than the number of switchers in most cases, the assumption is that the switchers will move toward the mean of the non-switcher population. If, however, switchers are different from nonswitchers at one point in time, their temporal health and use patterns may also be different from those of non-switchers.

AIMS

The overall aim of this study is to assess the extent of persistence of use in the nonaged population of HMO members and to model the underlying transition process. No single technique for modeling dynamic patterns of use is generally accepted in the literature as definitive. Because measuring use persistence requires many observations on each individual, time-series analysis is required. Time-series data present major methodological problems for traditional regression approaches because the longitudinal analysis of individual data results in autocorrelation in the residuals (McCall and Wai, 1983). In response to this problem, McCall and Wai propose an error components model. The error components model is appropriate to understanding the relative influence of different factors, but fails to measure change in patterns of use. The alternative approach, Autoregressive, Integrated, Moving, Average (ARIMA) modeling, is not feasible because of the long sequences required to estimate the parameters. We propose and test a simpler method based on Markov chain techniques as more appropriate to measuring changes in use patterns.

WHAT IS THE APPROPRIATE MEAN?

The first question is what constitutes the appropriate mean for an individual to regress toward? In studies of an aged Medicare population, the grand mean is likely to accurately represent the expected expense of most individuals. But in nonaged populations this is less likely to be true. We should not expect a teenaged male to have the same expected utilization as a 50-year-old female. If we define the expected mean as a population grand mean, we run the risk of missing exceptional utilization among naturally more or less expensive subgroups. A minimum level of discrimination can be achieved through simple age and gender classification. More viable tests of use persistence should adjust expected expense for permanent health status, health habits, and attitudes regarding use of medical care that are expected to influence future use (Hornbrook and Goodman, 1991b). This is the minimum requirement for a valid comparison of use patterns within a broadly defined population. Other studies focus on the problem of risk classification, which we have conceptualized in this paper as separation of use distributions; because our focus is on a methodological issue, we will employ a simple demographic risk taxonomy for heuristic purposes. We contend that whatever risk-assessment model is employed, both regression to the mean and use persistence effects are likely to be present. Any aggregation associated with a classification scheme will generate distributions for each group; the more the classification scheme captures differences in levels of permanent health status, the more likely that regression to the mean will be more salient than use persistence within groups. In a purely random classification scheme, use persistence effects would be relatively more important because the underlying risk factors are ignored.

Regression to the mean implies that, over time, an individual's health care utilization will become similar to some mean expense for a larger group. In the absence of underlying chronic disease and long-term disability, longitudinal variations in use would be expected to be purely random, characterized by randomly occurring episodes of acute disease which do not lead to long-term changes in use patterns. An individual with high expense in one year should not differ from the population in subsequent years. Similarly, individuals with low or no expense will become more expensive over time, on average. The question is what constitutes the appropriate mean (expected use) and how should it be estimated. This can be illustrated by considering the expected health care utilization of two individuals, one a 55-year-old male and the other a 20-year-old female. The expected health care use patterns by these two individuals is clearly different, all other things being the same. If we had a population composed entirely of the latter group, the mean would be lower than if we combined the two groups. The mean of the combined group would be an inaccurate predictor of future utilization for either group. In simplest terms, true expected utilization varies by age and gender—each age-gender subgroup has a separate distribution of expense. Adjustments for gender will recognize the implicit U shape of the male distribution with the added expense of maternity utilization for females.

Age and gender represent fundamental risk factors essential to understanding regression to the mean. Hornbrook, Goodman, and Bennett (1991) have shown that even using relatively complex diagnostic models, age and gender still provide significant improvement in prediction of future health care expense. In measuring persistence of use, they provide essential information for developing separate, reasonably homogenous subgroups.

Others factors appropriate to accurate definition of the expense distribution of each subgroup (that is, age and gender in our case) could be included. Measurement of regression to the mean requires, however, that the mean of the distribution represents the expected use for any member of the defined subgroup. For a broadly defined population, simple factors such as age and gender represent appropriate factors. More complex models may include family size, occupation, education, family health history, chronic disease states, and other factors (Hornbrook, Goodman, and Bennett 1991).

Expected expense is not difficult to operationalize. We can simply create a mean of the expense distribution for each defined population subgroup. The simplest method would be to define a priori, iso-risk groups, such as five-year or ten-year age cells by gender. Development of groups in this way should have a theoretical

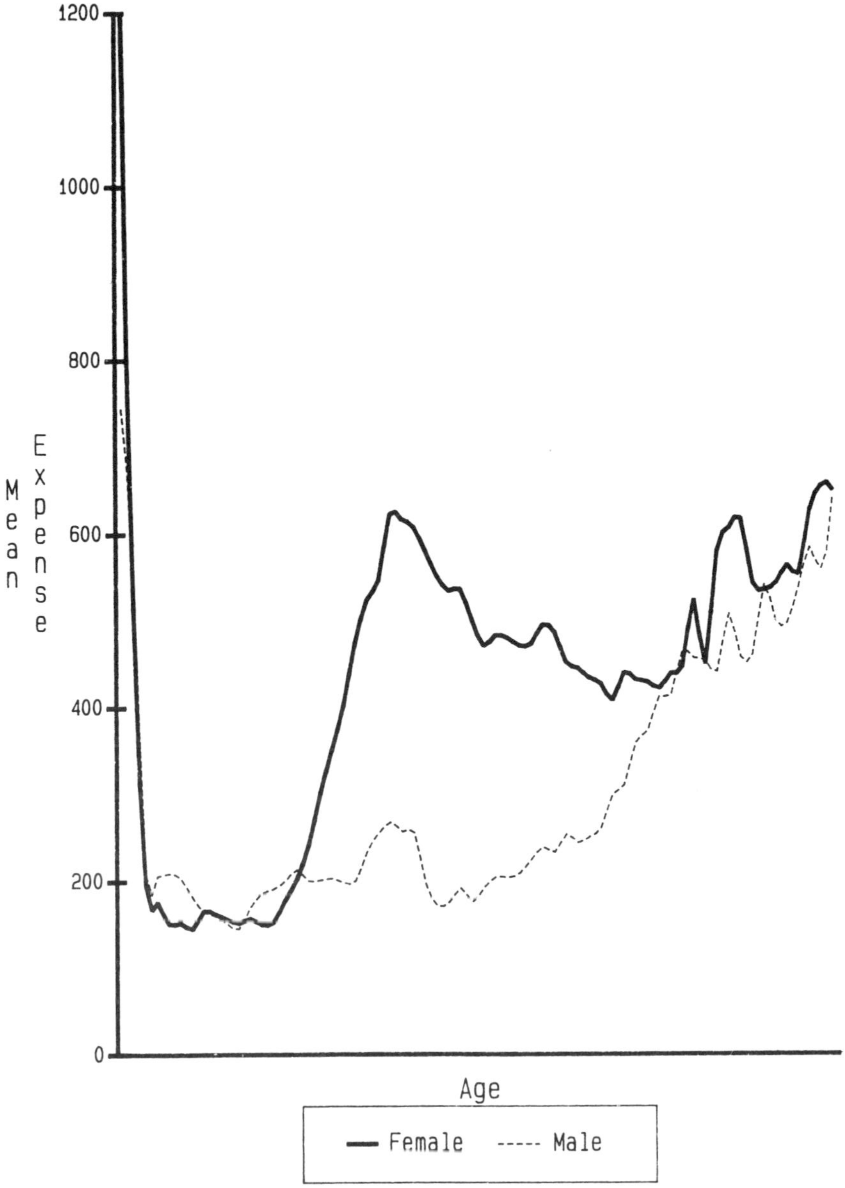

Figure 1. Average expected expense by age and gender.

basis related to predictable variance in future utilization. Characterizing five-year age/gender groups as "iso-risk" is somewhat misleading; this implies that, for example, in a 50- to 54-year-old group, a 50-year-old male is more like a 54-year-old male than a 49-year-old male. Such artificial boundaries, although better than using the overall population mean because they recognize the existence of separate expense distributions for different age-gender groups, still create some distortions at the discrete jumps from one group to the next. At any specific age, those in age groups surrounding the given age are likely to be more similar than persons who are much older or younger. For this reason, we calculate age- and gender-adjusted means employing five-year *moving* averages (except for the top and bottom of our distribution where this is impossible) to smooth out the distribution and avoid undue influence of outlier observations. This has an added benefit of producing more stable expected values through the use of larger numbers of observations. These five-year moving averages are plotted for each age and gender in Figure 1; the plots are not as smooth as we would like but they are sufficient to serve as the foundation for further analysis.

An alternative method of deriving these values would be to fit a curve to the data using regression techniques. This would smooth the observed curve. For males, with a U-shaped expense function, this process would not be too difficult. The female curve, however, would be quite difficult and potentially unreliable given the relatively small number of observations in our data set.

SAMPLE AND ESTIMATION PROCEDURE

The data for this study are derived from a sample of employed persons enrolled in the Kaiser Foundation Health Plan of the Northwest, a large prepaid group practice HMO, in the medium-sized metropolitan area of Portland/Salem, Oregon and Vancouver, Washington for the years 1980 through 1987. In 1980 through 1983, a 5% sample of the HMO membership was drawn; in 1984 through 1987, a 2% sample was drawn. To be included in the study, individuals could not have reached their sixty-fifth birthday by the end of a study year and they had to be members of employer groups. This study's eligibility criteria exclude Medicare beneficiaries (including aged, disabled, and ESRD groups), Medicaid recipients, and persons with individual (ID) coverage. From this larger group, a subsample of individuals *continuously* eligible for five-year periods was developed. An individual, therefore, could be included more than once. This sample included 7,666 observations.

For each age and gender, the expected mean expense (E_{ij}) was computed using a five-year moving average for each age (except in the very young and very old, where insufficient data were available); the five-year period was defined to bracket the individual's own age. For a 40-year old, the expense of those persons who were 38, 39, 40, 41, and 42 years of age in the same gender would be used. This yielded the expected mean expense in each year for each individual.

A deviation score was then computed to show the difference between actual and expected expense, adjusted for age and sex, as follows:

$$D_t = A_t - E_{ij}, \tag{1}$$

where D = Deviation score, A = Actual expense, t = time from 0 to 4, E = 5-year Age/Gender Group Moving Average, i = age group, and j = gender. A 60-year-old male with $1,000 in actual expense in one year will have a different deviation score than a 20-year-old male with the same actual expense. These deviation scores are used in all subsequent analyses.

This algorithm assumes that a secular trend is not present. A secular trend could be produced by either inflation or other factors relating to improvements in health care technology. Inflation is removed from the expense data by assigning a relative value to each procedure and then using cost weights that do not vary over time to assign expense over time. A test, using a standard regression, was made for a secular trend controlling for age and gender separately. In both formulations, year was not a significant predictor.

Bishop, Feinberg, and Holland (1975) suggest that when data can be classified into discrete categories at successive points in time, Markov models represent an appropriate analytic device. The key to this approach is a transition matrix that relates the distribution of states at time *t* to the distribution of states at time *t+1*. In this study, transition matrices show an individual's class of health care expense (state) in one year (time *t*) by expense class in a following year (time *t+1*). The transition probabilities—the percentage distributions across a given row—show the distribution percentages of a baseline expense group at time *t+1*. A sequence of transition matrices for succeeding pairs of years is a Markov chain.

The required discrete categories are defined by individuals' relative health care expense—for example, quartiles, quintiles, or deciles. The first transition matrix—for the distribution by quintiles—is shown in Table 1. Among individuals classed in the first quintile (the lowest utilizers) in year 1, for example, more than 60% remain in the first quintile in year 2.

Three characteristics of Markov chains are pertinent to the study of persistence of use: *order* of the chain; *stationarity* of the transition probabilities; and *symmetry* of the transition probabilities. Each of these properties is defined below.

The order of a Markov chain refers to whether the transition probabilities at one point in time are dependent on the transition probabilities at previous points in time. For example, in a first-order Markov chain, the transition

Table 1. Transition Matrix for Quintiles

Rank at Time 0	*Rank at Time 1*				
	1	*2*	*3*	*4*	*5*
1	61.8%	18.8%	4.0%	5.3%	10.1%
2	22.2	37.3	14.3	12.6	13.6
3	5.5	18.1	37.7	24.6	14.1
4	3.7	13.6	28.5	32.6	21.7
5	12.2	14.0	14.0	21.4	38.3

probabilities at one point in time depend only on one year and not on two or more prior years.

Stationarity refers to Markov chains that have transition probabilities that are independent of time. In a first-order, stationary Markov chain, transition probabilities in successive transition matrices are identical. Simply stated, for this case, if TM is the transition matrix, assuming stationarity, then the limiting distribution P is defined by the equation $P = TM * P$. A nonstationary chain would have varying transition probabilities over the length of the chain.

A transition matrix is symmetric if the transition probability for a change from state i at time t to state j at time $t+1$ is equal to the transition probability for a change from state j at time t to state i at time $t+1$, for all states i and j. In other words, the transition probabilities above the diagonal of identical states are the mirror image of the transition probabilities below the diagonal.

For cross-classified data, a first-order Markov chain can be represented by the log-linear model $I \times I \times T$, where I refers to the distribution of states in a time period and T refers to the number of separate $I \times I$ tables which can be constructed over the time series with the available data (Bishop, Fineberg, and Holland, 1975). In expanded form, the log-linear model for a first order Markov chain is:

$$\ln m_{ijt} = u + u_{1(i)} + u_{2(j)} + u_{3(t)} + u_{12(ij)} + u_{13(it)} \qquad (2)$$

where m_{ijt} is the expected number of subjects in state i at time t and state j at time $t+1$. The main effects are defined by $u_{1(i)}$, for the current state, $u_{2(j)}$ for the future state, and $u_{3(t)}$ for the trend or time coefficient. The interaction effects are specified in $u_{12(ij)}$ and $u_{13(it)}$. Higher order models can be similarly specified to determine the order of the Markov chain (Chen, 1988). A test of stationarity of a first-order Markov chain is simply the Chi-squared (or G-squared) statistic for this log-linear model (Bishop, Fineberg, and Holland, 1975).

After determining the order and stationarity of a Markov chain, the transition probabilities can be applied to predict the distribution of individuals in future periods. With a first-order, stationary Markov chain, simple matrix techniques will yield predictions of long-term outcomes. These predictions may be compared with observed distributions at future points in time to test the overall fit of the model.

DESCRIPTIVE ANALYSIS

Mean expense for each age-gender group was computed. A deviation score was constructed for each individual by subtracting the five-year age-gender mean from actual expense. The range of deviation scores is from −$1,156 to $30,487. Most deviation scores are negative because expensive cases were left in the calculation of the age-gender means. A negative score indicates low use relative to the mean for the person's age-gender group. For analytic purposes, we convert the deviation scores into an ordinal classification by quintile. Figure 2 shows annual mean score for each of the five cohorts. Each set of bars is one year. In the first year, cohort 1 had a mean deviation score of −$456. Cohort 5 had a mean deviation score of $1,001. By the fifth year, each cohort had moved closer to the expected mean—cohort 5's mean deviation score was $135. Cohort 1 had a deviation score of −$135 in the fifth year. In a classic sense, therefore, we observe regression to the mean—declining deviation scores over time.

Regression to the mean can also be seen descriptively by tracking changes in a cohort across time. Change is movement from one state to another. The first step in a Markov chain analysis is to define discrete states or categories of medical care expense deviation, such as quartiles, quintile, or deciles. Quintiles will be used for demonstration purposes throughout the remainder of the paper. At each discrete time point (that is, annually), each individual is classified into a mutually exclusive expense category. Figures 3, 4, 5, 6, and 7 show each quintile and the distribution by quintile in each subsequent year. Figure 3 displays those individuals in quintile 1 in year 0. Each bar represents one year of the remaining four years. More than 60% of those in the first quintile in year 0 are still in this group in year 1. Quintile 1 represents those with the largest negative deviation scores.

In the highest quintile (Figure 7), there is more movement away from the original position, which suggests a non-symmetric pattern of change across different expense groups. Among a population of relatively high utilizers, there is relatively little persistence of use. Conversely, low utilizers (quintile 1) show fairly strong persistence of use. This is consistent with data shown in McCall and Wai (1983). Even when the number of categories is large, the difference between the low and high users remains, suggesting that it does not represent movement within cells. This is also consistent with prior research on nonaged populations which implies that high-use patterns tend to be the result of

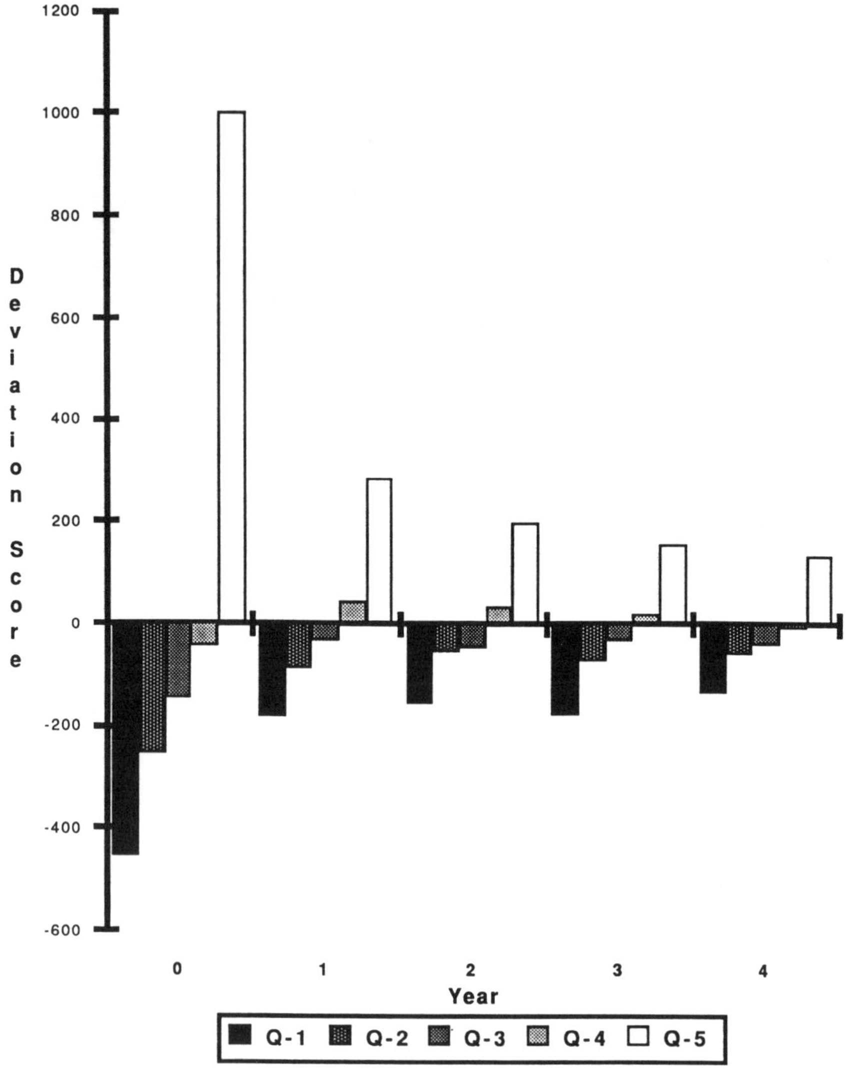

Figure 2. Mean deviation score by cohort.

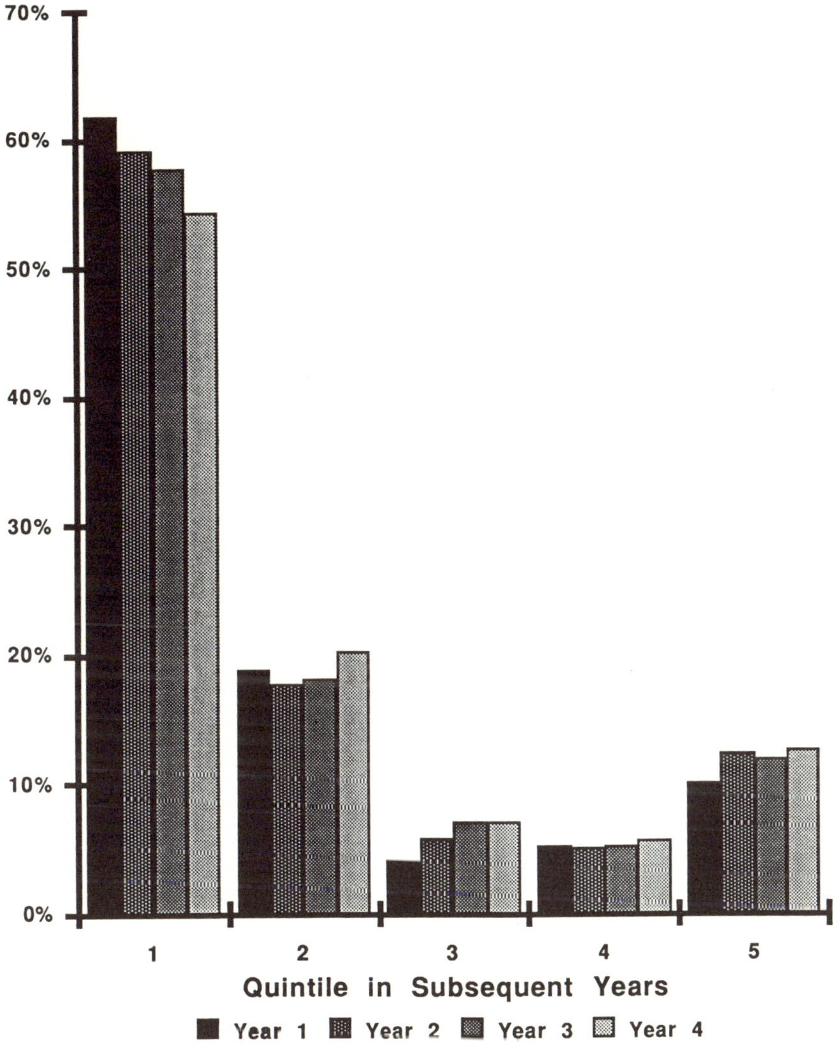

Figure 3. Distribution of first quintile: Years 1-4.

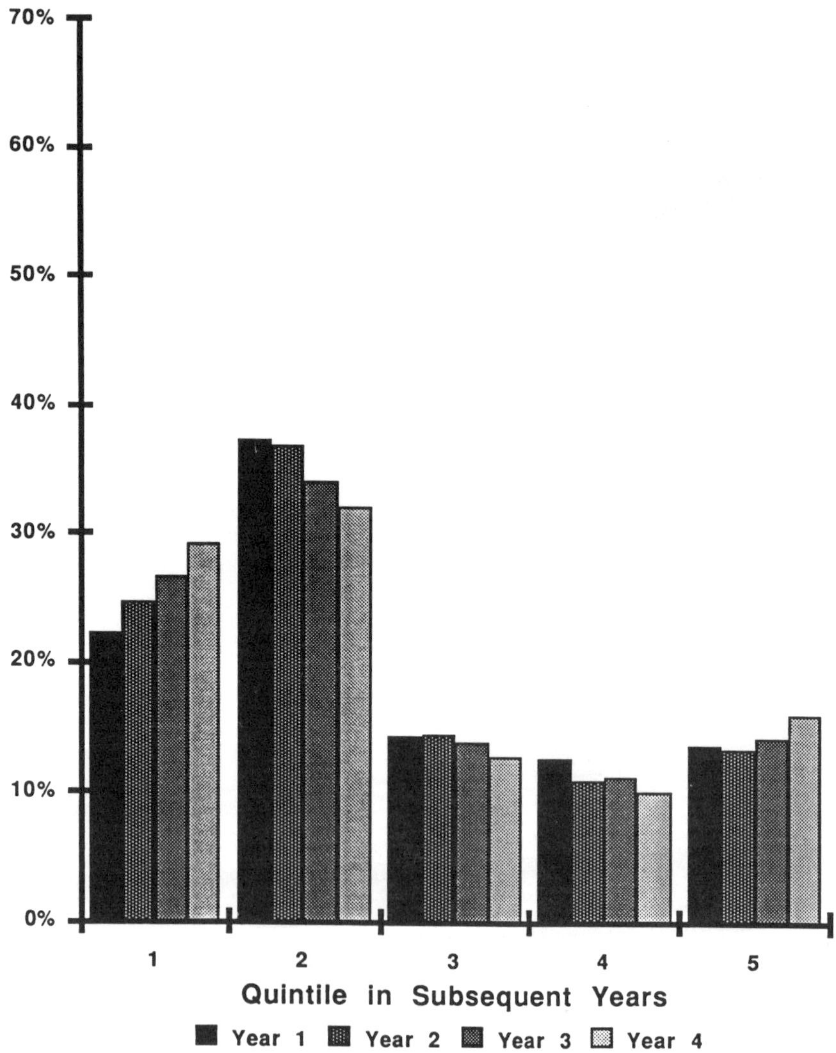

Figure 4. Distribution of second quintile: Years 1-4.

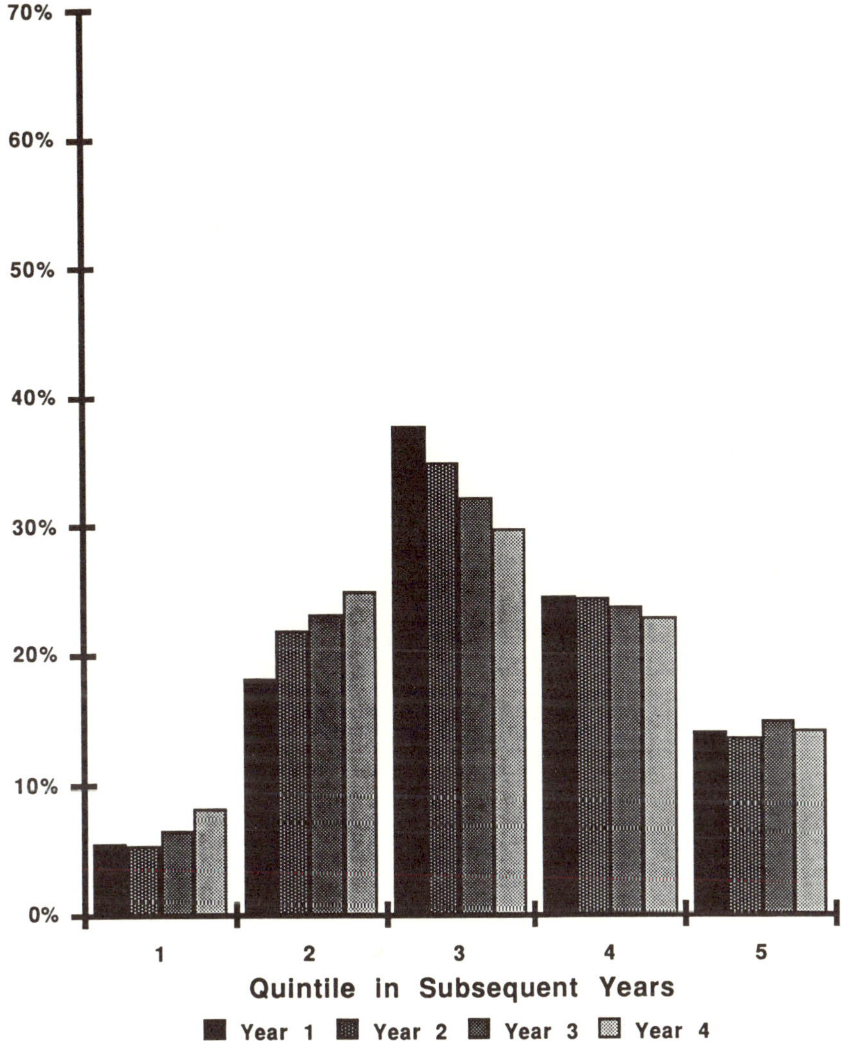

Figure 5. Distribution of third quintile: Years 1-4.

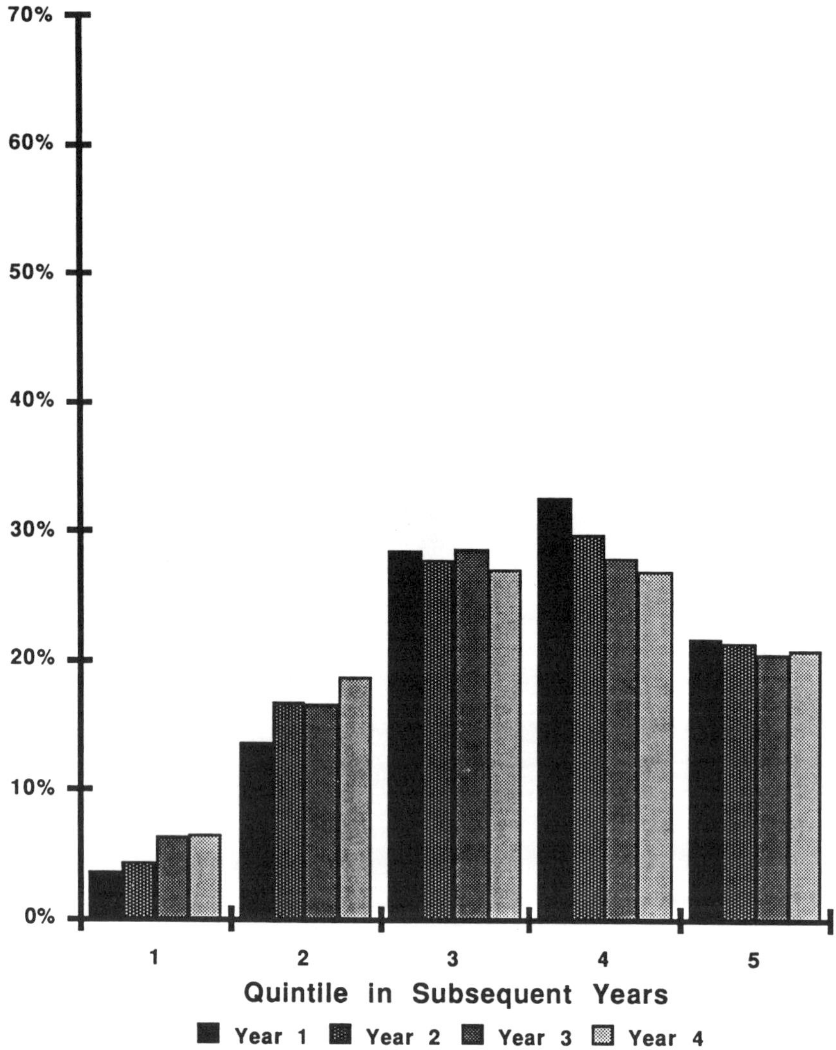

Figure 6. Distribution of fourth quintile: Years 1-4.

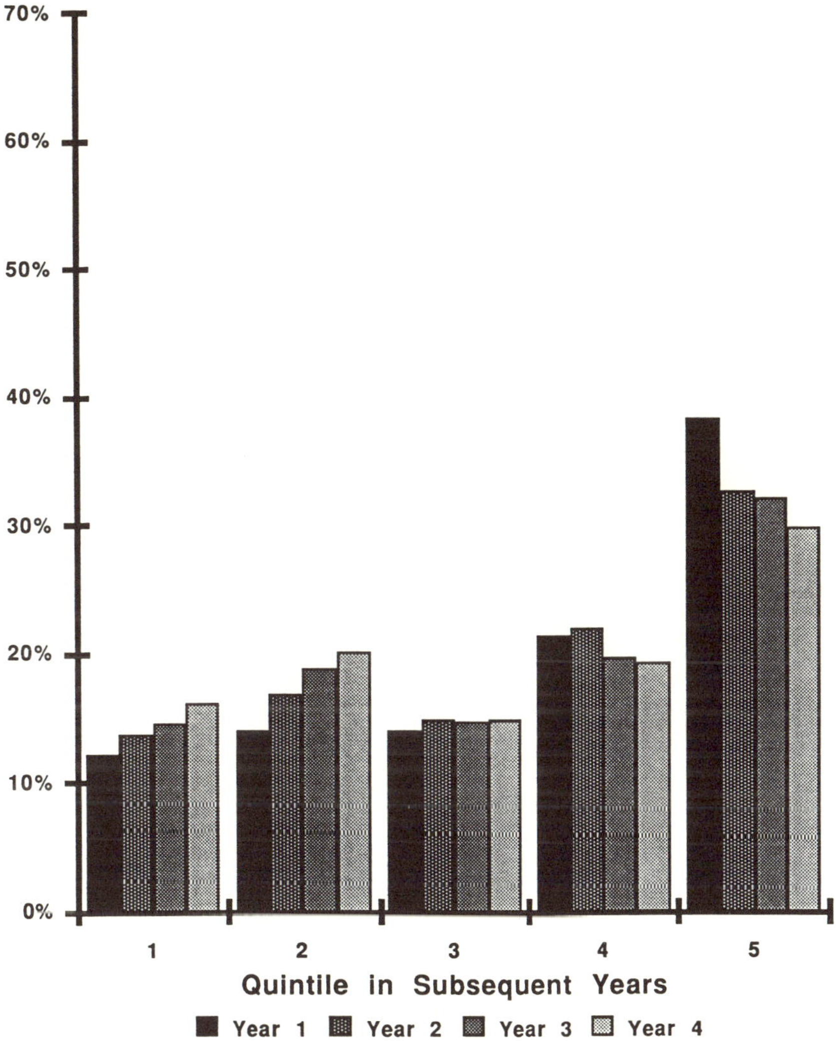

Figure 7. Distribution of fifth quintile: Years 1-4.

relatively random events such as child-bearing and trauma, rather than the result of long-term chronic conditions as in the aged (Hornbrook, Goodman, and Bennett, 1991). To summarize, these data seem to provide evidence that persistence of use is low in the high-use group and modest among the low-use groups.

Simply measuring the degree to which individuals remain in a cell in any year in the future is only one method of measuring persistence of use. An individual in a cell after the second time period could have been in any other cell in a previous time period. In fact, when the entire distribution is plotted, a much smaller percent are continuously in their original expense category. Table 2 shows for each year the percentage continuously in the same quintile. Only a small percent stay continuously in the same quintile through five time periods. The lowest quintile decays the least, but even in this cell only 20% are continuously in the lowest utilizing cell. Using this strict definition, we do not observe strong long-term persistence of use.

Freeborn et al. (1990) define high users as persons in the high expense category for four of the six study years. This standard is operationalized in Table 3, which shows the percent in the same expense category for any two, three, four, or five (including the base year) years. Under this more liberal standard, fewer than 50% of any cell remain in the same cell for four of the five study years. By this standard, modest persistence of use is observed.

Table 2. Percent of Quintile Continuously in Same Quintile (1 is lowest deviation score)

Rank at Year 0	*Year* 1	2	3	4
1	61.8%	41.3%	29.1%	21.3%
2	37.3	18.7	9.7	6.1
3	37.7	18.0	8.0	5.0
4	32.6	13.1	5.4	2.7
5	38.3	17.7	9.8	6.6

Table 3. Number of Years in Same Quintile
(Includes non-consecutive years)

Rank at Year 0	Number of Years			
	2	3	4	5
1	90.9%	72.9%	47.9%	21.3%
2	73.6	42.4	18.0	6.1
3	70.3	40.3	19.0	5.0
4	68.1	34.0	12.5	2.7
5	68.1	39.5	18.4	6.6

MARKOV CHAIN ANALYSIS

We now turn to some tests aimed at understanding more about the Markov chain. This section tests for different properties of the Markov chain. The first step will involve tests of stationarity (temporal independence of transition probabilities) assuming first- and second-order chains. The first step answers two questions: whether the transition matrices differ significantly over time, and whether the transition is dependent on only one or more than one previous time period. The second step will assess the order of the chain. This step is limited because only five time periods are present. With these few periods, tests for chains higher than a second-order chain would involve two or fewer time periods.

The likelihood ratio Chi-square values for each of the Markov chain analyses are presented in Table 4. The first column presents the generating classes, which are those terms used to estimate the model. The second column provides a model number. The third column indicates the number of states in each table. The fourth column provides the likelihood ratio Chi-square, which measures the overall fit.

We begin by testing for first-order stationarity, which assumes an I $\times$ I $\times$ T model. In this model, there are four time periods. If the likelihood ratio Chi-square of the overall model is significant, then we can reject the hypothesis of stationarity. None of the equations is significant, so we cannot reject this hypothesis. Thus, if the Markov chain is a first-order chain, it is stationary, and the I $\times$ I transition matrices do not change from one time period to another. Had we measured significance at the .10 level (instead of .05), model 1, with four states (quartiles) would have been significant. This indicates that, with a small number of categories, the transition matrices may change over time. Model 6, with only three states of high, medium, and no use, will be discussed below.

The next step is a test (Model 7), using quintiles, which asks: If the Markov chain is second order, is it stationary? This is shown in the second section of

Table 4. Likelihood Ratio Chi-Square Statistics Tests of Stationarity

Generating Class[a]	*Model Number*	*Number of States*	*Likelihood Ratio Chi-square*	*Degrees of Freedom*	*Goodness-of-Fit P Value*
A. Test of Stationarity Assuming First-Order					
DEV0 * DEV1, DEV0 * TIME	1	4	48.71	36	0.076
	2	5	52.56	60	0.742
	3	6	74.92	90	0.873
	4	7	73.41	126	0.999
	5	8	128.76	168	0.989
	6	3	11.57	18	0.867
B. Test of Stationarity Assuming Second-Order					
DEV0 * DEV1 * DEV2, DEV0 * DEV1 * TIME	7	5	102.82	200	1.000
	8	3	17.44	35	0.994

Notes: [a]Highest order interactions are specified; lower order interactions and main effects are implied.
DEV0 = Deviation Score in First Time Period.
DEV1 = Deviation Score in Second Time Period.
DEV2 = Deviation Score in Third Time Period.

Table 5. Test of Order if Assuming Second-Order Stationarity

Generating Class[a]	Model Number	Number of States	Likelihood Ratio Chi-square	Degrees of Freedom	Improvement-of-Fit P Value
First Order					
DEV0 * DEV1, DEV1 * DEV2	9	5	3219.53	80	
Second Order					
DEV0 * DEV1 * DEV2			662.54	64	
Difference			2556.99	16	0.000
First Order					
DEV0 * DEV1, DEV1 * DEV2	10	5	619.27	12	
Second Order					
DEV0 * DEV1 * DEV2			25.08	8	
Difference			594.19	4	0.000

Notes: [a]Highest order interactions are specified; lower order interactions and main effects are implied.
DEV0 = Deviation Score in First Time Period.
DEV1 = Deviation Score in Second Time Period.
DEV2 = Deviation Score in Third Time Period.

Table 4. The significance level indicates that if this is a second-order chain, it is stationary. When transitions are defined with three levels (I × I × I), the number of time periods is reduced to three. In summary, the tests for stationarity indicate that there is not a significant time trend.

Table 5 assesses the order of the chain (Model 10). Looking at the difference in the likelihood ratios between the first-order test and the second-order test, we see an improvement of almost 2,500 in the likelihood ratio Chi-square, while using only 16 degrees of freedom. This improvement indicates that the data are consistent with a second-order chain. With additional years of data, higher-order chains could be tested.

Given the limited number of time periods, the data are consistent with a stationary, second-order (or higher-order) Markov chain. For any state, therefore, the transition probability is determined by at least the two prior states. These three dimensional tables do not change significantly over time; the last three-period model is not significantly different from the first. While a first-order chain lends itself to simple matrix multiplication to determine whether it fits the actual data, higher order chains do not have this property.

This analysis demonstrates the ability of Markov chain techniques to provide insight into the nature of change in our data set. The following two brief analyses explore additional applications. The first examines Models 6, 8, and 10, using classes defined by high and low use. The second will examine the symmetry of the initial transition matrix. Symmetry, while straightforward in a two-dimensional table (such as Table 1), is much more difficult to describe and analyze at higher levels.

There is a general concern in health policy dating back to Densen et al. (1959) with select groups of high and low users. In order to apply these techniques to these groups, a Markov chain with three groups is analyzed. The groups are a high-using group (deviation from expected greater than $500), a non-using group, and those not in the first two groups. Model 6 in Table 4 shows a test for stationarity assuming a first-order chain. Model 8 provides a test for stationarity, assuming a second-order chain. As with the earlier models, the data are consistent with a second-order, or higher, Markov chain; there is no significant trend. Table 5 (Model 10) tests the order of the chain assuming it is second-order stationary. The improvement in the likelihood ratio of 594, with only four degrees of freedom, indicates that the chain is consistent with a second-order chain. The change in utilization, even with these broad definitions, is complex, requiring more than a single previous period.

Finally, we examine the inside of the matrix. The previous Markov chain analyses have dealt with the overall chain. This test, using the transition matrix from Table 1, looks at the changes within the matrix to see whether the pattern of change is different for high and low users. Visual analysis of those results indicates that change is not symmetric across groups. High users show less persistence of use than the low users. To test whether this is true, an I × I transition matrix is tested. The test for symmetry had a Chi-square value of 27.4 with 10 degrees of freedom. This indicates that change is not symmetric across the different subgroups. Intuitively, this is plausible when Figures 2-6 and the initial transition matrix are examined.

DISCUSSION AND CONCLUSIONS

This research demonstrates that there is only modest long-term persistence of use among nonaged, employed populations. Most of those in the highest use category do not exhibit persistently high expense. The lowest use category shows substantially greater persistence of use—healthy persons stay healthy and sick persons recover. In both cases, more than 50% of the individuals will be in a different use category over the study period. In all except the low-use group, persistence of use is low.

This work is consistent with past work on nonaged populations which shows that high use is often the result of random, short-lived acute illness events. The pattern of change in the highest utilizing group helps to confirm this.

The Markov chain analysis demonstrated that the pattern of utilization change is relatively complex. The data are consistent with at least a second-order, stationary Markov chain. This dependence on multiple time periods is an important finding for future risk-assessment research. If this is correct, individual risk assessment requires consideration of multiple predictor years to accurately characterize future health care expense. Specification of the correct functional form of these models will present an important challenge to future research. These implications also apply to "switcher" studies using short time periods to measure relative risk of health plans.

The present study is limited, exploring the appropriateness of Markov chain techniques for studies of persistence of use. Future studies should control for the effect of additional covariates related to health status. The population in the study includes only long-term members of a single HMO. Finally, the limited years of data prevented adequate examination of higher-order chains. Future research should use longer time periods so these questions can be answered.

An important policy implication emerging from these findings is the importance of longer enrollment periods. The use of enrollment for two or more years would eliminate some of the incentives health plans have to skim low users and disenroll high users. If very high use is mostly random, as indicated by this study, then longer enrollments would reduce the chance of loss on individual patients who engage in opportunistic switching. Similarly, the market for small groups could be enhanced through the use of longer contract terms. All of these enhancements stem from the lack of strong persistence of high use in nonaged health care use.

ACKNOWLEDGMENTS

This research was supported by a grant from Kaiser Foundation Health Plan, Inc. The views expressed in this paper are those of the authors, and no official endorsement by Kaiser Foundation Health Plan is intended or should be inferred. We would like to acknowledge the assistance of Margaret R. Sucec, who provided technical editing.

REFERENCES

Anderson, D. (1991). "Can Risk Assessment Tools Be Feasibly Used in the Health Benefits Marketplace?" In M. Hornbrook (Ed.), *Advances in Health Economics and Health Services Research: Vol. 12, Risk-Based Contributions to Private Health Insurance* (pp. 3-18). Greenwich, CT: JAI Press.

Anderson, G. and J.R. Knickman (1984). "Patterns of Expenditures among High Utilizers of Medical Care Services." *Medical Care* 22:143-149.

Beebe, J.C. (1988). "Medicare Reimbursement and Regression to the Mean." *Health Care Financing Review* 9:9-22.

Bishop Y.M.M., S.E. Feinberg, and P.W. Holland (1975). *Discrete Multivariate Analysis: Theory and Practice.* Cambridge, MA: MIT Press.

Buchanan, J.L. and S. Cretin (1986). "Risk Selection of Families Electing HMO Membership." *Medical Care* 24:39-51.

Chen, T.T. (1988). "Modelling the Liver Function Data in Diabetes." *Statistics in Medicine* 7:671-683.

Densen, P.M., S. Shapiro, and M. Einhorn (1959). "Concerning High and Low Utilizers of Service in a Medical Care Plan, and the Persistence of Utilization Levels over a Three Year Period." *Milbank Memorial Fund Quarterly* 37:217-236.

Eggers, P.W. and R. Prihoda (1982). "Pre-Enrollment Reimbursement Patterns of Medicare Beneficiaries Enrolled in "At-Risk" HMOs." *Health Care Financing Review* 4:55-73.

Freeborn, D.K., C.R. Pope, J.P. Mullooly, and B.H. McFarland (1990). "Consistently High Users of Medical Care Among the Elderly." *Medical Care* 28:527-540.

Hornbrook, M.C. and M.J. Goodman (1991a). "Adjusting Health Benefit Contributions to Reflect Risk." In M. Hornbrook (Ed.), *Advances in Health Economics and Health Services Research: Vol. 12, Risk-Based Contributions to Private Health Insurance* (pp. 41-76). Greenwich, CT: JAI Press.

Hornbrook, M.C. and M.J. Goodman (1991b). "Health Plan Case Mix: Definition, Measurement, and Use." In M. Hornbrook (Ed.), *Advances in Health Economics and Health Services Research: Vol. 12, Risk-Based Contributions to Private Health Insurance* (pp. 111-148). Greenwich, CT: JAI Press.

Hornbrook, M.C., M.J. Goodman, and M.D. Bennett (1991). "Assessing Health Plan Case Mix in Employed Populations: Ambulatory Morbidity and Prescribed Drug Models." In M. Hornbrook (Ed.), *Advances in Health Economics and Health Services Research: Vol. 12, Risk-Based Contributions to Private Health Insurance* (pp. 197-232). Greenwich, CT: JAI Press.

Hornbrook, M.C., M.J. Goodman, M.D. Bennett, and M.R. Greenlick (1991). "Assessing Health Plan Case Mix in Employed Populations: Self-reported Health Status Models." In M. Hornbrook (Ed.), *Advances in Health Economics and Health Services Research: Vol. 12, Risk-Based Contributions to Private Health Insurance* (pp. 233-272). Greenwich, CT: JAI Press.

McCall N. and H.S. Wai (1983). "An Analysis of the Use of Medicare Services by the Continuously Enrolled Aged." *Medical Care* 21:567-585.

Roos N.P. and E. Shapiro (1981). "The Manitoba Longitudinal Study on Aging: Preliminary Findings on Health Care Utilization by the Elderly." *Medical Care* 19:644-657.

Roos N.P., E. Shapiro, and R. Tate (1990). "Does a Small Minority of Elderly Account for a Majority of Health Care Expenditures?: A Sixteen Year Perspective." *Milbank Quarterly* 67:347-369.

PART III

RISK-ASSESSMENT MODELS

DEMOGRAPHIC RISK FACTORS DERIVED FROM HMO DATA

Stephen T. Hayes

INTRODUCTION

When employers offer a range of health benefit options, some plans inevitably experience biased selection. This is due to the range of benefits and prices (employee contributions) available on the one hand, and each employee's perceived need for health services, financial situation, and personal preferences, on the other. In some situations this will encourage health plans to compete on the basis of risk selection rather than their quality of care and cost-effectiveness.

One way employers can compensate for biased selection is to shift a larger portion of their contribution dollars to plans with higher risk employees, that is, risk adjustment of employer contributions. After risk adjustment, any remaining differences in employee contributions should be due to efficiency and/or benefits. This should stabilize the annual cycle of selective disenrollment of lower risk employees (from the adversely selected plan), followed by a high premium rate increase.

Advances in Health Economics and Health Services Research, Vol. 12, pages 177-196.
Copyright © 1991 by JAI Press Inc.
All rights of reproduction in any form reserved.
ISBN: 1-55938-241-4

The purpose of this study was to examine the feasibility of using routinely available data to access the average risk of employees enrolled in competing health plans. The specific objectives of the study were to evaluate several alternative risk-assessment models (that is, functional forms) and predictors of health care costs. A discussion of risk adjustment methods can be found elsewhere (Bowen and Slavin, 1991).

The study described in this paper was conducted by Kaiser Permanente's Northern California Region. This analysis served as a basis for developing an actuarial model which uses demographic factors to measure relative risk. The paper discusses several alternative approaches that were evaluated and concludes with a discussion of some of the practical uses and limitations of these risk-assessment models.

METHODS

Overview

Three risk-assessment models were developed: an actuarial model, an individual-subscriber-level regression model, and an employer-group-level regression model. The models generally use two years of "prior" inpatient utilization and "current year" subscriber demographics and length of enrollment to predict "next year's" costs. In each case, a baseline model was specified using type of contract (single, double, or family). The baseline model represents a typical situation in which the costs associated with family size are reflected in the health plan's pricing structure. We attempted to improve the baseline model by adding subscriber demographics (age, sex, and retiree status), length of plan enrollment, and nondiscretionary admissions. These variables were added sequentially, beginning with those that are relatively inexpensive for employers to obtain. Finally, the test of the models was not how well they predicted the cost of each individual subscriber unit, but how well they performed at the employer-group level.

Two random samples of equal size were used, an estimation sample and a validation sample. The estimation sample was used to estimate the model parameters (that is, either cost weights or regression coefficients) and the validation sample was used to evaluate the models' prediction errors. The reason for dividing the study population into halves was to find out how well the models performed when applied to a population of employer groups other than the one used to estimate them in the first place.

Study Population

The study population consisted of subscribers and dependents enrolled in Kaiser Permanente's Northern California Region during the period from July

1984 through June 1988. The Northern California Region includes the San Francisco Bay Area and Sacramento Area. Excluded from the study were employer groups without continuous enrollment during the four-year study period or with fewer than 50 subscribers. We also excluded individual direct-pay (non-group) accounts and beneficiaries of Medicare and Medi-Cal. If any member of a family was covered by Medicare, the entire family was excluded. After the exclusions, 1,086 employer groups remained. In the final year of the study period, these groups represented 587,659 subscribers and approximately 1.4 million enrollees. The distribution of demographic characteristics of these subscribers is presented in Table 1.

Unit of Observation

The basic unit of observation was the subscriber unit, that is, the employee and all covered dependents (if any). Individual enrollee-level risk-assessment models have the advantage of controlling for the number of dependents in families and for the risk factors of each individual. This approach was considered but was rejected since many employers do not have data describing the dependents and therefore could not take advantage of a model with these requirements.

Dependent Variable

The dependent variable was the cost per subscriber unit during the expense period, July 1987 through June 1988. The costs of subscribers with partial year enrollment were annualized and these observations were weighted accordingly. Costs were based on inpatient and outpatient utilization of services provided by plan providers plus the amount paid for services referred to non-plan providers. Costs for emergency and out-of-area claims and regional administration were excluded because these data were not available.

Since Kaiser Permanente does not currently capture patient-level costs for services provided in-house, these costs were estimated. Inpatient costs were estimated by first defining patient categories using Diagnosis Related Groups (DRGs), SysteMetrics' Disease Staging (Gonnella, 1987), and length of stay. These categories were weighted using non-Kaiser hospital charges obtained from the California Individual Hospital Discharge Data Set (OSHPD 1986), so that a share of total inpatient costs for Kaiser Foundation Hospitals could be estimated and attributed to individual inpatients. Outpatient costs were estimated based on the average cost per visit.

The distribution of costs—that is, both the total annual cost (July 1987-June 1988) of individual subscriber units and the employer group average cost

Table 1. Distribution of Study Population by Type of Contract and Subscriber Sex, Age, and Retiree Status

	Type of Contract			
	Single	*Double*	*Family*	*Total*
Female				
00-24	2.55	0.60	0.37	3.52
25-29	3.17	1.34	1.59	6.10
30-34	2.37	1.34	2.80	6.51
35-39	1.90	1.22	3.43	6.55
40-44	1.71	1.17	2.89	5.77
45-49	1.58	1.11	1.62	4.31
50-54	1.56	1.06	0.74	3.35
55-59/Active	1.39	0.84	0.28	2.51
55-59/Retired	0.26	0.11	0.02	0.39
60-64/Active	1.23	0.52	0.07	1.81
60-64/Retired	0.68	0.14	0.01	0.83
65+	0.35	0.11	0.01	0.47
Subtotal	18.76	9.55	13.82	42.14
Male				
00-24	2.73	0.38	0.43	3.54
25-29	3.76	1.21	2.24	7.21
30-34	2.91	1.21	4.34	8.46
35-39	2.19	1.96	5.61	8.76
40-44	1.65	0.87	5.68	8.20
45-49	1.15	1.09	4.15	6.39
50-54	1.02	1.70	2.67	5.39
55-59/Active	0.84	1.91	1.35	4.10
55-59/Retired	0.19	0.49	0.19	0.88
60-64/Active	0.61	1.54	0.48	2.63
60-64/Retired	0.41	1.04	0.21	1.66
65+	0.17	0.40	0.08	0.64
Subtotal	17.63	12.80	27.43	57.86
Total	36.39	22.35	41.25	100.00

Notes: Study period covers July 1987-June 1988.
$N = 587,659$

per subscriber—is described in Table 2. The mean cost of the study population, estimation and validation samples combined, was $1,464. Notice that the distribution of individual costs is extremely wide and highly skewed.

The distribution of group average cost is much narrower simply because of averaging and because small groups were excluded. Later we will see that

Table 2. Distribution of Subscriber Cost

Individual Subscriber (Total Cost)	
Number of Observations	587, 659
Mean	1,464
Median	555
Minimum	0
Maximum	1,762,559
99th Percentile	15,957
Standard Deviation	8,765
Cost Equal to Zero	
Number of Subscriber Units	64,055
Percent of Subscriber Units	10.9
Employer Group (Average Cost)	
Number of Observations	1,086
Mean	1,464
Median	1,289
Minimum	237
Maximum	4,486
99th Percentile	2,940
Standard Deviation	483
Cost Equal to Zero	
Number of Groups	0
Percent of Groups	0

Note: Study period covers July 1987-June 1988.

while it is virtually impossible to predict the costs of individuals, their predicted values can be aggregated to yield reasonable prediction errors at the group level. Previous studies have truncated the cost distribution by capping individual costs at $25,000 (Cave, Schweitzer, and Lachenbruch, 1988; Robinson, Luft, Gardner, and Morrison, 1991), assuming that a reinsurance program was in effect. Like averaging, this makes it easier to explain the remaining variance. In this study, we used the entire range of costs because no such reinsurance program is in effect for Kaiser Permanente. For comparison purposes only, we capped subscriber costs at $25,000 and re-fit our individual regression model.

Independent Variables

Demographic Risk Classes

Demographic risk classes were defined using four-way interactions among type of contract (that is, single, double, or family), subscriber age category, subscriber sex, and subscriber retiree status. An example of a risk class is "single party contract males between the ages of 60 and 64 who are retired." The risk classes were defined based on subscriber characteristics as of December 1986, six months before the start of the period for which costs were predicted. This models the lead time necessary for employers to assess plan risks, calculate contributions, and hold open enrollment.

Length of Enrollment

In a separate study of Kaiser Permanente members, the utilization propensity of recent joiners was found to be higher for obstetric services and lower for non-obstetric services, followed by regression towards the mean (Hayes, 1991). Thus, we believed that length of enrollment would play an important role in predicting utilization. In this study, four length-of-enrollment categories were defined: (1) less than or equal to one year; (2) greater than one year but less than or equal to two years; (3) greater than two years but less than or equal to three years; and (4) greater than three years. Length of enrollment was determined as of December 1986, six months prior to the expense period.

Non-Discretionary Hospital Admissions

An important objective of the study was to determine how well prior hospital use predicted future costs. We believed that individuals with a history of certain chronic diseases would have higher utilization in the future. However, there was a concern that any risk assessment/adjustment formula that used total utilization (both discretionary and non-discretionary) would discriminate against efficient health plans and providers who control the number of discretionary admissions. An admission was considered to be discretionary if the criteria for determining whether a patient should be hospitalized are not well established among physicians (Anderson et al., 1986). A detailed listing of non-discretionary principal diagnoses was developed based on a review of the literature (Anderson et al., 1986, Ellis and Ash, 1988; Roos, Wennberg, and McPherson, 1988). These diagnoses were reviewed by the Permanente Medical Group and consolidated into fourteen major diagnostic categories. Admissions, excluding re-admissions, that occurred during a two-year period, July 1984 through June 1986, were used to develop diagnostic markers. The remaining cases represented approximately 40% of all (non-newborn) admissions during this period.

Discussion of Prediction Models

Actuarial versus Regression Model

Two methodological questions arose during the initial stages of the study. The first question was, "Should we develop a simple actuarial model or a more sophisticated regression model?" Simple actuarial models that use widely available data are relatively easy to implement, making this a very practical approach for employers to pursue in the short term. However, regression models have some potential advantages that we wanted to explore. First, they can accommodate a large number of predictors such as chronic disease markers. Second, a time-series regression approach for predicting next year's cost using baseline population characteristics seemed applicable to risk assessment. Thus, we decided to develop both actuarial and regression models.

Individual versus Group (Ecological) Approach

The second question was, "If we develop a regression model, should it be based on the characteristics of individual subscribers or employer groups?" We believed that both individual and group effects were involved in determining risk. For example, individuals with a history of certain chronic diseases will have high utilization in the future. Furthermore, certain ecological dynamics of the group give rise to medical needs such as treatment of heart disease. Moreover, these medical needs do not necessarily involve the same individuals in each time period. Whereas the individual-level regression assumes that employees who are in the group during the baseline period will remain in the group during the subsequent expense period, the group-level regression assumes that employees who leave the group and/or plan are replaced by persons with similar characteristics. We decided to develop both individual and group regression models.

Description of Prediction Models

Three alternative prediction models were developed: an actuarial model, an employer-group-level regression model, and an individual-subscriber-level regression model. These models were used to estimate either actuarial cost weights or regression coefficients which were then used to predict the mean cost of employer groups in the validation sample.

Actuarial Model

The actuarial model is essentially a standard rate table approach to determining risk. Cost weights were developed by classifying subscribers by demographic risk class and calculating a mean or expected cost. Length of plan enrollment and non-discretionary admissions were not used because many of the resulting risk class weights would have been based on an insufficient number of observations.

Employer Group-Level Regression Model

This is an ordinary least-squares multivariate regression model with a single observation representing each employer group. The dependent variable represented the group's average cost per subscriber. The independent variables specified the percentage of subscribers: (1) in each of twenty-four demographic risk classes, (2) in each of four length of enrollment categories, and (3) with one or more hospital admissions for each of the fourteen categories of non-discretionary diagnoses. We reduced the number of age categories from ten (as listed in Table 1) to three because the regression coefficients initially exhibited large standard errors.

Individual Subscriber-Level Regression Model

This is an ordinary least squares, multi-variate regression model with a single observation representing each subscriber unit. The dependent variable represented the total annual cost of subscriber units. Independent dummy variables specified: (1) the subscriber's demographic risk class (among all seventy-two categories), (2) the subscriber's length of enrollment, and (3) the presence or absence of a previous hospitalization for each non-discretionary diagnosis within the subscriber unit. The model was estimated using only those subscribers who were enrolled during both December 1986 and one or more months during the expense period year, July 1987 through June 1988, that is, "stayers."

Evaluation Criteria

Earlier we stated that the purpose of this paper was to develop a method for assessing risk in an employer group. We also stated that the test of such a model is not how well it predicts the cost of each individual subscriber, but how well it predicts the mean cost of the group. Thus, the models were tested to determine which minimized the prediction error at the group level. If our intention had been to explain the variance in cost across individuals, we would have used the R^2 statistic (from the individual regression).

Our measure of prediction error was the percent root mean square error (PRMSE). This measure reflects the range of errors across all employer groups in a sample. For example, a PRMSE of 10% means that for 65% of the groups (one standard deviation), the predicted cost was within 10% of actual. The PRMSE was derived by summarizing employer group-level error ratios as follows: (1) for a single group, % error = ((actual − predicted) ÷ predicted) × 100; and (2) for many groups, PRMSE = SQRT(Σ (% error)^2 ÷ N).

Using the PRMSE, several comparisons were made:

1. *Actuarial versus regression models.* This would indicate whether the actuarial model or the more complex regression model (with the additional predictors) was more effective in reducing prediction error.
2. *Individual versus group regression model.* This would indicate which of the regression models was most effective. As indicated, the individual model was estimated using stayers only; the group (ecological) model assumes that the leavers are replaced by joiners with similar characteristics.
3. *Estimation versus validation sample.* Upon estimation, a model can over-fit the data, capitalizing on chance (Hornbrook, Goodman, and Bennett, 1991). Upon validation, the PRMSE would then deteriorate. This comparison would thus indicate which model was most robust.
4. *Large versus small groups.* We anticipated that the models would perform better for large groups than for small groups. However, we wanted to identify break points above which we could have more confidence in the predicted value of an employer group of a certain size. We compared prediction errors of groups with 50-99, 100-499, 500-999, and 1,000+ subscribers.

RESULTS

This section presents the results of the study. First, we present the estimation results, which include a description of the cost weights of the actuarial model and the parameter estimates and R^2 statistics of the regression models. Then we present the validation results, which compare the prediction errors (PRMSEs) as described above.

A total of ten models were examined: two actuarial models, four group-level regression models, and four individual-level regression models. Abbreviations and descriptions of the four different types of models are as follows:

1. Model 1 (Baseline) includes independent variables for type of contract.
2. Model 2 (Demographic) adds subscriber age, sex, and retiree status.
3. Model 3 (LOE) adds length of plan enrollment.
4. Model 4 (Admission) adds non-discretionary hospital admissions.

Estimation Results: Actuarial Model

Estimation results for the actuarial models consist of a table of cost weights by type of contract (Model 1) and by demographic risk class (Model 2). The cost weights are presented in Table 3a. The mean cost per subscriber unit for all 286,071 subscribers in the estimation sample was $1,458, which is equal to a weight of 1.000.

The salient characteristics of the cost weights are as follows:

1. The mean cost of only one group of subscribers, single party contract males, increases linearly with age. This suggests that age alone is a poor measure of risk and underscores the importance of controlling for sex and family composition (or type of contract as a proxy).
2. The costs of single party contract females are relatively constant. This is because medical and surgical care are substituted for maternity care as they age.
3. Employees with double and family contracts experience a distinctive "U-shaped" cost curve. Driven initially by maternity utilization, the cost curve bottoms out near age forty and increases thereafter, as utilization of medical and surgical care increases.
4. Early retirees' costs are generally higher than those of active employees. Female retirees with double and family contracts are an exception, however. Their costs are generally lower than those of their active counterparts.
5. In some cases, active employees who are 65 years old or older appear to be relatively healthy (compared to their 60-64 year old counterparts). This is consistent with what would be expected for a population that remains in the work force beyond the typical age of retirement. (As mentioned earlier, Medicare beneficiaries were excluded from the study population; thus, virtually all of the remaining subscribers over the age of 65 were working.)

Estimation Results: Group Regression Model

The estimation results of the group regression model are presented in Table 3b. The R^2 statistics were .402, .506, .516, and .515 for the baseline, demographic, LOE, and admission models, respectively. Essentially all of the improvement in explained variance over the baseline model came from adding demographics. Length of enrollment and non-discretionary admissions did not explain any of the variance. These R^2 statistics are much higher than those generally reported in the literature. This is simply due to averaging subscriber units at the employer group level which reduced the variance in the dependent variable. (Most other studies have been based on individual-member-level observations.)

Table 3a. Actuarial Model Relative Cost Weights (Estimation Sample)

	Type of Contract		
	Single	*Double*	*Family*
Total	0.478	1.135	1.390
Female			
00-24	0.507	1.240	1.645
25-29	0.460	0.977	1.523
30-34	0.498	1.005	1.247
35-39	0.492	0.896	1.297
40-44	0.480	0.793	1.263
45-49	0.591	0.998	1.323
50-54	0.596	1.137	1.412
55-59/Active	0.760	1.400	1.473
55-59/Retired	1.058	1.236	1.879
60-64/Active	0.802	1.807	1.982
60-64/Retired	0.944	1.642	1.132
65+	0.603	1.505	3.877
Male			
00-24	0.206	1.022	1.647
25-29	0.240	0.884	1.596
30-34	0.281	0.791	1.457
35-39	0.358	0.672	1.365
40-44	0.412	0.713	1.299
45-49	0.512	0.860	1.324
50-54	0.525	1.147	1.386
55-59/Active	0.715	1.327	1.629
55-59/Retired	0.982	1.548	2.186
60-64/Active	0.921	1.721	1.863
60-64/Retired	1.223	2.045	1.953
65+	1.269	1.507	1.382

Notes: Study covers July 1987-June 1988.
$N = 286{,}071$.
Mean = $1,458.

Table 3b. Group Level Model Estimation Results (Estimation Sample)

	Model			
Variable	*1*	*2*	*3*	*4*
Intercept[a]	593**	308	437*	412*
% Double	24**			
% Family	8**			
% Single, F, 00-39		2	3	4
% Single, F, 40-54		7	6	5
% Single, F, 55+, Active		7	7	5
% Single, F, 55+, Retired		2	−9	−10
% Single, M, 40-54		12	10	9
% Single, M, 55+, Active		25*	25*	25*
% Single, M, 55+, Retired		55	71	68
% Double, F, 00-39		15*	16*	15*
% Double, F, 40-54		5	1	1
% Double, F, 55+, Active		19	18	19
% Double, F, 55+, Retired		30	30	30
% Double, M, 00-39		8	9	12
% Double, M, 40-54		2	6	6
% Double, M, 55+, Active		36**	35**	31**
% Double, M, 55+, Retired		26*	22*	19
% Family, F, 00-39		18**	16**	15**
% Family, F, 40-54		18**	19**	18**
% Family, F, 55+, Active		−9	−8	−10
% Family, F, 55+, Retired		−88	−113	−118
% Family, M, 00-39		18**	18**	16**
% Family, M, 40-54		13**	10**	10**
% Family, M, 55+, Active		3	4	−4
% Family, M, 55+, Retired		23	26*	21
% ≤ 1 year in Group			−1	−1
% > 1 year, ≤ 2 years in Group			−7**	−7**
% > 2 years, ≤ 3 years in Group			2	2

(*continued*)

Table 3b. (Continued)

	Model			
Variable	*1*	*2*	*3*	*4*
Infections, Parasites				1961
Neoplasms				-2918
Endocrine, Nutritional				-2475
Blood, Blood Forming				8064
Nervous, Sensory				6655
Circulatory				7545
Respiratory				7519
Digestive				5195
Genitourinary				293
Child Birth				509
Skin, Subcutaneous Tissue				-2004
Musculoskeletal				421
Congenital Abnormality				-7186
Injury, Poisoning				3144
Adj. R^2	.402	.506	.516	.515
F-Ratio	183	25	23	15
Mean	1458	1458	1458	1458

Notes: Study covers July 1987-June 1988.
$N = 544$.
[a]The intercept represents all subscribers with single party contracts for Model 1 and single contract males age 0-24 for Models 2 through 4.
$*p < .05$.
$**p < .01$.

Estimation Results: Individual Regression Model

The estimation results of the individual regression models are presented in Table 3c. As expected, the R^2 statistics were much lower than those of the group regression model. The R^2 statistics were .0085, .0114, .0114, and .0150 for the baseline, demographic, LOE, and admission models, respectively. Approximately half of the improvement in explained variance over the baseline model came from adding demographics and approximately half came from adding non-discretionary admissions. LOE did not explain any of the variance. To illustrate the impact of a few high cost subscriber units, we truncated the cost distribution at $25,000 (replacing 2,280 observations). This gave us R^2 of .0274, .0341, .0342, and .0430, respectively.

Table 3c. Subscriber Level Model Estimation Results (Estimation Sample)

Variable	*Model*			
	1	*2*	*3*	*4*
Intercept	820**	458**	514**	448**
Double	910**			
Family	1197**			
Single, F, 00-24		438**	439**	436**
Single, F, 25-29		378**	361**	364**
Single, F, 30-34		553**	527**	533**
Single, F, 35-39		312**	281**	289**
Single, F, 40-44		320**	287**	293**
Single, F, 45-49		439**	404**	402**
Single, F, 50-54		492**	454**	438**
Single, F, 55-59, Active		726**	686**	674**
Single, F, 55-59, Retired		1088**	1042**	1007**
Single, F, 60-64, Active		809**	768**	743**
Single, F, 60-64, Retired		943**	896**	846**
Single, F, 65+		407	364	381
Single, M, 25-29		39	23	39
Single, M, 30-34		81	56	75
Single, M, 35-39		164	131	150
Single, M, 40-44		185	150	166
Single, M, 45-49		343**	307*	306*
Single, M, 50-54		505**	466**	455**
Single, M, 55-59, Active		697**	657**	617**
Single, M, 55-59, Retired		729*	686*	622*
Single, M, 60-64, Active		1067**	1026**	944**
Single, M, 60-64, Retired		1401**	1354**	1282**
Single, M, 65+		1896**	1854**	1859**
Double, F, 00-24		1387**	1382**	1323**
Double, F, 25-29		1141**	1121**	1083**
Double, F, 30-34		981**	952**	922**
Double, F, 35-39		917**	883**	867**
Double, F, 40-44		677**	641**	624**
Double, F, 45-49		1003**	965**	907**
Double, F, 50-54		1291**	1252**	1186**
Double F, 55-59, Active		1809**	1768**	1700**
Double, F, 55-59, Retired		1152**	1105**	1050**
Double, F, 60-64, Active		1924**	1881**	1750**

(*continued*)

Table 3c. (Continued)

	Model			
Variable	*1*	*2*	*3*	*4*
Double, F, 60-64, Retired		1791**	1741**	1666**
Double, F, 65+		1751**	1708**	1638**
Double, M, 00-24		1007**	1004**	1000**
Double, M, 25-29		957**	940**	939**
Double, M, 30-34		930**	905**	899**
Double, M, 35-39		527**	495**	496**
Double, M, 40-44		636**	599**	590**
Double, M, 45-49		868**	828**	794**
Double, M, 50-54		1304**	1263**	1197**
Double, M, 55-59, Active		1689**	1647**	1578**
Double, M, 55-59, Retired		1894**	1853**	1764**
Double, M, 60-64, Active		2439**	2397**	2285**
Double, M, 60-64, Retired		2740**	2697**	2561**
Double, M, 65+		2248**	2205**	2125**
Family, F, 00-24		2041**	2033**	1837**
Family, F, 25-29		1576**	1552**	1362**
Family, F, 30-34		1383**	1353**	1229**
Family, F, 35-39		1344**	1311**	1235**
Family, F, 40-44		1405**	1368**	1307**
Family, F, 45-49		1492**	1452**	1374**
Family, F, 50-54		1638**	1596**	1532**
Family, F, 55-59, Active		1651**	1605**	1533**
Family, F, 55-59, Retired		989	937	790
Family, F, 60-64, Active		1920**	1874**	1756**
Family, F, 60-64, Retired		685	636	456
Family, F, 65+		1687	1632	1426
Family, M, 00-24		1934**	1929**	1757**
Family, M, 25-29		1837**	1815**	1634**
Family, M, 30-34		1662**	1631**	1496**
Family, M, 35-39		1543**	1506**	1420**
Family, M, 40-44		1441**	1400**	1332**
Family, M, 45-49		1474**	1431**	1363**
Family, M, 50-54		1604**	1559**	1483**
Family, M, 55-59, Active		2034**	1988**	1885**
Family, M, 55-59, Retired		1748**	1705**	1591**
Family, M, 60-64, Active		2077**	2031**	1895**
Family, M, 60-64, Retired		2908**	2862**	2700**
Family, M, 65+		1371	1325	1343
$\leq$ 1 year in Group			−74	7
$>$ 1 year, $\leq$ 2 years in Group			−29	−16
$>$ 2 years, $\leq$ 3 years in Group			−2	1

Table 3c. (Continued)

Variable	*Model* 1	2	3	4
Infectious, Parasitic				830**
Neoplasm				900**
Endocrine, nutritional				3274**
Blood, Blood Forming				1395**
Nervouse, Sense				1893**
Circulatory				1762**
Respiratory				1896**
Digestive				736**
Genitourinary				1261**
Child Birth				551**
Skin, Subcutaneous				1182**
Musculoskeletal, Connective				731**
Congenital				765**
Injury, Poisoning				656**
Adj. R^2	.0085	.0114	.0114	.0150
F-Ratio	1057	41	39	44
Mean	1542	1542	1542	1542

Notes: Study covers July 1987-June 1988.
$N = 246{,}251$.
[a]The intercept represents all subscribers with single party contracts for Model 1 and single contract males age 0-24 for Models 2 through 4.
$*p < .05$
$**\ p < .01$

As mentioned earlier, individual regression models were estimated using only those subscribers in the estimation sample with plan eligibility during December 1986 and one or more months during the subsequent expense year (stayers), that is, 246,251 subscribers. Thus, 14% of the original estimation sample, persons who enrolled or disenrolled during the intervening period, were excluded. The average cost of the remaining subscribers (stayers) was $1,542, which was $84 (5.8%) higher than the complete estimation sample ($1,458). This is because joiners and leavers in Kaiser Permanente are generally younger than stayers and their overall age/sex adjusted utilization is lower (Hayes 1991). This "joiner/leaver effect" (caused by excluding their costs) introduces bias into the individual regression model.

Validation Results

As stated earlier, the models were tested to determine which minimized the prediction error at the group level. Either actuarial cost weights or regression coefficients (derived from the estimation sample) were applied to the employer groups in the validation sample. Predicted values were calculated and summed to the group level (where necessary). An error ratio was calculated for each group and a PRMSE was calculated across groups. Values for the PRMSEs are listed in Table 4.

A brief summary of the validation results is as follows. First, the actuarial model (based on demographics, Model 2) performed better than either of the regression models. The PRMSE was 16.0%, meaning that the predicted cost was within 16.0% of actual for 65% of the groups in the validation sample of 542 groups. Second, the individual regression model performed slightly better than the group regression model, although neither offered much of an improvement compared to the actuarial model. Third, as expected, prediction errors were consistently higher for groups in the validation sample, compared to the estimation sample). PRMSEs for the

Table 4. Prediction Results, Percent Root Mean Squared Error (PRMSE) (Validation Sample)

Type of Model	*Number of Employer Groups*	*Model*			
		1	*2*	*3*	*4*
Actuarial					
All Groups	542	17.2	16.0	NA	NA
Group Size					
50 - 99	222	42.2	39.9	NA	NA
100 - 499	240	24.7	23.9	NA	NA
500 - 999	41	18.9	15.9	NA	NA
1000 +	39	9.3	8.3	NA	NA
Group Regression					
All Groups	542	17.2	16.6	16.8	16.9
Group Size					
50 - 99	222	44.1	40.9	42.2	43.5
100 - 499	240	23.5	25.1	25.0	25.2
500 - 999	41	16.5	15.9	16.2	16.0
1000 +	39	9.9	8.7	8.8	8.4
Individual Regression					
All Groups	542	17.4	16.5	16.4	16.3
Group Size					
50 - 99	222	42.6	40.8	41.1	40.7
100 - 499	240	25.5	24.4	24.3	24.3
500 - 999	41	19.2	17.3	17.1	17.1
1000 +	39	9.5	8.8	8.7	8.5

estimation and validation samples were as follows: actuarial model (15.7%, 16.0%), group regression (15.1%, 16.6%), and individual regression (15.6%, 16.5%). This is based on the demographic variables (Model 2). Although the group regression model performed best initially, it performed worst upon validation. The actuarial model appeared to be most robust. Fourth, prediction performance varied substantially by group size. The PRMSEs of the actuarial model (based on demographics, Model 2) were 39.9%, 23.9%, 15.9%, and 8.3% for groups with 50-99, 100-499, 500-999, and 1,000 subscribers, respectively. All models similarly produced very unreliable results for small groups but produced very reliable results for large groups.

CONCLUSION

Many employers are beginning to ask: "Is there is a selection problem in my company?", "How serious is it?", and "What should be done about it?" Risk assessment provides a way of determining how much of the difference in the premium cost of plans is due to risk selection versus other factors such as benefits and efficiency. This study evaluated several risk-assessment models that could be used by employers using routinely available data.

To summarize the results of the study, we found that both demographic characteristics and prior hospitalizations for selected conditions were useful predictors of the health care costs of individual subscribers. However, prior hospitalizations did not improve the model's ability to predict the average cost of employer groups. The actuarial model, based on demographic variables, performed better than either of the more complex regression models when tested using a validation sample of 542 employer groups.

While this study evaluated the performance of several risk-assessment models derived from enrollees of Kaiser Permanente, questions regarding the application of these models to enrollees of traditional fee-for-service plans remain. Fee-for-service plans differ in benefits, utilization, and underlying characteristics of the population. Thus, the Kaiser Permanente cost weights are not an appropriate yardstick for the entire industry, but may serve as one of several points of reference.

While very large companies may consider conducting their own all-carrier risk-assessment studies, these efforts require a high degree of commitment, cooperation, and trust among participants. In the absence of employer group and plan specific weights, the Kaiser Permanente weights can be used, either alone or in conjunction with weights derived from a large fee-for-service population. This should approximate the magnitude of the selection problem. Moderate-size and smaller companies may consider using this approach.

This study points to the need to concentrate our next efforts in several related areas:

1. Several technical refinements can be made to the actuarial model. These include: (a) expanding the population base to include the entire membership of Kaiser Permanente's Northern California Region; and (b) updating the weights to include four consecutive years of experience, (representing more than 3 million subscriber-years and 8 million member-years). We plan to share these factors with interested employers in our service area.
2. Cost weights derived from a large fee-for-service population should be compared to the Kaiser Permanente weights in order to evaluate the degree of similarity between cost weights derived from Kaiser Permanente and those from indemnity insurers.
3. Similar risk-assessment models should be developed using the experience of several carriers, including HMO, PPO, and traditional fee-for-service plans, within the context of a single large employer group. This would provide an indication of how well the Kaiser Permanente factors measure relative risk compared to plan-specific factors.
4. This and other studies have found that the overall cost of recent joiners is relatively low. This suggests the need to develop a way to address situations where a significant amount of plan switching has taken place.

ACKNOWLEDGMENTS

I would like to thank the many people who contributed valuable advice and assistance. Karl Iorio and Brit Harvey developed the statistical models and conducted much of the analysis. Greg Lieberknecht moved enormous amounts of data to create the study data base. The contributions of Karl and Greg are especially appreciated. Jerry Fleming and Bill Kramer established the project and provided guidance along with Bruce Bowen, Ann Evans, Doug Roblin, and Jim Taul. The views expressed in this paper are those of the author and no official endorsement by the Kaiser Permanente Medical Care Program should be inferred.

REFERENCES

Anderson, G.F., et al. (1986). "Capitation Pricing: Adjusting for Prior Utilization and Physician Discretion." *Health Care Financing Review* 8(2):27-34.

Bowen, B. and E. Slavin. (1991). "Adjusting Contributions to Address Selection Bias: Three Models for Employers." In M. Hornbrook, (Ed.), *Advances in Health Economics and Health Services Research: Vol. 12. Risk-Based Contributions to Private Health Insurance* (pp. 97-108). Greenwich: JAI Press.

Cave, D.G., S. O. Schweitzer, and P. A. Lachenbruch. (1988). "Community Rating by Class as a Method of Adjusting Community Rated Employer Group Capitation Premiums." *GHAA Journal* 9(1):80-96.

Ellis R.P. and A. Ash. (1988). *Refining the Diagnostic Cost Group Model: A Proposed Modification to the AAPCC for HMO Reimbursement.* Final Report, Grant No. 18-C-98526/1-03, Baltimore, MD: Health Care Financing Administration.

Gonnella, J.S. (1987). *Disease Staging Clinical Criteria.* Santa Barbara, CA: SysteMetrics/McGraw-Hill.

Hornbrook, M.C., M.J. Goodman, and M.D. Bennett. (1991). "Assessing Health Plan Case Mix in Employed Populations: Ambulatory Morbidity and Prescribed Drug Models." In M. Hornbrook, (Ed.), *Advances in Health Economics and Health Services Research: Vol. 12. Risk-Based Contributions to Private Health Insurance* (pp. 197-232). Greenwich: JAI Press.

Hayes, S.T. (1991). Relative Risk of Joiners and Leavers in Kaiser Permanente. Oakland, CA: Kaiser Foundation Health Plan, Inc. (internal memorandum).

Office of Statewide Health Planning and Development (OSHPD), California Hospital Discharge Data Set (1986), Sacramento, CA:OSHPD.

Robinson, J.C., H.S. Luft, L. B. Gardner, and E. M. Morrison. (1991). "A Method For Risk-Adjusting Employer Contributions to Competing Health Insurance Plans." *Inquiry,* 28:107-116.

Roos, N.P., J. E. Wennberg and K. McPherson. (1988). "Using Diagnosis-Related Groups for Studying Variations in Hospital Admissions." *Health Care Financing Review* 9(4):53-62.

ASSESSING HEALTH PLAN CASE MIX IN EMPLOYED POPULATIONS:

AMBULATORY MORBIDITY AND PRESCRIBED DRUG MODELS

Mark C. Hornbrook, Michael J. Goodman, and Marjorie D. Bennett

INTRODUCTION

Efficient functioning of a competitive market for health insurance is an important determinant of the overall performance of the health care sector. Since 1977, when about 18% of employees had a choice of health plans (Farley and Wilensky, 1983), multi-option health benefit programs have flourished. Over 44% of employers, including more than 70% of large employers, now offer their employees a choice of several health plan options which more often than not include prepaid group practice health maintenance organizations (HMOs), preferred provider organizations (PPOs), independent practice associations (IPAs), employer self-funded plans, and managed fee-for-service (FFS) indemnity plans (Gabel et al., 1988). Variation in the premiums of these

Advances in Health Economics and Health Services Research, Vol. 12, pages 197-232.
Copyright © 1991 by JAI Press Inc.
All rights of reproduction in any form reserved.
ISBN: 1-55938-241-4

plans can derive from differences in benefits, risk, or efficiency. Consumers have difficulty knowing whether a high-priced plan is actually a good value because of better benefits, or a poor value because of a higher proportion of sick enrollees.

If sicker persons are disproportionately attracted into a specific health plan, a more resource-intensive output is produced and the premium will increase relative to other plans. This will induce some of the healthier enrollees, for whom the plan has now become relatively less attractive because the premium is such a large share of their total health care expenses, to switch to another plan, so the remaining membership has an even higher expected annual per capita expense. This cost-premium spiral, whether caused by known or unknown factors, is an early symptom of market failure (Price and Mays, 1985; Luft, Trauner, and Maerki, 1985).

Possible health plan responses to this cost-premium spiral are reducing benefits (to reduce costs), marketing to healthy persons, and screening out unhealthy persons. Unfortunately, these actions also reduce the overall level of coverage in a community. Risk differentials among competing health plans create incentives for competition by risk skimming rather than by efficiency in internal operations.

Evidence (or even presumption) of risk differentials often leads employers to question whether managed care options actually generate savings or simply skim high health status persons from traditional fee-for-service (FFS) indemnity plans. Many employers have been pressuring community-rated HMOs to experience-rate to obtain rates that reflect the actual risk of their own enrolled employees. By narrowing risk pools in search of lower health benefit costs, firms impose higher costs on other groups in society. Experience rating pushes the financial burden of illness back to the sick, thus defeating the social risk-sharing function of health insurance.

An alternative response by employers to the problem of selection bias is to seek methods of modifying their health benefit contribution formulas to redistribute risk differentials and provide incentives for the equalization of risk across health plans. Such techniques can potentially alleviate the social inefficiencies of risk skimming even when it does occur. Ideally, health plans should receive payments that reflect an informed risk rating, and consumers should face relative prices that reflect differences in efficiency among the options (Hornbrook and Goodman, 1991a). In this manner, both payers and consumers would face appropriate signals on which to base their decisions.

AIMS

The overall aim of this study is to develop improved methods for assessing relative risks of various health plans under multi-option health benefit programs. The specific aims of this study are: first, to derive alternative approaches to measuring risk related to permanent health status and propensity to use medical care in a defined population; second, to derive the criteria for evaluating different risk-assessment models; third, to explore the prediction performance of alternative risk-assessment models; and finally, to suggest priorities for future research.

PREVIOUS RESEARCH

Medicare's Adjusted Average Per Capita Cost (AAPCC) methodology for determining capitation payment rates under risk contracts with HMOs is the major example of a risk-status adjustment. The AAPCC formula adjusts payments under risk contracts with Medicare HMOs to reduce selection bias between risk and non-risk beneficiaries and among various risk contractors. The adjustment factors are county, age, sex, welfare, and institutional status. Several studies that have examined the accuracy of this prediction model for adjusting rates paid to HMOs found it to be highly unstable and very inadequate in accounting for the variance in annual per capita medical expense (Lubitz, 1987). The studies generally find that AAPCC risk factors explain less than 1% of the variance in expenses per beneficiary (Hornbrook, Bennett, and Greenlick, 1989).

The AAPCC's policy importance to Medicare risk contracting, combined with its relative inefficiency, has focused the majority of studies of individual risk prediction on the aged population. For example, in a survey of studies published from 1970-1985, Epstein and Cumella (1988) found 42 studies examining different risk factors for aged populations.

Actuarial research on the nonaged population has concentrated on alternatives to community rating, such as Community Rating by Class (CRC) and Adjusted Community Rating (ACR), as intermediates to experience rating (Wrightson, 1990).

The majority of selectivity and selection-bias literature is not aimed at predicting future health care expense. Rather, it argues that individuals joining HMOs differ from individuals staying in indemnity plans on some fundamental predictive attribute (Wilensky and Rossiter, 1986). The interest in this subject ignores two important factors. First, only a small proportion of a population actually switches health plans in any year (Neipp and Zeckhauser, 1985), with the majority of the population remaining with their plans. Thus, focus on the switchers may be misplaced (Goodman et al., 1991). Second, because this work is rarely predictive in the sense of using a validation sample or checking future against predicted expense, it ignores the fact that individuals with utilization above and below the mean in one year will regress toward the mean in future years. The regression to the mean would become clear using a prediction methodology (Goodman et al., 1991).

Perhaps more important, almost all studies of prediction with nonaged populations have used the family or subscriber unit as the unit of analysis. This ignores individual attributes which more accurately describe the underlying structure of risk. The usual method of aggregation to subscriber unit level (subscriber plus dependents) also loses information on age, gender, family structure, and health status which can prove useful in simple demographic models.

The previous studies of risk can provide more than a sense of predictable versus unpredictable (random) variance. The variety of predictors in these analyses provides a rich source of information on risk-assessment methods. Sources of data include self-reported health status gathered via survey methods, behavioral risk factors, measures of physiological health or diagnoses, and prior use of health care services.

An example of the use of aggregate survey data is Garfinkel, Riley, and Iannacchione (1988) who, in examining high-cost utilizers using data from the National Medical Care Utilization and Expenditure Study, found that the best predictors of high cost were the number of restricted activity days, number of chronic conditions, age, and employment status. Employed individuals were less likely to be high utilizers.

Using data from the Framingham Heart Study, Howland et al. (1987) found that risk-factor measurements such as EKG, blood sugar, hematocrit, and skinfold tests did not accurately predict the frequency of hospitalization in a subsequent two-year period. Note that this study is based strictly on explained variance (R^2), not on a split-half methodology as used in the present study.

Newhouse et al. (1989), using data from the RAND Health Insurance Experiment for individuals 14-years and older, found that the AAPCC variables plus a dichotomous physiological health indicator based on claims explained 31% of "explainable" variance (this is an R^2 of .045 (.045/.145 = .31, where .145 = maximum attainable R^2 if every individual were perfectly controlled)). Continuous physiological health plus AAPCC explained 29% of the explainable variance ($R^2 = .042$).

Ellis and Ash (1988, 1989) and Hornbrook, Bennett, and Greenlick (1991) have studied the use of Diagnostic Cost Groups (DCGs) as a replacement for the AAPCC demographic factors. Using a classification based on age, gender, and prior inpatient morbidities, they conclude that the DCGs perform better than the AAPCC demographic model; however, risk classes based on inpatient data are unstable. For nonaged populations, a much smaller proportion are likely to be hospitalized, reducing the utility of these models. Hayes (1991) estimates prediction models using demographic and inpatient morbidity variables for an employed HMO population.

At the family or subscriber level, prediction can be more accurate because one high-cost case in a clustered unit is typically offset by one or more ordinary cases. For example, Cave, Schweitzer, and Lachenbruch (1989) showed that an experience-rated model containing age, sex, family size, marital status, and prior-year expense could explain 38% of the variance in total family health care expense. Although the demographic variables explain 21% of the variance in a traditional community rating by class (CRC) model, when combined with prior utilization, they provide only 4.5% additional explanation of variance at the family level (Cave, Schweitzer, and Lachenbruch 1989).

On an individual level, analysis of the Medicare AAPCC formula has indicated that the maximum explainable variance may be much lower. McCall and Wai (1983) have shown that only 15% of the variance in total per capita expense can be explained in the Medicare population. Explanation of overall variation in individual health care expense is quite low because a significant portion of the expense involves inpatient stays, which are more difficult to predict accurately at the individual or family level in a nonaged population.

One method of reducing the variance is to change the shape of the distribution by removing non-users from the estimation equations. Duan et al. (1983) have developed several versions of multi-part models. These work by predicting, first, who will use any medical care services and, with that prediction in hand, how much expense users will have. This approach can be modified in numerous ways. In four-part models, the users at the second level are divided into hospitalized or not hospitalized. This has been further modified by separating hospitalized cases into high- and low-cost cases in a six-part model (Robinson et al., 1991). Although these methods are appealing, truncating the prediction distributions generated by these models still fails to reflect the true structure of the risk. In actual distributions, a large number of persons will be observed to have no use; but no individual has a zero probability of use. Similarly, at the high end, a few very high-cost cases will be observed, but no single individual is predicted to be an outlier, by the very nature of the statistical techniques employed. These models, therefore, fail to exhibit significant prediction returns for the increased computational complexity.

In this study, we opt for simplicity of models and focus our efforts on measuring disease risk and developing validation tests.

DEFINITION OF RISK

"Risk" is defined as the expected value of the per capita cost distribution of efficiently provided health care inputs required to deliver preventive, diagnostic, and treatment outputs to a defined group of enrollees for a specific future period (Hornbrook and Goodman, 1991b). Future aggregate medical care expense is a function of, among other things, the health status of the population treated, the quality of the care delivered, the pricing practices of providers, and the prices of inputs. For the purposes of this paper, we assume that access problems have been solved—all consumers have comprehensive health insurance coverage and face no financial or physical access barriers to medical care providers. Further, we assume that these providers deliver care of acceptable technical quality and that their pricing practices and input costs are constant. These assumptions enable us to focus on health status as the dominant factor in variations of use patterns in a defined population. One population that is likely to satisfy these assumptions is the membership of a large mature prepaid group practice health maintenance organization (HMO).

Variation in total health care expense is determined by the behavior interactions of the various actors—consumers, providers, health plans, and employers. Elsewhere we argue that variations in enrollee health status and use propensity are the only two sources of expense variation that should be systematically shifted from specific health plans to larger risk pools (Hornbrook and Goodman, 1991b). While population health status may be viewed as endogenous to the medical care system, relatively simple linear models of disease risk may prove useful in improving incentives for health plan performance in the intermediate run. Valid and powerful risk-assessment models are necessary for successful risk adjustment to remove incentives for skimming healthier enrollees. Development of risk-assessment methods that separate and quantify only variation associated with the two sources of risk is not a simple task. In this paper, we explore alternative indicators of exogenous permanent health status and use propensity in an attempt to understand the nature of risk in an employed population using individualistic forecasting techniques.

When individuals become ill or injured, they demand medical care. Thus, explaining current patterns of use requires information on the nature of the disease or injury. Forecasting this utilization requires information on the likelihood that these diseases or injuries will occur. Prior morbidity data can provide useful epidemiologic information in eight ways. First, chronic diseases, by definition, have a long duration, giving rise to need for care and management in a future period. Thus, presence or absence of a chronic disease will differentiate future use patterns, with more severe chronic conditions requiring more care than mild cases.

Second, serious acute disease may incur longer-term sequelae that require treatment; for example, a severe injury may require months of physical therapy. Moreover, an acute disease may lower immune system functioning or other physiologic reserves and, as a result, increase the probability of subsequent infections or health problems.

Third, conversely, a disease may confer immunity, so that future health status can be expected to be better, other things being the same.

Fourth, persons with a higher frequency of disease episodes may simply be less able to resist disease. Thus, recurrence of disease or a succession of various other diseases, related or not, may be predictive of a pattern that will continue.

Fifth, acute disease episodes incurred at the end of the risk period may persist into the prediction year. This applies particularly to conditions diagnosed in the early stages of their episodes.

Sixth, persons who incur very serious diseases that require extensive and invasive treatment will be likely to experience a reduction in their treatment intensity in the next year. Either they will improve as a result of the treatment or they will not be able to withstand further treatment at the same level.

Seventh, non-disease reasons for contact with the medical care system may indicate positive health. Preventive services may themselves confer protection against future expense, and persons who seek these services may be expected to be healthier than average.

Eighth, prior-use patterns may reflect habits that will persist, such as doctor office visits for treatment of symptoms of viral illnesses. Whatever the nature of a symptom, some persons are more likely to seek medical care than others.

Provider practice style and system-related inefficiencies in prior treatment may contaminate the measurement of illness. Diagnostic measures differ from prior use in that they measure the existence of a condition, not the actual treatment. Using the disease episode as the unit of analysis further separates the risk measurement from prior use by filtering out practice patterns of hospitalization, tests, or return visits—the episode is counted the same regardless of the intensity of treatment. Treated morbidity data reflect the propensity to seek care because individuals must obtain treatment to assign a diagnosis; illnesses of persons who do not seek care remain undocumented.

Information on diseases and other health status factors may be obtained from two original sources—the provider or the patient. In this study, we focus on the diagnoses recorded in outpatient medical records. A separate study was conducted using patient self-reported health status information (Hornbrook, Goodman, Bennett, and Greenlick, 1991).

Prescribed drugs work on a principle similar to morbidities—they capture underlying disease validated by a doctor's drug order. Unlike diagnoses, however, drug orders are much closer conceptually to patterns of practice, especially given the expectation by many patients that the output of a doctor office visit should be a prescription.

One of the problems with predicting health care expense stems from the non-normal shape of the distribution of annual individual expense. Most people have little or no health care use in a particular year. A very small percentage have extremely high use in any time period. This gives rise to a skewed distribution of expense. No individual, however, has a zero probability of having expense in a future year and it is not appropriate to predict future zero expense for current nonusers, nor is it appropriate to predict catastrophic expense for current high-cost users. Prediction models will overpredict for the nonusers and underpredict for very high-cost cases.

By definition, outliers are difficult to predict. This is not bad, per se, because the purpose of insurance is to share the risk of high expense. Perfect prediction is not possible, or desirable, because this would violate the principles of an insurable event. The essence of risk sharing is that the risk is unpredictable for the individual, but becomes predictable for the group via the law of large numbers. Risk assessment addresses the intermediate problem of groups whose mean expenses are stable but different from each other for underlying systematic reasons.

METHODS

Data and Sample

Data for a sample of employed persons enrolled in the Kaiser Foundation Health Plan of the Northwest, a large prepaid group practice HMO, for the years 1980-1987 in the medium-sized metropolitan areas of Portland/Salem, Oregon, and Vancouver, Washington, were employed for this study. In 1980-1983, a 5% sample of the HMO membership was drawn; in 1984-1987, a 2% sample was drawn. To be included in the study, individuals could not have reached their 65th birthday by the end of a study year, and they had to be members of employer groups. These study eligibility criteria excluded Medicare beneficiaries (including aged, disabled, and ESRD groups), Medicaid recipients, and persons with individual (ID) coverage. The latter group was eliminated because they were not participating in an employment-related multi-option health benefit program. Because ID enrollees may differ from group enrollees in health and use patterns, we elected to avoid the possibility of selection-bias effects in the risk-assessment models for this analysis. Future research can examine the question of whether a group-based model is unbiased for ID enrollees.

The analysis is limited to individuals with at least one month of eligibility in each of two consecutive years. This results in 51,633 observations in the pooled time-series cross-section sample. The same person can be included in the analysis multiple times over the study period because of the pooling of data from multiple years. The majority of the study population had 12 months of eligibility—79.5% in Year 0 (baseline period) and 81.6% in Year 1 (expense period).

The sample ages slightly over time, reflective of the aging of the overall HMO membership. The mean age in 1980 was 26.1 years, increasing to 28.5 years by 1986. The overall mean age of the population in the baseline year (Year

0) was 26.8 years, with a median age of 27 years. Newborns accounted for around 2% of the sample in each year; infants and children up to age 14 accounted for about 25%; women ages 20 to 39 accounted for another 20%; 49.2% of the sample was male.

Data on the demographic characteristics and eligibility status of the sampled beneficiaries were obtained from the HMO's membership accounting system. Data on hospital use for these beneficiaries were derived from the HMO's inpatient discharge abstract data system. This data system was used in computing annual hospital care expenses for the sampled members.

Data on ambulatory care services were derived from the Outpatient Utilization System (OPUS) maintained by the Center for Health Research for special research populations. Highly trained medical records technicians abstracted information on all ambulatory services and procedures provided to sampled members in HMO facilities, as documented in their medical charts. These included surgical procedures, medical services, laboratory tests, and imaging (radiology, CAT scans, and so forth) procedures. A description of this data system can be found in Greenlick, Freeborn, and Pope (1988). These data were used to measure morbidities, prior use, drug orders, and annual ambulatory expenses for each person.

Measurement of Total Annual Expense

The dependent variable for this analysis, total annual expenses for medical care, was constructed on the basis of a comprehensive utilization profile for each HMO member. Utilization data were obtained from inpatient and ambulatory records. Services obtained outside the health plan were excluded, comprising out-of-area emergency services, referral for services not provided by the HMO, and self-referral to non-HMO providers. Brown (1991) found that 13% of this population reported using some out-of-plan services. These exclusions do not necessarily undermine the validity of this data set for testing risk-assessment models because they represent a very small proportion of total use by this population, and the distribution of annual use of HMO services is quite similar to the distribution of total annual use because most cases of outside use are expected to have an HMO complement as part of the illness episode.

Departmental costs were obtained from the HMO's Medicare cost reports. A relative cost coefficient was developed for each utilization parameter. Total HMO costs were first split into two areas—inpatient and outpatient. Inpatient utilization parameters comprised the following: days in the critical care units (ICU/CCU), days in intermediate care, minutes of operating room (OR) and recovery room (RR) time, and admissions from the emergency department (ED). Four special inpatient cost centers were defined, corresponding to intermediate care, critical care, OR, and ED. All indirect costs and physician

Table 1. Distribution of Total Expenses by Analysis Year

	Year 0	*Year 1*
Mean	$321	$323
Maximum	$46,859	$45,409
Median	$97	$96
Number of individuals with expenses greater than 0	39,760	39,190
(Percent)	(77%)	(76%)

costs were allocated proportionately to the daily cost centers. ED costs attributable to inpatient admissions were allocated proportionate to those admissions. Thus, we were able to estimate an average cost per routine day, per critical care day, per minute of OR/RR time, and per admission from the ED.

Ambulatory expenses were allocated on the basis of relative-value units (RVUs), employing a special version of a relative-value scheme developed by the Center for Health Research for measuring the costliness of ambulatory services and procedures in an HMO setting. Total departmental outputs of RVUs were estimated for each year and then used to compute average cost per RVU for each of four major outpatient cost centers—laboratory, surgery, medicine, and radiology. These RVU-cost conversion coefficients enable all use elements to be summed to a total annual cost for each sampled HMO member.

Day surgery performed in the hospital was treated the same as inpatient surgery in assigning direct cost expense weights. Indirect costs were less than for inpatient surgery. Day surgery performed in the physician's office was treated the same as ambulatory services.

All utilization was converted to 1982 dollars by using the cost conversion coefficients for that year. This eliminated the effects of inflation on expenses and removed the burden of predicting inflation from the risk-assessment models. The distributions of total expenses in Year 0 (baseline year) and Year 1 (expense year) are summarized in Table 1. The means are nearly identical, indicating that inflation has been removed from the data. The median expense is just under $100, with a mean of nearly $325. About 24% of the cases had no expense. The maximum annual expense was around $45,000.

The dependent variable for this study is a measure of real use of services. While we label the variable total per capita expense, no pricing variation is included because fixed dollar weights are used to convert the various use units into a commensurable dollar unit. The significance for this study is that any variation in annual per capita expense reflects only differences in the use of services, as contrasted with other risk assessment studies that employ claims data (for example, Ellis and Ash 1988, 1989; Cave, Schweitzer, and Lachenbruch, 1989).

Regression to the Mean

On an individual level, prediction of future health care expense is heavily influenced by the random nature of illness. The majority of the variance in nonaged, individual total health care expense appears to be purely random. In the study population, the correlation between total expense in Year 0 and Year 1 is only .0266. The outliers—those who are very expensive or have no expense in one year—regress toward the mean in the succeeding year. Persons with no expenses are unlikely to remain nonusers indefinitely. Similarly, those with extremely high expense in one year are likely to have substantially lower expense the following year. Within the study population, for example, those with no expense in Year 0, had an average expense of $133 (1982 dollars) in the following year. Of this total study population without expense in Year 0, 52% had some expense in Year 1. Similarly, those above the 95th percentile, who had a mean of expense of $2,229 in Year 0, had an average expense of $674 in Year 1. Those above the 99th percentile, the true outliers with a mean expense of $7,370 in Year 0, had a mean expense of only $1,459 in the succeeding year.

Is it possible to predict the high-cost outliers? Within the nonaged population, the high expense cases are more likely to be unpredictable catastrophes, such as automobile accidents. These events cannot be predicted for individuals. Within the study population, the major causes of high-cost cases (above $15,000 in 1982 dollars), were trauma, cancer, and heart disease. Examination of a time series of individuals in this group is instructive. In the year prior to the high-cost year, the mean expense for this group (excluding ineligibles) was $815, with a range from $0 to $7,247. In the following year, the mean expense of this group was $21,100. In the next year, again excluding ineligibles, the mean expense fell to $2,066, with a range from $0 to $16,136. The individual with two consecutive years above $15,000, had an expense of only $500 in the following year. Thus, although high-cost individuals contribute significantly to health care expense and significantly change the shape of the expense distribution, their individual utilization is largely random and unpredictable. The question for this study is whether knowing about underlying health status factors like morbidity helps to predict these use patterns.

Independent Variables

Four types of independent variables are employed as predictors in the empirical analyses: demographic variables, such as age and gender; prior use

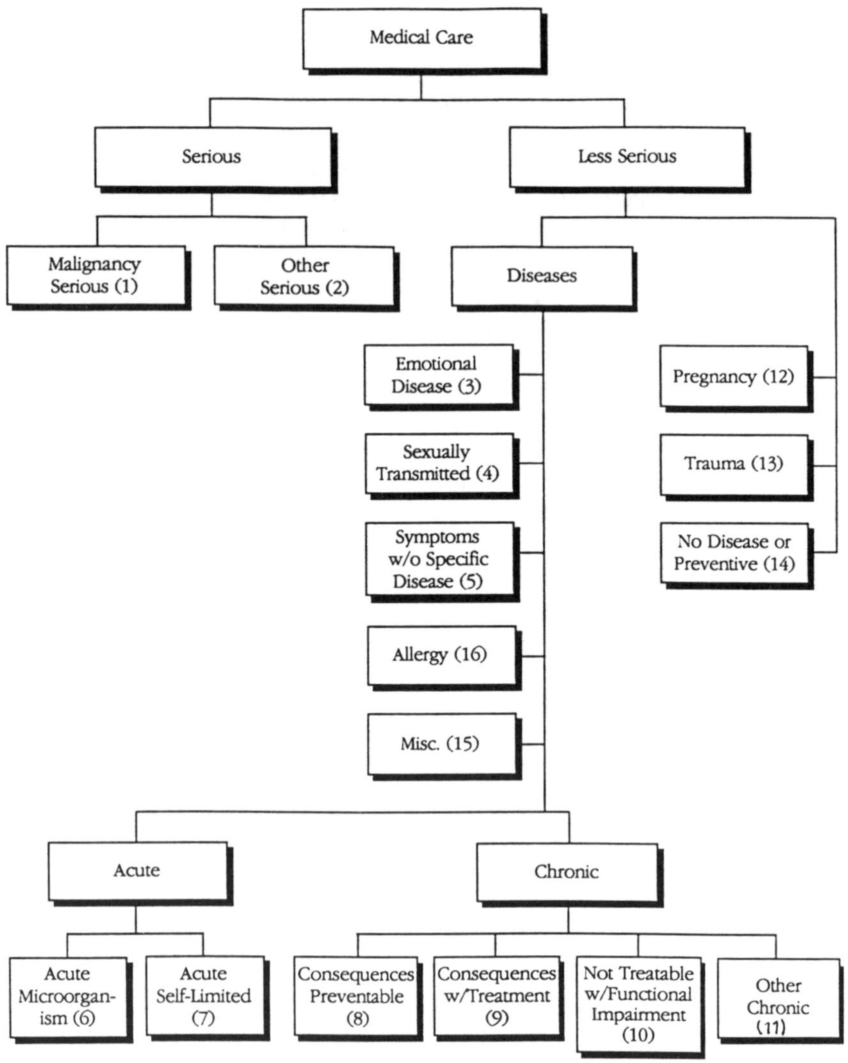

Figure 1. Clinical-behavioral disease classification system.

within the previous calendar year; treated outpatient morbidity episodes within the prior calendar year; and prescription drug orders within the prior calendar year.

The definitions and criteria for measuring treated morbidity episodes have been described by Hornbrook, Hurtado, and Johnson (1985). Briefly, a medical care episode begins when a patient formally requests treatment from the HMO and continues for as long as care is provided for the morbidity that was the reason for the initial visit. Thus, chronic diseases may have lifelong episodes. Individuals may have multiple simultaneous episodes, one for each treated co-morbidity. Recurrences of the same disease are defined on the basis of the clinical notation in the patient's chart or, in the absence of any evidence to the contrary, minimum elapsed time between contacts for the same problem. A diagnosis code is assigned to each morbidity episode. Diagnoses have been aggregated into 16 classes using an updated version of the clinical-behavioral classification scheme developed by Hurtado and Greenlick (1971). The overall structure of this classification scheme is diagrammed in Figure 1. The complete listing of 99 revised clinical-behavioral classes is available from the authors. This diagnostic taxonomy classifies diseases according to the nature and intensity of the expected response from the medical care system. This scheme is based solely on clinical judgment; no empirical clustering algorithms were used to define the morbidity groups.

Prior use is measured as the total per capita expense in the previous year (Year 0). Drug order data are derived from physician notations in patients' medical records. This information assesses the clinician's response to a disease or health problem. The data do not measure whether the patient had the prescription filled or complied with the medication instructions. Drugs are classified into 27 therapeutic classes (the classification system is available from the authors). Only the number of drug orders is counted, not the number of doses, the size of the dosages, or routes of administration. This measure captures the general therapeutic action desired by the physician, from which can be inferred the nature of the disease under treatment—for example, antineoplastic drugs are prescribed for cancer. Counts of drug orders by therapeutic class also assess the *variety* of drugs prescribed for an individual and the overall *intensity* of prescribing activity.

Estimation Technique

The models in the present study are developed using two techniques, one linear and one nonlinear. The linear technique employs ordinary least squares regression to estimate single equation forecasting models. Variables expected to be nonlinear in their effects are tested via transformation into a series of dummy variables.

The general risk prediction hypothesis is that expense in Year 1 is predicted by morbidities, drug orders, and demographics in Year 0, where time is defined in calendar years:

$$\text{Total Expenses}_1 = a + b\ Dx(i)_0 + c\ Rx(j)_0 + d\ Age_0 + e\ Sex + u_0 \quad (1)$$

where i = 1 to 16 (or 1 to 99) disease classes, j = 1 to 27 therapeutic classes, Total Expenses_1 = Total health plan expense in Year 1, $Dx(i)_0$ = number of episodes of Diagnosis Class *i* in Year 0, and Rx(j)0 number of drug orders in Therapeutic Class *j* in Year 0. Each type of predictor is run separately and in concert with each of the others as shown in the equation above. The separate runs with only a single class of predictor allow us to examine the independent effects of each class.

A second class of prediction models was developed to investigate two problems. First, traditional regression techniques assume homogeneity (linearity) among variables—that one unit of a dependent variable contributes the same amount of future expense throughout the range of the variable. In medical care, homogeneity may be a faulty assumption. The effect of pneumonia is different for someone with chronic respiratory disease than for someone without chronic disease. This is normally handled in regression through a priori specification of interaction terms. Specification of interactions among medical risk factors is difficult because of the large number of diseases and the highly variable nature of disease classification systems. With a large number of variables, the n-way interactions become too numerous to handle and their interpretation problematic. The second problem, related to this point, is that part of the investigative process is to discover new relationships between predictors and future expense. Reliance on a priori assumptions and hypotheses may preclude discovery of important new relationships that may help to explain risk.

Hierarchical variance (regression tree) analysis allows variables to behave differently under different conditions. Three regression trees were generated using the Automatic Interaction Detector (AID) software developed by the Michigan Survey Research Center (Sonquist and Morgan, 1964). The analysis was run using a relatively early version of the software. (A number of new, more robust packages now exist, including THAID, CART, and FACT. Preliminary analysis was also done with CHAID. The difficulty with CHAID software was the requirement that the dependent variable be categorical, which is not the case in our analysis.) The AID software limited the size of the sample to approximately 5,000 observations, and the number of variables to approximately 35 (with this sample size). Technically, with smaller samples the number of variables could be larger and, with much smaller numbers of variables, the sample size could be increased by about

25%. Despite the relatively smaller sample size, however, the models are relatively stable. That is, tested with a different sample, they generate similar trees. To compare tree models with pure regression models, the classes defined by AID were converted into dummy variables and a prediction model estimated on the full data set. Hence, the class definitions are derived from about 5,000 observations, but the risk coefficients are derived from over 25,000 observations.

Criteria for Evaluation

Split-half validation methods are used to measure the performance of prediction models. Each random split-half subsample has about 25,816 observations. Prediction performance is overstated for the estimation data set because of overfitting, or capitalizing on chance. Testing models on an independent data set, the reserved half, reveals the degree of overfit.

As an initial performance screen, the proportion of explained variance in the estimation dataset, R^2, is useful. Given two alternative sets of a priori risk factors, the set that accounts for more variation in expense is preferred because it will generate more variance in the prediction distribution. If we expect a variable to account for risk, its validity is supported by the degree of expense variation it accounts for. The estimation R^2 is the traditional measure to show model performance in previous studies, so we offer it to allow comparisons.

An ideal risk-assessment model would accurately predict the mean expense of any group, no matter how the population group is chosen (except on an *ex post* basis). The purpose of risk assessment is to capture the relevant effects of a systematic selection process. This suggests that one way of validating these models is to test them against deliberately biased samples. With large samples, most models can predict the overall mean with reasonable accuracy, although some subgroups are overpredicted and some subgroups are underpredicted. If the subgroup prediction errors are acceptable, the model can be an improvement over using the overall population mean as the predictor. Large subgroup prediction errors reveal that the model is biased and generate misleading predictions under some conditions.

A criterion for judging a risk-assessment model is the size of internal cross-subsidization among selected subgroups in a validation data set. For example, are expenses for older persons underpredicted while expenses for younger persons are consistently overpredicted? We have operationalized this in a two-step process. To test for age cross-subsidy, a scatter plot of mean prediction error (predicted minus actual expense in the validation data set) by age is produced to visualize systematic patterns, such as cross-subsidy from young to old or old to young and heteroscedasticity. Note that age is only one potentially relevant dimension of cross-subsidization. Gender, marital status, social class, race, ethnicity, county of residence, and other personal characteristics are other possible classifications whose subsidy effects may be policy relevant. We employ age and gender as primary internal cross-subsidy tests to discriminate among different models. Any model that fails on these criteria is likely to be unacceptable to employers whose workforces are older (or younger) or have a higher share of women than their competitors.

The second step is a regression of prediction error on age in years. If the coefficient on age is significantly different from zero (using a t-test), then the direction and approximate magnitude of the subsidy is quantified. This coefficient can also be compared across models as a measure of relative prediction performance for age-related cross-subsidy bias. This is a conservative test because it is restricted to a linear functional form; non-linear forms may better describe the pattern of residuals.

Success in subgroup prediction leads, inevitably, to success in predicting the overall mean, as measured by the overall prediction error when the model is applied to the validation data set. This, in practice, is not useful as a stand-alone criterion because models can fail to predict subgroups but predict the mean accurately.

The goodness-of-fit between the predicted and the actual values for the validation data set can be measured by the R^2 of a linear regression of predicted on actual values of expenses in Year 1 in this data set. This replicates the subgroup standard on an individual basis. The higher this value, the better the overall model because it generates a prediction distribution more closely approximating the observed distribution of per capita expense. One measure of stability is the change in R^2 between the estimation and validation datasets.

RESULTS

Twelve models are developed in the following analysis: nine pure regression models and three AID tree models. The estimation results are reported first for the regression models, followed by the tree models. The prediction analyses are reported in the third section.

Estimation: Regression Models

The pure demographic model (Model 1 in Table 2) explains about 2% of the variance in annual per capita expense. Age and gender are grouped into a series of dummy variables for 5-year intervals, with the exception of newborns and infants less than 1 year of age, who are placed in their own gender-specific classes. Females, aged 15-19 years, are the omitted class, and form the comparison group. Relative to this group, males aged 1-39 are less expensive, as are females aged 1-14. All other groups exhibit greater expenses. All of the age/gender cells are statistically significant except newborn males, 40- to 44-year-old males, and 45- to 49-year-old males.

Table 2. Estimation Results:
Total Expenses, Year *t* (Estimation Data Set)

	Model					
Variable	*1*	*2*	*3*	*4*	*5*	*6*
Intercept	318.46*	151.88*	230.20*	172.99*	231.00*	170.64*
Male, 0	109.11			45.03	62.81	44.42
Male, 1-4	−142.64*			−122.02*	−133.60*	−109.10*
Male, 5-9	−166.25*			−103.59*	−118.22*	−92.11*
Male, 10-14	−148.07*			−84.78*	−87.18*	−70.44
Male, 15-19	−101.98*			−48.94	−50.89	−37.29
Male, 20-24	−161.74*			−103.02*	−121.56*	−99.70*
Male, 25-29	−132.33*			−80.88*	−93.52*	−76.10
Male, 30-34	−106.00*			−68.06	−76.71*	−65.89
Male, 35-39	−81.81*			−56.14	−50.59	−49.22
Male, 40-44	5.80			8.38	25.80	14.74
Male, 45-49	30.34			−26.50	28.72	−19.99
Male, 50-54	135.05*			33.09	128.09*	52.91
Male, 55-59	217.41*			95.40	209.19*	114.59*
Male, 60-64	338.27*			164.79*	320.90*	186.39*
Female, 0	129.09*			86.78	93.39	87.37
Female, 1-4	−145.87*			−123.70*	−142.04*	−114.03*
Female, 5-9	−166.14*			−95.77*	−119.05*	−86.01*
Female, 10-14	−135.62*			−77.90*	−83.15*	−65.27
Female, 15-19			Omitted Class			
Female, 20-24	168.27*			111.98*	123.60*	96.58*
Female, 25-29	221.71*			157.83*	176.27*	150.54*
Female, 30-34	127.79*			84.20*	95.01*	80.56*
Female, 35-39	120.54*			66.31	88.39*	65.89
Female, 40-44	140.50*			76.97	104.67*	72.03
Female, 45-49	224.46*			76.62	150.63*	64.42
Female, 50-54	138.28*			2.28	55.52	−9.50
Female, 55-59	224.32*			91.11	145.40*	86.83
Female, 60-64	392.52*			224.02*	304.37*	213.93*
Diagnosis Classes						
Dx01		645.71*		608.55*		499.34*
Dx02		222.54*		225.86*		219.98*
Dx03		78.41*		72.90*		60.14*
Dx04		278.81*		268.49*		232.39*

(*continued*)

Table 2. (Continued)

	Model					
Variable	*1*	*2*	*3*	*4*	*5*	*6*
Dx05		44.04*		35.03*		21.26*
Dx06		13.36*		20.98*		13.33
Dx07		71.58*		85.67*		37.05*
Dx08		125.70*		96.03*		126.25*
Dx09		362.14*		341.53*		329.38*
Dx10		45.95		77.91		75.02
Dx11		82.21*		66.91*		52.96*
Dx12		124.68*		93.20*		75.68*
Dx13		41.53*		50.98*		42.31*
Dx14		9.47		3.02		−2.17
Dx15		33.09*		21.62		18.09
Dx16		22.86		25.05		13.20
Drug Classes						
Rx01			67.37*		63.88*	40.70*
Rx02			−1.58		2.31	1.71
Rx03			−42.16*		−41.21*	−45.18*
Rx04			22.66*		27.82*	5.62
Rx05			41.13*		40.82*	36.27*
Rx06			49.19*		41.61*	18.05
Rx08			35.00*		23.26*	−31.58*
Rx09			19.93*		16.03	−6.01
Rx10			66.91*		61.78*	30.61
Rx11			79.01*		48.05*	31.79*
Rx12			20.53		18.39	1.33
Rx14			−0.06		−21.60	−41.64*
Rx17			105.91*		90.73*	48.37*
Rx19			90.18*		76.09*	50.02*
Rx21			93.53		86.47	58.17
Rx22			227.22*		182.02*	60.50
Rx24			226.71*		209.25*	163.19*
Rx25			97.19*		89.56*	62.41*
Rx26			60.97*		47.71*	22.69*
Adj. R^2	.0212	.0557	.0388	.0613	.0498	.0689
F-Ratio	21.694*	96.142*	55.861*	40.230*	30.382*	31.799*
n	(25,816)	(25,816)	(25,816)	(25,816)	(25,816)	(25816)

The age/gender profile of risk reveals the characteristic U-shape, with males and females ages 5-9 years having the lowest risk, and females age 60-64 years having the highest risk. Childbearing activities create a steeper risk gradient for females relative to males from age 15 up, with men catching up to women by age 50. Women age 60-64 are somewhat more expensive than males in this age group. These results meet our expectations regarding the demographic structure of risk in a nonaged population.

The pure morbidity model (Model 2 in Table 2) explains over 5.5% of the variance in total expense, supporting our hypothesis that direct measures of health status provide more homogeneous risk categories than demographic measures. The risk measure here is the number of episodes experienced by an individual in each morbidity class. The coefficients represent the incremental contribution to next year's expense of one episode (or a continuing episode) of a disease type in the previous year. Thirteen of the 16 classes achieve statistical significance. The most expensive class is Dx01, serious malignancies, adding about $645 (1982 dollars) to expense in the ensuing year. Note that this is likely to represent a mixture of effects, including continued treatment of the same episode(s), metastases, effects of adverse reactions to cancer therapy, and the incidence of other disease episodes. The next highest risk class is chronic diseases with serious consequences even if the disease is controllable by therapy (Dx09). This class has about half the risk effect as serious malignancies. Other high risk disease classes include sexually transmitted diseases (Dx04), serious illness with risk of death or disability (Dx02), and chronic diseases with serious consequences if not controlled (Dx08).

The drug use model (Model 3 in Table 2) explains about 4% of the variance in next year's expense, again an improvement over the pure demographic model. Each variable is the count of different drug orders (new and refill prescriptions authorized by the physician) in each therapeutic class. Eight classes had no utilization in the study population and were omitted from the analysis; 15 of the 19 included classes were statistically significant. Of these, all but one represent increased risk next year. This class, antihistamines (Rx03), offers a protective effect—significantly lower expenses next year. This result suggests that persons with seasonal allergic rhinitis, who likely comprise the majority of users in this class, are otherwise healthier than average. The drug classes carrying the highest risk are Rx22, hypoglycemics, and Rx24, therapeutic nutrients. The former variable is an indicator of persons with diabetes, and the latter is an indicator of persons with hypertension (potassium replacement) and persons with other serious diseases requiring nutritional supplements.

Model 4 (Table 2) combines demographic and morbidity predictors to achieve an R^2 of 0.061, an improvement over either demographics or morbidities alone. This indicates that age and gender contribute additional prediction to the disease model. Indeed, only one of the disease classes (Dx15,

Miscellaneous) loses statistical significance by inclusion of the age/gender dummies, but the older age groups for both men and women lose significance by inclusion of the disease factors. This suggests that disease may be more important for predicting expense for older adults than for children and young adults. The fact that age and gender are important for the latter groups shows that the disease factors are unable to account for the heterogeneity of expenses in these subgroups.

Model 5 (Table 2) combines demographic and drug order factors to achieve an R^2 of .05, larger than for either set of factors alone. Only one drug class, Rx09 (Tranquilizers) loses significance by inclusion of the demographic factors. The inclusion of the demographic factors reduces the effects of the drug factors on future use, but age and gender contribute independent prediction power across a wide range of ages, especially for females where only a single age group loses significance.

Model 6 (Table 2) includes all three sets of predictors—demographics, morbidity classes, and drug orders. This model achieves the highest R^2 of all the models, nearly 7%, but the collinearity among the large number of variables begins to take a toll on the statistical significance and stability of the coefficients. Age retains significance mainly in the youngest and oldest groups; gender appears to make a difference in the childbearing years. Serious malignancy (Dx01) remains a strong predictor, as do serious illness with a high likelihood of death and disability (Dx02), sexually transmitted diseases (Dx04), chronic diseases with serious consequences if not controlled (Dx08), and serious chronic diseases with serious consequences even if controlled (Dx09). The coefficient on Dx02 remains nearly unchanged even when demographic and drug use variables are entered, suggesting that this predictor may operate independently of either factor. Conversely, some of the initial effect of Dx01 declines when other factors are entered, suggesting that this is correlated with age and drug use. The coefficient on use of hypoglycemics (Rx22) drops in both magnitude and significance, most likely because the chronic disease diagnosis class picks up most of the risk associated with this disease. Therapeutic nutrients (Rx24) retains some of its importance for prediction, declining by about one-third in Model 6. Of interest is the fact that controlling for diagnosis, use of cardiovascular drugs (Rx08), and diuretics (Rx14), are associated with lower risk of future expense. Antihistamines (Rx03) also are associated with lower risk.

Model 7 (Table 3) expands the diagnostic classification scheme used in Model 2. This scheme has a total of 99 classes, but not all are relevant to this analysis. Disease classes with both substantively (coefficients smaller than +/− $25) and statistically insignificant risk coefficients were omitted to achieve parsimony in this presentation. This leaves 46 disease classes in the model; three of these (Dx04, Dx10, Dx16) are 16-class categories because no sub-classification from that category met the criteria above. Miscarriage is associated with the largest risk of expenses next year (Dx12-04), followed by chronic musculo-skeletal diseases with serious consequences possible even if controlled (Dx09-04), severe malignancy usually requiring surgery (Dx01-01), and birth injuries, malformations, and metabolic abnormalities in newborns (Dx11-06). Five disease classes are associated with lower risk, but they do not reach statistical significance in this specification. These results confirm the usefulness of assessing the appropriate dimensions of diseases for prediction purposes, although the improvement in R^2 over the 16-class model is only slight.

Model 8 (Table 3) adds the demographic dummy variables to the expanded morbidity model, which raises the R^2 to .064. The results are similar to those obtained for Model 4.

Model 9 (Table 3) includes demographic, expanded morbidity, and drug use predictors. This is the most elaborate model with the highest proportion of variance explained, over 7%. In general, the effect of adding more variables is to reduce the size of the coefficients compared to the previous model, as their effects are shared among a larger number of variables. This indicates a degree of multicollinearity among the predictors, but the standard errors are sufficiently small on 45 of the included variables to reach statistical significance.

Model 10 (Table 3) is a simple prior use model, which includes only one predictor—last year's total expense, a type of individualistic experience rating. This model performs relatively poorly, accounting for about 2.2% of the variance.

Estimation: Tree Models

Two of the models described above—4 and 5—are re-analyzed using empirical variance branching, specifically Automatic Interaction Detector (AID) (Sonquist and Morgan, 1964). Figure 2 shows the tree produced when only age, gender, and the 16 clinical-behavioral classes are available for splitting. Each box represents a subset of the population from the next higher (left) branch. Inside each box, N is the number of individuals in a cell and X is their estimated mean expense. Because cells are built from a subsample of about 5,000 cases from the estimation data set, the overall mean is slightly different than in the remainder of the paper. In this tree, seven terminal groups are identified. The criteria for groupings are three-fold. First, a grouping must have more than 25 individuals. This means that a cell with fewer than 50 cases cannot be split. Second, the proportion of variation of a grouping relative to the total variation of the sample must be large enough to attempt another split; homogeneous groupings are not subdivided any further. Third, any predictor in the analysis must be capable of reducing the unexplained variation in that group sufficiently to form an additional split (Sonquist and Morgan, 1964). The goal of AID is to produce groupings with homogenous variance.

Table 3. Estimation Results (including Expanded Diagnostic Classes and Prior Use): Total Expenses, Year *t* (Estimation Data Set)

Variable	*Model* 7	8	9	10
Intercept	160.86*	175.92*	170.49*	272.37*
Male, 0		63.08	50.18	
Male, 1-4		−108.43*	−105.62*	
Male, 5-9		−102.79*	−93.96*	
Male, 10-14		−84.04*	−71.49	
Male, 15-19		−43.88	−34.37	
Male, 20-24		−99.94*	−96.54*	
Male, 25-29		−80.47	−74.58	
Male, 30-34		−65.24	−61.63	
Male, 35-39		−52.90	−45.43	
Male, 40-44		11.57	19.46	
Male, 45-49		−21.15	−15.59	
Male, 50-54		36.13	56.29	
Male, 55-59		110.51*	123.78*	
Male, 60-64		164.68*	178.37*	
Female, 0		84.65	75.60	
Female, 1-4		−119.15*	−118.08*	
Female, 5-9		−88.04*	−82.20*	
Female, 10-14		−71.47	−62.71	
Female, 15-19	Omitted Class			
Female, 20-24		111.49*	99.15*	
Female, 25-29		153.57*	146.42*	
Female, 30-34		83.40*	79.32*	
Female, 35-39		70.01	67.63	
Female, 40-44		86.96*	79.18	
Female, 45-49		102.46*	85.01	
Female, 50-54		20.27	−0.92	
Female, 55-59		113.34*	103.79*	
Female, 60-64		238.36*	220.70*	
Diagnosis Classes				
Dx01-01	656.79*	607.13*	540.11*	
Dx02-01	395.72*	391.30*	367.93*	
Dx02-02	269.58*	265.14*	270.19*	

(*continued*)

Table 3. (Continued)

Variable	*Model* 7	8	9	10
Dx02-03	131.22*	144.03*	125.37	
Dx02-04	83.51	92.51	75.99	
Dx02-05	254.24*	269.25*	267.50*	
Dx02-10	116.07	102.79	102.43	
Dx03-01	27.09	4.75	−21.97	
Dx03-02	111.38*	120.94*	115.72*	
Dx03-06	−54.25	−60.81	−67.54	
Dx03-08	121.76*	117.28*	120.09*	
Dx04	266.13*	264.33*	227.90*	
Dx05-01	54.34*	45.20*	28.22*	
Dx05-03	109.43	57.61	65.78	
Dx06-01	−58.32	−38.63	−49.41	
Dx06-02	45.66*	44.52*	29.59*	
Dx06-03	69.24	49.55	28.78	
Dx06-08	−142.82	−155.60	−171.46	
Dx07-01	76.71*	63.45	32.91	
Dx07-02	133.23*	131.48*	86.00*	
Dx07-03	31.54	32.37	20.59	
Dx07-05	42.38	40.19	6.67	
Dx07-06	48.19	26.00	−0.99	
Dx07-07	225.43*	183.16	207.78*	
Dx08-02	140.59*	102.74*	145.09*	
Dx08-03	63.28	15.26	29.66	
Dx08-04	280.62*	268.05*	214.04*	
Dx09-01	271.47*	247.67*	208.97*	
Dx09-02	336.72*	312.87*	344.97*	
Dx09-04	743.73*	718.33*	563.33*	
Dx10	40.06	67.46	65.32	
Dx11-02	115.98*	84.47*	64.04*	
Dx11-03	47.25*	36.79*	13.07	
Dx11-04	108.90*	95.23*	88.63*	
Dx11-06	394.10*	422.13*	354.90*	
Dx11-13	128.47*	115.84*	111.91*	
Dx12-01	138.68*	100.51*	84.07*	
Dx12-02	58.62	54.75	45.74	

(continued)

Table 3. (Continued)

Variable	*Model* 7	8	9	10
Dx12-04	820.92*	792.50*	686.87*	
Dx13-01	43.43*	53.25*	44.54*	
Dx13-02	47.03	43.69	24.26	
Dx13-03	−32.75	−18.77	−26.10	
Dx14-02	28.90*	24.43*	15.66	
Dx14-04	77.96	72.63	39.65	
Dx14-06	85.96	96.43	72.40	
Dx15-01	83.22*	78.21*	65.16*	
Dx16	28.26	30.62	13.26–	
Drug Classes				
Rx01			36.93*	
Rx02			−0.94	
Rx03			−41.16*	
Rx04			9.13	
Rx05			37.25*	
Rx06			12.91	
Rx08			−36.07*	
Rx09			−1.04	
Rx10			34.33	
Rx11			23.21	
Rx12			7.51	
Rx14			−36.46*	
Rx17			37.79*	
Rx19			53.26*	
Rx21			55.45	
Rx22			115.56	
Rx24			169.42*	
Rx25			59.57*	
Rx26			17.25	
Expense in Year 0				0.16*
Adj. R^2	.0591	.0649	.0723	.0224
F-Ratio	35.503*	25.194*	22.628*	591.602*
n	(25,816)	(25,816)	(25,816)	(25,816)

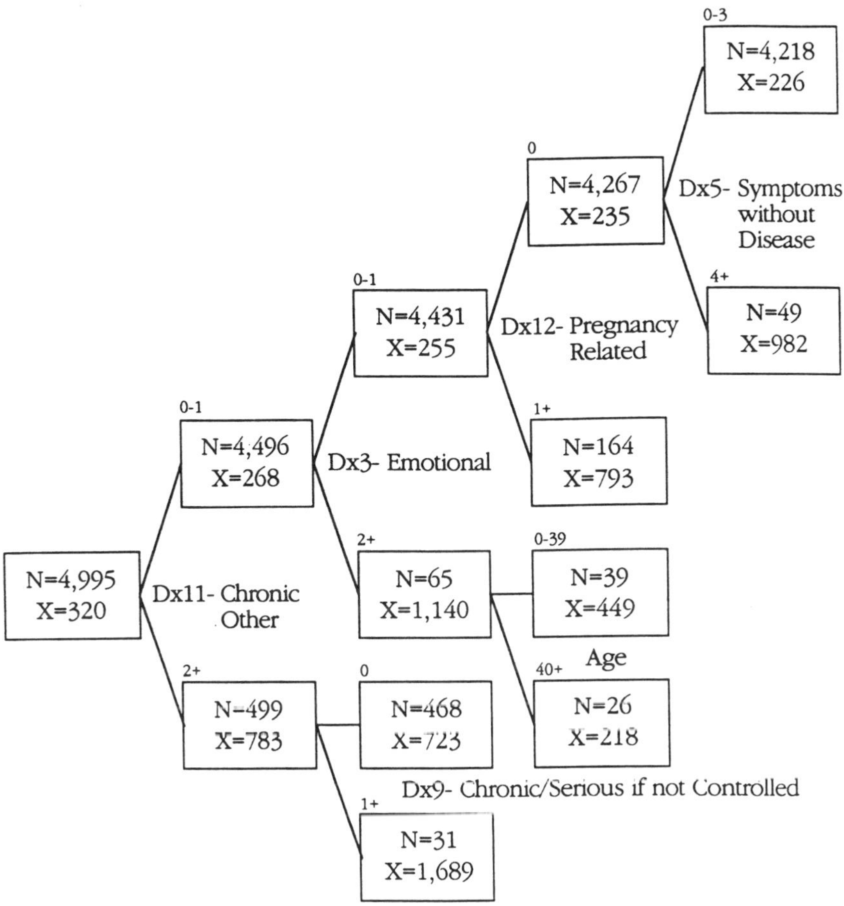

Figure 2. Tree analysis of variables in model 4.

The first terminal grouping, starting from the top of the figure, is persons who had 0 or 1 episodes of other chronic disease (Dx11), 0 or 1 episodes of emotional disease (Dx03), no pregnancy-related episodes, and 0 to 3 episodes of symptoms without active disease (Dx05). The second terminal group differs on the number of episodes of Dx05, that is, 4 or more. The third terminal group, moving back down the tree, differs on the existence of pregnancy. Note that in other branches of the tree, pregnancy does not enter; pregnancy defines a terminal group only for persons with little or no emotional diseases and other chronic diseases. The fourth and fifth terminal groups split on two or more episodes of emotional diseases (Dx3), and then split into old and young age groups, respectively. The final two groups include those with two or more episodes of chronic disease, and then split further on the presence of one or more episodes of serious controllable chronic disease. In sum, the AID analysis points to chronic disease, emotional diseases, and undiagnosed symptom episodes as important risk factors. The symptom episodes could be interpreted as psychosomatic utilization; if this type of episode represents an underlying emotional problem, higher use rates in the future are expected, as observed here. The classification is very concentrated, with 84% of the cases falling into the first terminal group, and another 9% in group 6. This analytic technique produces four terminal groups with less than 50 cases each. Hence, a majority of the classes discriminate rather few cases.

The AID analysis of age, gender, and drug factors produces five terminal groups based on age, analgesics, tranquilizers, and anti-infectives (Figure 3). The fact that age enters first attests to the relative inability of drug-use patterns to capture risk. Thus, patterns of diagnosis are more important than patterns of prescribing for predicting future health risk. This classification is somewhat less concentrated than the previous one, with the largest class—younger persons who received fewer than two drug orders for analgesics and no orders of tranquilizers/sedatives—about 75% of the cases, and the second largest—older persons who received two or more orders of anti-infective drugs—another 19%.

A third tree was developed to explore all three types of predictors, but did not differ from Figure 2, confirming that prescription drug predictors are relatively weak. In sum, age enters prior to any drug order variable. Age enters into only one branch of the diagnostic model. Second, the empirically derived groupings are highly concentrated. The variance within the largest cells is not homogeneous, mostly because pertinent splitting variables were not available.

Validation: Regression Models

The overall mean prediction error in each of the models is positive and small. All of the models overpredict mean per capita expense by less than 2%, which represents less than $6 per person per year (see Table 4). Thus, all of the models provide extremely accurate overall prediction for the validation sample.

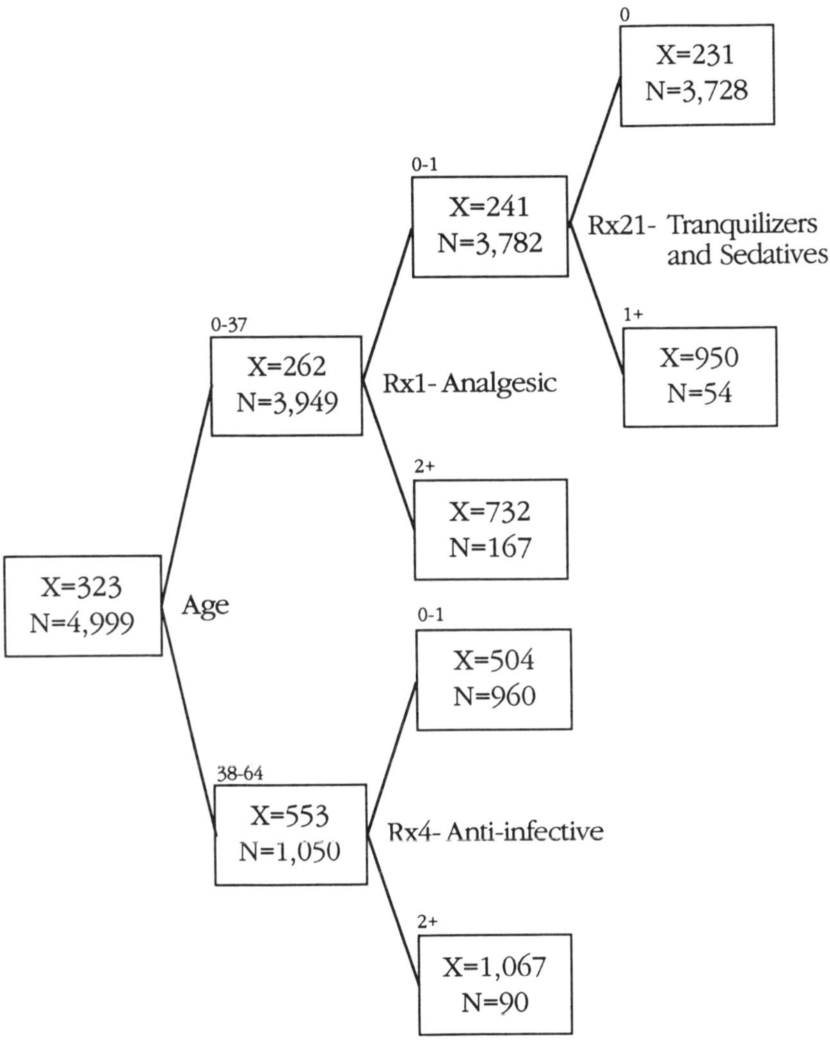

Figure 3. Tree analysis of variables in model 5.

Table 4. Prediction Results: Total Expenses, Year t (Validation Data Set)

	Model									
Variable	*1*	*2*	*3*	*4*	*5*	*6*	*7*	*8*	*9*	*10*
Under- /Over-Payment	4.64	3.39	1.58	3.77	2.11	2.74	3.64	3.93	5.97	3.49
Under- /Over-Payment as Percent of Mean	1.44%	1.05%	0.49%	1.17%	0.66%	0.85%	1.1%	1.0%	1.9%	1.1%
Intercept	−17.14	−41.74*	2.76	−33.20*	−2.76	− 17.33	−14.75	−8.75	7.69	−41.42*
Predicted Expense	1.04*	1.12*	0.98*	1.09*	1.00*	1.05*	1.03*	1.01*	0.96*	1.12*
Adj. R^2	.0269	.0822	.0396	.0877	.0547	.0889	.0749	.0807	.0821	.0316
F-Ratio	713.69*	2312.34*	1065.50*	2483.53*	1495.60*	2520.16*	2090.85*	2266.44*	2308.76*	842.14*
n	(25,816)	(25,816)	(25,816)	(25,816)	(25,816)	(25,816)	(25,816)	(25,816)	(25,816)	(25,816)
Age										
Prediction Error (Slope)	−1.89	−4.40	−6.77	−1.51	−1.83	−1.49	−4.58	−1.60	−1.62	−7.90
Gender										
Prediction Error										
Male	.92	38.03	44.69	−0.17	2.20	0.33	39.36	0.39	3.59	62.03
Female	8.21	−29.03	−39.86	7.57	2.02	5.07	−30.72	7.34	8.26	−52.81

The goodness-of-fit of the predicted and the actual distributions of expense for the validation data set are summarized by the R^2 statistics. They are in the general neighborhood of their respective estimation R^2 values. That is, the distribution of the predictions from the demographic model (Model 2) has the poorest fit with the observed expenses, and the prediction distribution from the combined morbidity/drug order/demographic model (Model 6) offers the best fit to the observed values.

While all prediction R^2 values appear to be slightly higher than the R^2 obtained in the initial estimations, they can not be directly compared because the number of predictors differs. Only one predictor variable is used in the prediction validation, which inflates the adjusted R^2 statistics.

If the predicted distributions fit closely to the actual distributions, the regression line of actual on predicted expenses would have an intercept of 0 and a slope of 1. The negative intercepts *and* slopes greater than 1 for Models 1, 2, 4, 6, and 10 indicate that at higher values of expense, the models cannot produce equivalent predictions so the line of best fit is rotated above unity. Models 3, 5, 7, 8, and 9 have relatively good overall fit on this measure.

Despite the fact that these models are extremely accurate for a large, representative population, they may be subject to selection bias for small, selected populations. The sensitivity of the models to age-related selection bias is explored with scatter plots and regressions of predicted values on age for each of the ten models. The first finding is the negative slope of the regression of prediction error on age (Table 4). Ideally, the prediction error should be random, so the slope in this plot would be 0. Thus, the smaller the absolute value of the slope, the better the model. On this criterion, Models 1, 4, 5, 6, 8 and 9 have the least age bias. These models all include age as a predictor. To illustrate age bias, the plot of predicted values by age for Model 10 is shown in Figure 4. In a model without age bias, there would be minimal slope to the plot. The error of overpredicting for infants and children compounds the error of underpredicting for older adults, creating substantial intergenerational transfer.

The second finding is the heteroscedasticity of the models; the variance increases as age increases. The models that do the worst on this test are those not containing age, Models 2, 3, 7, and 10. This is confirmed by the values of the slopes of these models, -4.40, -6.77, -4.73, and -7.90 respectively.

The gender bias test is simpler. If there is a large difference between the residual for each gender and the differences have different signs, the models have a subsidy by gender. The worst models, as above, are those that do not explicitly include gender—Models 2, 3, 7, and 10 (as reported in Table 4). The best model is Model 5, where males subsidize females by only $0.20 per year. The remaining models all have a relatively small gender cross-subsidy.

To summarize, none of the ten models are unbiased with respect to age and gender. The best results appear to be obtained in Models 4, 5, 6, and 9, all

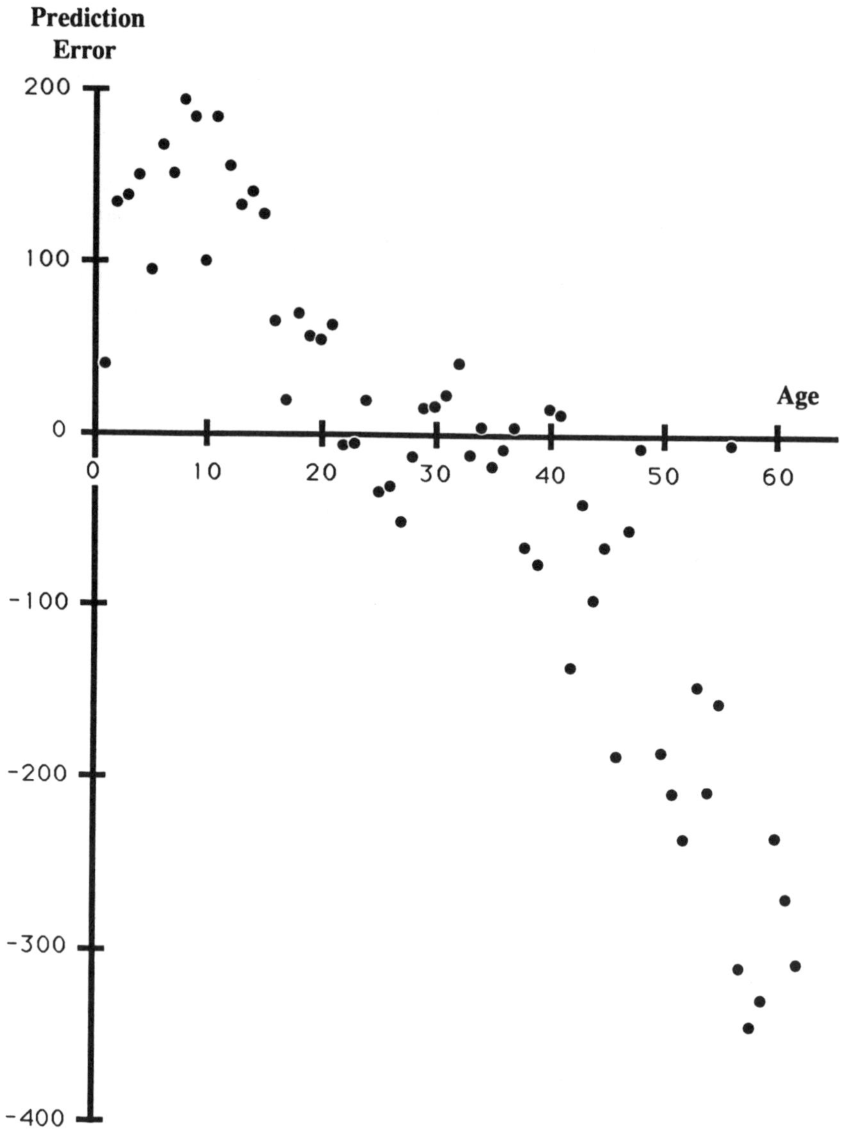

Figure 4. Scatter plot of average prediction error by age, model 10.

Table 5. Regression Tree Analysis

Estimation Results	*Model 4*	*Model 5*
Intercept**	1359.56*	748.64*
Node 1	−1111.74*	−490.17*
Node 2	−666.18*	−153.95
Node 3	−508.19*	−88.67
Node 4	−738.45*	−323.61*
Node 5	−251.39*	
Node 6	−704.49*	
Adj. R^2	.0350	.0131
F-Ratio	156.96*	86.69*
n	(25,816)	(25,816)
Intercept	11.54	−23.47
Predicted Expense	0.94*	1.06*
Adj. R^2	.0366*	.0167
F-Ratio	981.92*	439.55*
n	(25815)	(25815)
Under- / Over- Payment	6.93	4.16
Under- / Over- Payment as Percent of Mean	2.16%	1.30%
Age Prediction Error (Slope)	−6.27	−4.60
Gender Prediction Error		
Male	40.84	68.72
Female	−25.68	−57.94

Notes: #Nodes do not correspond between models; see Figures 2 and 3 for definition of nodes.
*Significant at .05 level.
**Intercept represents last terminal group.

of which include both factors. This suggests that, as measured here, drug orders and morbidity episodes are not sufficient to capture age-related expenditures across the lifespan.

Validation: Tree Models

Prediction results for the two tree models are reported in Table 5. The R^2 value for the morbidity/demographic tree model, .035, is about 3 times higher than that obtained for the drug order/demographic tree model. Both models overpay from 1 to a little over 2% of total mean expenses, with the morbidity/demographic tree having the highest overpayment of all models estimated. Both tree models exhibit substantial age and gender bias, with older persons subsidizing younger persons and females subsidizing males. This is consistent with the finding that omission of these variables leads to greater bias. This complex modeling approach does not yield dramatic improvements in unbiasedness or goodness of fit.

The tree models exhibit significant age bias. The scatter plot of age-related prediction error is nearly identical to that shown in Figure 4, which is based on a model without age as a predictor. This is true because age does not enter the tree as a predictor until relatively deep in the tree. At that point it only divides into two classes, resulting in the observed pattern. The pattern of heteroscedasticity observed with other models which do not include age as a predictor is obvious as age increases, as is the substantial incidence of under-prediction for older working adults. The same pattern is observed for Model 5.

CONCLUSIONS AND DIRECTIONS FOR FUTURE RESEARCH

Several major conclusions and implications emerge from this analysis. First, treated morbidities and drug use offer substantial improvement in prediction performance over age and gender. The morbidity and drug models are plausible, account for substantially more of the variance in risk than pure demographic models, and are less biased.

Second, age and gender still contribute to prediction power independent of disease and drug use factors as measured here. This indicates that further exploration of the morbidity experience of infants and younger adults is needed. Age and gender appear to work where the risk may be more stochastic; hence, "group" characteristics are more predictive than individual attributes.

Third, interactive modeling produces simpler models than a priori regression models, but their performance appears to suffer correspondingly. We have not yet identified by this process any prediction tools that will adequately substitute for the more complex morbidity episode regression models.

Fourth, interactive modeling does not discover functional forms that significantly improve prediction performance, and interpreting them is more difficult than a priori models. A given level of expense can be produced by a wide variety of health care utilization patterns; when hierarchical variance analysis encounters this variance, it attempts to derive classes that place these heterogeneous utilization patterns into the same iso-expense group. Hence, classes are difficult to interpret. A variety of other alternatives exists which may provide equally valid prediction. The regression tree technique is not very successful in capturing the high cost tail of a distribution or the truncation at 0 (nonusers). Groupings produced by this algorithm have substantial overlap and heterogeneity. Our results with interactive modeling offer reassurance that a priori modeling efforts have not missed a useful specification.

Fifth, morbidities are significantly more powerful than drugs in predicting risk. The underlying epidemiology is more predictive of future risk than patterns of drug prescribing. Alternatively, the structure of therapeutic classes may discard important disease information available at the product-specific level.

Sixth, prior use is not a powerful predictor in the nonaged population. Chronic morbidities are a more accurate risk factor rather than undifferentiated prior use.

Seventh, a disease classification system designed specifically for nonaged expense prediction may improve the predictive power of morbidity models. The system used in this study is only one of many possibilities. As additional diagnostic information becomes available via enhanced utilization data systems, this modeling can be improved.

The data requirements for morbidity risk modeling are substantial. The episode structure of disease and all comorbidities must be documented for all persons in a population. Such data are not likely to be widely available until medical records become routinely automated. Indeed, it is likely that laboratory and pharmacy information systems will be automated before clinicians are converted to an electronic charting system. One research direction should, therefore, focus on modeling risk from laboratory test results and prescription drug use and on developing social surveys to measure morbidity episodes on a self-report basis. With more attention to refinements in classification, these sources may provide a reasonably close proxy measure of the epidemiologic structure of the population captured in medical records.

Finally, this analysis focused on a twelve-month baseline period for assessing risk. Future research should examine longer time periods in assessing predictors. Lagged risk factors, from one, two, and three or more years past, may contain useful prediction information. Certainly, longer baseline periods will help to smooth the clustered nature of medical care use and obtain a more accurate measure of permanent health status. Along the same lines, models that include a medical condition variable for the existence, at any time in the person's lifetime, of specific chronic diseases might be useful in the longer time frame. Moreover, the pattern of risk weights over time, indicating increasing or decreasing risk as a function of time since onset of a disease, should be explored for common chronic and acute diseases.

ACKNOWLEDGMENTS

This research was supported by a grant from the Kaiser Foundation Health Plan, Inc., Oakland, California. The views expressed in this paper are those of the authors and no official endorsement by Kaiser Foundation Hospitals or the Kaiser Foundation Health Plan is intended or should be inferred. We are grateful for the assistance of the following persons: Barbara J. Mendius, who provided all the computer programming required to create the data files for this study; Susan Reedy, who provided able assistance in conducting the statistical analyses; and Margaret R. Sucec, who provided technical editing. This paper benefitted from discussions with the Technical Subcommittee of the Kaiser Permanente Risk Adjustment Task Force and from comments by Arlene Ash, Nelda McCall, Richard Scheffler, Bill Thomas, and Pete Welch. An earlier version of this paper was presented at the Workshop on Risk Adjustment of Employer Contributions, sponsored by the Kaiser Permanente Center for Health Research, Otter Rock, Oregon, July 16, 1990.

REFERENCES

Abraham, K.S. (1986). *Distributing Risk.* New Haven, CT: Yale Press.

Brown, J.B. (1991). Personal Communication.

Cave, D.G., S.O. Schweitzer and P.A. Lachenbruch (1989). "Adjusting Employer Group Capitation Premiums by Community Rating by Class Factors." *Medical Care* 27:887-899.

Duan, N., W.G. Manning, C.N. Morris, and J.P. Newhouse (1983). "A Comparison of Alternative Models of the Demand for Medical Care." *Journal of Business and Economic Statistics* 1:115-126.

Ellis, R. P. and A. Ash (1988). Refining the Diagnostic Cost Group Model: A Proposed Modification to the AAPCC for HMO Reimbursement. Final Report, Grant No. 18-C-98526/1-03. Baltimore, MD: Health Care Financing Administration.

Ellis R.P. and A. Ash (1989). The Continuous-Update Diagnostic Cost Group Model. Final Report, Grant No. 18-C-98526/1-03. Baltimore, MD: Health Care Fianancing Administration.

Epstein, A.M. and E.J. Cumella (1988). "Capitation Payment: Using Predictors of Medical Utilization to Adjust Rates." *Health Care Financing Review* 10:51-69.

Farley, P.J. and G.R. Wilensky (1983). "Options, Incentives, and Employment-Related Health Insurance." In R. M. Scheffler and L. F. Rossiter (Eds.), *Advances in Health Economics and Health Services Research,* (Vol. 4, pp. 57-82). Greenwich, CT: JAI Press Inc.

Gabel, J., C. Jajich-Toth, G. de Lissovoy, T. Rice, and H. Cohen (1988). "The Changing World of Group Health Insurance." *Health Affairs* 7:48-65.

Garfinkel, S.A., G.F. Riley, and V.G. Iannacchione (1988). "High-Cost Users of Medical Care." *Health Care Financing Review* 9:41-52.

Goodman, M.J., D.W. Roblin, M.C. Hornbrook, and J.P. Mullooly (1991). "Persistence of Health Care Expense in an Insured Working Population." In M. Hornbrook (EWd.), *Advances in Health Economics and Health Services Research: Vol. 12. Risk-Based Contributions to Private Health Insurance* (pp. 149-173). Greenwich, CT: JAI Press.

Greenlick, M.R., D.K. Freeborn, and C.R. Pope (1988). *Health Care Research in an HMO: Two Decades of Discovery.* Baltimore, MD: Johns Hopkins University Press.

Hayes, S. (1991). "Demographic Risk Factors Derived from HMO Data." (1991). In M. Hornbrook (Ed.), *Advances in Health Economics and Health Services Research: Vol. 12.*

Risk-Based Contributions to Private Health Insurance (pp. 177-196). Greenwich, CT: JAI Press.

Hornbrook, M.C., M.D. Bennett, and M.R. Greenlick (1989). "Adjusting the AAPCC for Selectivity and Selection Bias Under Medicare Risk Contracts." In R. M. Scheffler and L. F. Rossiter (Eds.), *Advances in Health Economics and Health Services Research,* (Vol. 10, pp. 111-149). Greenwich, CT: JAI Press.

Hornbrook, M.C., M.D. Bennett, and M. R. Greenlick (1991). "Adjusting for Health Status Under Medicare Risk Contracts Using Prior Inpatient Morbidities: The Diagnostic Cost Groups." Final Report, Grant No. 18-C-99804-1/04. Baltimore, MD. Health Care Financing Administration.

Hornbrook, M.C. and M.J. Goodman (1991a). "Adjusting Health Benefit Contributions to Reflect Risk." In M. Hornbrook (Ed.), *Advances in Health Economics and Health Services Research: Vol. 12. Risk-Based Contributions to Private Health Insurance* (pp. 41-76). Greenwich, CT: JAI Press.

Hornbrook, M.C. and M.J. Goodman (1991b). "Health Plan Case Mix: Definition, Measurement, and Use." In M. Hornbrook (EWd.), *Advances in Health Economics and Health Services Research: Vol. 12. Risk-Based Contributions to Private Health Insurance* (pp. 111-148). Greenwich, CT: JAI Press.

Hornbrook M.C., M.J. Goodman, M.D. Bennett, and M.R. Greenlick (1991). "Assessing Health Plan Case Mix in Employed Populations: Self-Reported Health Status Models." In M. Hornbrook (Ed.), *Advances in Health Economics and Health Services Research: Vol. 12. Risk-Based Contributions to Private Health Insurance* (pp. 233-272). Greenwich, CT: JAI Press.

Hornbrook, M.C., A.V. Hurtado, and R.E. Johnson (1985). "Health Care Episodes: Definition, Measurement and Use." *Medical Care Review* 42:163-218.

Howland, J., J. Stokes, S.C. Crane, and A.J. Belanger (1987). "Adjusting Capitation Using Chronic Disease Risk Factors: A Preliminary Study." *Health Care Financing Review* 9:15-23.

Hurtado, A.V. and M.R. Greenlick (1971). "A Disease Classification System for Analysis of Medical Care Utilization, with a Note on Symptom Classification." *Health Services Research* 6:235-250.

Lubitz, J. (1987). "Health Status Adjustments for Medicare Capitation." *Inquiry* 24:362-375.

Luft, H.S., J.B. Trauner, and S.C. Maerki (1985). "Adverse Selection in a Large, Multi-option Health Benefits Program: A Case Study of the California Public Employees' Retirement System." In R. M. Scheffler and L. F. Rossiter (Eds.), *Advances in Health Economics and Health Services Research.* (Vol. 6, pp. 197-230). Greenwich, CT: JAI Press Inc.

Manning, W.G. and M.S. Marquis (1989). *Health Insurance: The Tradeoff Between Risk Pooling and Moral Hazard.* Santa Monica, CA: Rand Corporation, R-3729-NCHSR.

McCall, N. and H.S. Wai (1983). "An Analysis of the Use of Medicare Services by the Continuously Enrolled Aged." *Medical Care* 21:567-585.

Neipp, J. and R.J. Zeckhauser (1985). "Persistence in the Choice of Health Plans." In R. M. Scheffler and L. F. Rossiter (Eds.), *Advances in Health Economics and Health Services Research,* (Vol. 6, pp. 47-74). Greenwich, CT: JAI Press.

Newhouse, J.P., W.G. Manning, E.B. Keeler, and E.M. Sloss (1989). "Adjusting Capitation Rates Using Objective Health Measures and Prior Utilization." *Health Care Financing Review* 10:41-54.

Price, J.R. and J.W. Mays (1985). "Selection and the Competitive Standing of Health Plans in a Multiple-Choice, Multiple-Insurer Market." In R. M. Scheffler and L. F. Rossiter (Eds.), *Advances in Health Economics and Health Services Research* (Vol. 6, pp. 127-148). Greenwich, CT: JAI Press.

Robinson, J.C., H.S. Luft, L.B. Gardner, and E.M. Morrison (1991). "A Method for Risk-Adjusting Employer Contributions to Competing Health Insurance Plans." *Inquiry* 28:107-116.

Sonquist, J.A. and J.N. Morgan (1964). *The Detection of Interaction Effects: A Report on a Computer Program for the Selection of Optional Combinations of Explanatory Variables.* Monograph No. 35. Ann Arbor, MI: University of Michigan Institute for Social Research. Survey Research Center

Wilensky, G.R. and L.F. Rossiter (1986). "Patient Self-Selection in HMOs." *Health Affairs* 5:66-80.

Wrightson, G.A. (1990). *HMO Rate-Setting.* Ann Arbor, MI: Health Administration Press.

Zeckhauser, R.J. (1970). "Medical Insurance: A Case Study of the Trade-off between Risk Spreading and Appropriate Incentives." *Journal of Economic Theory* 2:10-26.

ASSESSING HEALTH PLAN CASE MIX IN EMPLOYED POPULATIONS:

SELF-REPORTED HEALTH STATUS MODELS

Mark C. Hornbrook, Michael J. Goodman,

Marjorie D. Bennett, and Merwyn R. Greenlick

INTRODUCTION

By itself, voluntary health plan choice does not always promote efficiency in the insurance market. Some evidence correlates risk with health plan choice; that is, plan characteristics chosen by relatively sicker people differ from those chosen by relatively healthy people (Wilensky and Rossiter, 1986). If premium structures and employer contributions do not compensate for this difference, a cost-premium spiral results in market failure. If health status differences, or risk, can be assessed prospectively, then health plan revenues or employer contributions can be adjusted to protect health plans and their members from adverse selection, especially when caused by factors beyond health plan control (Hornbrook and Goodman, 1991a, 1991b).

Advances in Health Economics and Health Services Research, Vol. 12, pages 233-272.
Copyright © 1991 by JAI Press Inc.
All rights of reproduction in any form reserved.
ISBN: 1-55938-241-4

One of the principal obstacles to successful risk adjustment is a lack of useful data on risk factors and validated prediction models. The available methods are either overly general or difficult to implement. Demographic factors are readily available and easy to collect but are poor predictors of future health status (Lubitz, 1987; Hornbrook and Goodman, 1991b; Newhouse et al., 1989). Risk classes formed by pure demographic factors do not differentiate between sick and well persons. Classification systems relying on contact with medical providers are difficult to implement. Prior use factors, which depend on contact with the medical system, are likely to be biased by differences in treatment patterns between independent fee-for-service providers and managed care organizations. Morbidity factors obtained from medical records, while much more accurate than demographics or prior use (Hornbrook, Goodman, and Bennett, 1991), are very expensive to collect. Because data systems in indemnity plans and health maintenance organizations (HMOs) differ considerably, methods that depend on claims records are very complex and expensive to implement.

AIMS

This study specifies the conceptual framework for risk assessment via self-report, examines some simple prediction models based on self-reported health status, and derives implications for future research on self-report as a risk-assessment technique.

An individual's knowledge of his or her own health status, health history, and behavioral risk factors may provide a useful and valid foundation for risk-assessment models. Self-administered health surveys are now well-developed and can be applied consistently across different types of health plans. These surveys allow individuals to provide information on risk factors, such as family health history or tobacco use, that are difficult to obtain from other sources. Moreover, enrollees can provide information on their attitudes about use of health care and perceived risk of illness that are not available from any other source. Individuals can also provide information on recurrent and chronic diseases. For these reasons, it is important to explore the potential of self-reports from enrollees to obtain information on risk factors.

PREDICTION HYPOTHESES

We hypothesize that self-reported measures of health status and the propensity to use medical care can be used to predict future health care expense via several relationships. In general, we assume that individuals can validly and reliably report their own salient chronic health conditions, including perceived signs and symptoms, and conditions diagnosed by their physicians. A high degree of recall of diagnosed and treated chronic conditions can provide useful prediction information because these conditions and their associated treatments are likely to persist. We also assume that patients can assess the relative severity and stability of various chronic conditions. The latter may be related to the likelihood of acute flare-ups. In a similar vein, individuals can report functional and structural deficits that require ongoing medical intervention and support, such as implants, transplants, and maintenance of protheses and other medical devices (for example, ostomies and pacemakers). Reliable reporting may also extend to observations about dependents so that efficiencies can be gained by administering a single questionnaire per family.

In addition, self-reported health status can predict future expenses because the awareness of illness often predates contact with the medical system. Individuals may experience significant symptoms, for example, shortness of breath and chronic pain, with sufficient severity and duration to signify a need for medical care, but without having yet obtained it. They may also experience vague, recurring symptoms that are prodromal events to more serious episodes.

Individuals can also report on their habits and attitudes about using the health care system. In fact, they may be the most valid data source for these factors because individuals are most aware of their own willingness to seek and comply with medical regimens.

Individuals can assess their own propensity toward behaviors that expose them to infectious agents (unsafe sexual practices, drinking untreated water), to trauma (operating machinery under the influence of alcohol or drugs), to various hazardous substances (illicit drugs, solvents, poisons), or to environmental risk factors (volatile gases, dust, asbestos, automobile exhaust fumes).

The usefulness of these factors for assessing risk depends on the willingness of individual patients to provide reliable and valid information via social survey methods. While such methods are well-established, respondents may be encouraged to "game" a survey when they are coached to answer in specific ways. The success of self-reporting is also affected by an individual's understanding of the medical implications of particular conditions. One person may understand chest pain to signal impending heart failure, while another may pass off the same symptom as heartburn. Thus, serious conditions can be reported as non-serious and, conversely, non-serious ones can be reported as serious. A survey, in the absence of objective medical evaluation, may not validly measure disease. Finally, survey research inevitably involves measurement error because respondents interpret individual items differently.

PREVIOUS RESEARCH

An excellent literature review on the validity of recall of conditions and drug use is contained in Harlow and Linet (1989). They found 15 studies of health condition recall and 13 studies of drug recall. The studies of morbidity recall looked at several issues, including chronic conditions, hospitalization, and surgical procedures. They found that minor conditions, such as hay fever or asthma, were more likely to be reported but not confirmed in the medical record, and that major conditions such as malignant neoplasms or thyroid disease were more likely to appear in the medical record but not be reported. Of the studies on drug use, only two dealt with nonhormonal, nonpregnancy-related medication. One of these, a study by Paganini-Hill and Ross (1982), found that drug reports varied significantly depending on the class of drugs. Drugs with a negative social stigma, such as tranquilizers, tended to have a low correlation between record and report. Based on their review, Harlow and Linet concluded that people accurately recall their use of hormonal medications, hospitalization, and pregnancy-related events, but not their diagnostic radiographs and history of specific chronic illness.

The literature consistently demonstrates the long-term predictive validity of self-rated health questions. Garfinkel, Riley, and Iannacchione (1988), in an examination of high-cost utilizers of health care using National Medical Care Utilization and Expenditure Survey (NMCUES) data (National Center for Health Statistics, 1983), found that the best predictors of high cost were the number of restricted activity days, number of chronic conditions, age, and employment status. Looking at Michigan Medicare elderly, Lichtenstein and Thomas (1987a, 1987b) compared self-reported functional indicators (for example, ADL, IADL) with self-reported perceived health status (evaluation of total health as excellent, good, fair, poor). They concluded that functional measures are better predictors of expense than perceived health status. This is an especially pertinent finding because, unlike other studies, this project predicted expense for a prospective six-month time period.

Whitmore et al. (1989) examined four types of direct health status measures as predictors for Medicare reimbursements: perceived health status, activity limitations, functional limitations, and chronic conditions associated with high costs. These predictors were shown to be more accurate than the AAPCC demographic model using data for a sample of 1,068 aged Medicare beneficiaries responding to the NMCUES in 1980.

In a 12-year follow-up study, Idler and Angel (1990) found that self-rated health was associated with mortality for middle-aged males, but not for elderly males nor for females. Mullooly, Vogt, and Pope (1989) have shown that self-rated health is a significant predictor of subsequent objective health status over the next 15 years. In a study of the elderly in Iowa and Connecticut, Idler,

Kasl, and Lemke (1990) found that poor self-perceived health status was a significant predictor of future mortality.

Using data from the RAND Health Insurance Experiment on people under age 65, Newhouse et al. (1989) found that subjective health measures, including functional health status, do not account for as much of the variation in total health care expense as physiological measures (such as serum cholesterol, blood pressure, blood glucose, hemoglobin, electrocardiogram, and forced expiratory volume). However, they did not assess the accuracy of their models for predicting future expense.

Thus, previous research has shown an association between self-reported health status and long-term health outcomes. Unfortunately for the purposes of this study, the research has been dominated by studies of aged populations, who are likely to have relatively predictable health care expense (Hornbrook, Goodman, and Bennett, 1991). Except for Lichtenstein and Thomas (1987a, 1987b) and Newhouse et al. (1989), the studies all take a long-term perspective, predicting use over a period of years. When applying risk assessment to employers' needs, adjustments must be made for a fixed future time period, usually the forthcoming year. Therefore, previous research does not say whether self-reported health status will provide effective predictors for employed populations.

METHODS AND DATA

Analytic Approach

Using data from two samples of employed HMO members drawn five years apart, this study examines the predictive power of self-reported health status and demographic factors. Each sample is split randomly into two halves: one is designated an "estimation" data set and the other a "validation" data set. Employing individualistic linear regression techniques, this study estimates the relative prediction performance of alternative measures of risk. Research has shown that the simple linear approach is as robust as any other specification in predicting future expense (Hornbrook, Bennett, and Greenlick, 1991).

Measures from year *t-1* determine the risk classification of each person in the estimation data set. Observations from year *t* provide the total annual medical expense for each person in that data set. These expenses are regressed against the predictor variables to determine their relative risk weights. To test the risk weights, the risk factors in year *t-1* are entered in a model to predict expenses in year *t* for the validation data set. The actual expenses in year *t* are compared to the predicted expenses for that year. All expense variables are expressed in constant dollars.

Criteria for Risk-Assessment Models

A good risk-assessment model should include measures of the beneficiary's health status and propensity to seek care that are expected to influence future medical care use. All potential risk factors should be measured before the beginning of the reimbursement period and they should relate to permanent or semi-permanent dimensions of health and use habits. The model's health status dimensions should be pertinent to clinical decision making within the risk period (usually the forthcoming year).

Unless a risk-assessment model perfectly captures all the dimensions of health status, and as long as health status is correlated with the decision to enroll in an HMO, the coefficients from a model estimated on *either* FFS or HMO populations *alone* will be biased for the purposes of risk payment (Hornbrook, Bennett, and Greenlick, 1989). Special techniques have been developed to correct for this bias (Heckman, 1979; Olsen, 1980, 1982; Lee, 1983; Hornbrook, Bennett, and Greenlick, 1989). Validation in this context requires that a model contain only a small amount of bias as compared to much larger effects of measurable health status characteristics on future expense. In this manner, a good risk-assessment model identifies groups of people whose health status requires greater (or lesser) care and support, regardless of health plan type. For example, an insulin-dependent diabetic will require more clinical management in the future than a healthy person whose only chronic complaint is seasonal allergic rhinitis, whether seen by an HMO or FFS physician. We contend that improvements in predicting future expenses by current health status variables will be useful regardless of data source—FFS or HMO. Additional assumptions are required to address the biases inherent in applying risk weights derived from HMO data to FFS enrollees and vice-versa.

This study asumes that the diagnostic and treatment technologies of HMO and FFS sectors are sufficiently similar that severe diseases are treated with similar *relative* intensity compared to mild diseases across various types of organizational arrangements as long as quality assurance programs are effective. It also assumes that the study HMO's medical care is of acceptable quality so the predominance of the observed variation in use patterns will be related to actual medical need, not poor physician performance or access barriers. A good risk-assessment model should identify the structure of disease/injury risk in a well-insured population (such as HMO beneficiaries), even without randomly assigning beneficiaries to HMO and FFS modes of care.

Another criterion for a risk-assessment model is that it should predict the appropriate overall payment for any subgroup identified with baseline information. Cross-subsidization will occur within subgroups, but none should occur across these groups. Therefore, while it is virtually impossible for a risk-assessment model to predict the appropriate payment for an *individual* 55-year-old married male subscriber, a good model will identify the correct relative risk for that class of individuals.

Finally, a good risk-assessment model should reasonably predict revenue flow to health plans. HMOs in particular need to start the fiscal year with a budget that accurately predicts the HMO's revenues during the coming year. Instability and uncertainty about the budget usually leads to inefficiency in HMO operations.

If HMOs are included in a health benefit program, physician characteristics should be excluded from the model because they are controlled by the health plan. One might hypothesize that an HMO with more physicians per capita might be treating a population with greater needs, and that a health plan with a higher ratio of specialists to primary-care providers may have a sicker membership base than one with relatively fewer specialists. An alternative possibility is that the latter plan contracts with outside physicians for more of its specialty services. Rather than assessing HMO management practices as proxy variables for members' health status, risk-assessment models should employ direct measures of enrollee permanent health status whenever feasible.

A risk-assessment model relates the incidence of, say, lung cancer in a defined population last year to medical care costs this year. It does not show whether lung cancer itself is costly to treat. Contemporaneous prediction or explanation is akin to retrospective cost reimbursement—a high payment is required because lung cancer is expensive to treat. A system of prospective payment should encourage providers to develop methods for disease prevention and early detection as cost containment measures.

Measures of Model Performance

We employ several measures for judging the "goodness" of empirical risk-assessment models. First, health status indicators that account for a greater portion of the variation in expense (R^2) are preferred to those that account for less. While pursuit of maximum R^2 is not valid (because some expense variation results from provider characteristics), in choosing among models containing only risk factors determined a priori to fit conceptual requirements, models are preferred that account for more of the variation in expense. This enables models to generate more variation in their prediction distributions.

Second, models should generate distributions of predicted expenses that, when applied to a beneficiary group, are close fits to the realized distribution of future expenses. We employ linear regression techniques and simple mean difference scores to assess this goodness-of-fit. In general, a model should not under-predict or over-predict expenses for a defined group. For example, if a model over-predicts for older women relative to younger males, it contains internal bias. (Note that a post hoc definition of subgroups can always defeat risk-adjustment models because of asymmetric information.)

Third, predictions for the various subgroups should not reveal a systematic pattern of cross-subsidization based on factors included in the model. This is assessed using the validation data set via regression of prediction error on the included risk factors.

Fourth, prediction models ought to be relatively stable over time and place when there is no reason to suspect that the composition of the beneficiary group has dramatically changed or that medical technology has advanced significantly. We test this property by applying the models to a separate, but contemporaneous, data set.

Data and Samples

This study used data from two samples of HMO members who were enrolled in the Kaiser Foundation Health Plan of the Northwest, a large prepaid group practice HMO in the medium-sized metropolitan areas of Portland, Oregon/Vancouver, Washington and Salem, Oregon. One sample, for 1980-1981, represents a 5% random sample of all members of the HMO enrolled in both years. The other sample, for 1985-1986, represents a 2% random sample of all members of the HMO enrolled in both years. The study excluded individuals over the age of 64, those enrolled in Medicaid, and those enrolled as individuals (that is, non-group). Although the surveys were conducted to gauge member satisfaction, they also gathered information on perceived and functional health status.

The 1980 survey population was a 5% simple random sample of subscriber units drawn from the total membership with at least three months' eligibility. Originally drawn from the 1975 total membership, the sample is routinely updated each month by adding a 5% random sample of new enrollees. Thus, at any point, the sample accurately represents the entire health plan membership. The survey was addressed to subscriber units rather than individuals, although many of the survey questions seek information specific to a subscriber and his or her spouse. Each month, approximately one-twelfth of the sample received questionnaires with cover letters. Postcard reminders were mailed two weeks later. For those still not responding, another letter and questionnaire were sent two weeks after the postcard reminder. These mailings took place between mid-1980 and April 1981, with a response rate of 53.7%.

The 1985 Membership Survey population consisted of the same 5% sample of subscriber units, altered by new additions and terminations since 1981. A 40% random subsample was selected to obtain the 2% sample. It, too, was addressed to subscriber units rather than individuals. Each month, approximately one-eighth of the sample received questionnaires with cover letters. Postcard reminders were mailed ten days later. For those still not responding, another letter and questionnaire were sent two weeks later. These mailings took place between September 1985 and March 1986, with a response rate of 54.4%.

Our models are only estimated on respondents. This is appropriate if health care expenses are adjusted only for those who respond voluntarily, which is probably not a realistic implementation element. In applying risk adjustment, response would likely be mandated as an enrollment condition for any health plan. The alternative requires an assumption not usually required with other approaches to risk assessment. One can assume, for example, that those not responding closely resemble those who did respond, or that the nonrespondents are most like the lowest (or, perhaps, average) risk group. We make no attempt to test either approach. Because we use only respondent data, we are implicitly assuming mandatory response.

Measurement of Total Annual Expense

To construct the dependent variable for this analysis—total annual expenses for medical care—we used a comprehensive utilization profile for each HMO member. Inpatient and ambulatory records provided utilization data. The HMO's inpatient discharge abstract data system provided data on hospital use, which we used to compute annual expenses for hospital care for the sampled members.

Ambulatory care data were derived from the Outpatient Utilization System (OPUS), which is a data base maintained by the Center for Health Research for special research populations (Greenlick, Freeborn, and Pope, 1988). The OPUS sample is identical to the 1980 Membership Survey sample. For 1985, however, the OPUS sample was reduced to a 40% subsample of the 5% sample used for the Membership Survey, or 2% of the total HMO membership. Thus, the effective sample sizes were 1,545 and 842 cases for 1980 and 1985, respectively.

For OPUS, experienced medical records technicians trained in research medical records abstraction, abstracted information on all ambulatory services and procedures provided to sampled members in HMO facilities, as documented in their medical charts. This included surgical procedures, medical services, laboratory tests, and imaging procedures (radiology, CAT scans, and so forth). This data system and its use in past research is detailed in Greenlick, Freeborn, and Pope (1988). These data were used to measure each person's annual ambulatory expense.

Services obtained outside the HMO were excluded. The latter comprise out-of-area emergency services, referral for outside services not provided by the HMO, and self-referral to non-HMO providers. Previous research by Brown (1991) found that 13% of the respondents to the 1985 survey reported using out-of-plan services. We assume that most outside use episodes have an HMO complement as part of the illness episode, resulting in their capture in the ambulatory utilization database.

Departmental costs were obtained from the HMO's Medicare Cost Report. A relative cost coefficient was developed for each utilization parameter. First, total HMO costs were split into two areas—inpatient and outpatient. The five inpatient utilization parameters included days in the critical care units (ICU/CCU), days in intermediate care, minutes of operating room (OR) and recovery room (RR) time, and admissions from the emergency department (ED). Four special inpatient cost centers were defined corresponding to intermediate care, critical care, OR, and ED. All indirect costs and physician costs were allocated proportionately to the daily cost centers. ED costs attributable to inpatient admissions were allocated proportionate to those admissions. This enabled us to estimate average cost per routine day, per critical care day, per minute of OR/RR time, and per ED admission.

Ambulatory expenses were allocated on the basis of relative value units (RVUs), employing a special version of a relative value system developed by the Center for Health Research. Total departmental output of RVUs was estimated for each year and then used to compute average cost per RVU for each of four major outpatient cost centers—laboratory, surgery, medicine, and radiology. These RVU-cost conversion coefficients enabled all use elements to be summed as total annual cost for each sampled HMO member.

All utilization costs were converted to 1982 dollars by using the cost conversion coefficients for that year. This eliminated inflation effects on expenses over time and removed that prediction burden from the risk-assessment models. Therefore, any variance in the dependent variable represents differences in levels of resource use only; no pricing variation is included. This means that the risk coefficients estimated in this study are not confounded by any correlation between risk and pricing practices.

Unweighted regressions were employed in this study. Because relatively few persons experience the cluster of utilization associated with terminal illness in nonaged populations, the importance of weighting to adjust for partial periods of eligibility is not as important to capturing the variation in expense.

Measurement of Risk Factors

The demographic characteristics and eligibility status of the sampled beneficiaries were obtained from the HMO's membership accounting system. Measures of perceived and functional health status, education, behavioral risk factors, occupation, and satisfaction with care were obtained from the 1980 and 1985 Membership Surveys. (Copies of the pertinent items from these survey instruments are available from the authors upon request.)

The 1980 and 1985 Membership Surveys were designed with the subscriber unit as the unit of data collection. This differs from the individual level of our risk-assessment analyses. To maximize the population used in this analysis, we attempted to assign responses from the Membership Survey to all members within a subscriber unit without sacrificing the integrity (and predictive power) of the questionnaire items.

In the 1980 survey, four types of responses require special mention. In all cases, we assumed that the respondent knew who the subscriber was, so subscriber-specific responses were assumed to pertain to the correct person. We further assumed that respondents did not switch the definition of the subscriber and the spouse within the context of the same questionnaire; internal consistency is critical to validity of personal risk measures.

For items worded in terms of the subscriber unit (for example, *family* income), all members of the unit were assigned the same value for that variable. The same is true for self-rated health status since it, too, was worded for subscriber unit level in the 1980 survey. When the respondent was asked about overall satisfaction with KP, we assumed that the respondent was speaking for all family members.

Other questions allowed separate responses for the subscriber and spouse with no reference to other dependents. For some questions, such as the number of doctor visits in the past twelve months and the number of workdays missed, it was not possible to apply the responses of either the subscriber or the spouse to the children. In other cases, however, logic allows for assigning values to dependents. For example, we assumed that years of education correlated perfectly to age, and that dependents did not drop out of school before completing high school. Including children in this way may confound interpretation of the education variable, because children who by their ages are still in school and whose parents are college-educated, may use services more like their parents than like adults whose educational attainment is at the elementary or high school level. This alternative perspective has been operationalized in the case of occupation, where a value for children's occupation was assigned by giving the dependents the "highest" occupational level of either parent.

Finally, one item—whether or not "you or anyone else in your family have a regular doctor"—allowed a separate yes/no response for children. We applied this response to all children in the family.

Unlike 1980, the 1985 Membership Survey questionnaire included, for the most part, separate response categories for subscriber, spouse, and children, making it much easier to assign values to all family members, though some assumptions were still required.

Responses to questions of overall satisfaction with the HMO and size of family income were generalized to all family members. Workdays missed was asked only of subscriber and spouse since, as in 1980, this item is usually not relevant for dependents. Since the number of visits was asked for children as a group, it was not possible to break down this response for families with more than one child. Hence, this value was assigned only to a dependent in single-child families. Similarly, the "activities of daily living" requested a response for the "least healthy child." We could therefore only assign this response to single-child families. In other questions requesting responses for children as a group, we applied the responses to all children in the subscriber unit. An example of this is the self-rated health status question, which allowed for separate responses for subscriber, spouse, and children. For some variables (for example, education), values for dependents were deduced as they were in 1980.

Eligibility

To be included in the estimation and validation analyses, an individual had to respond to the Membership Survey, have at least one month of eligibility in both 1980 and 1981 for the 1980 analysis or have at least one month of eligibility in both 1985 and 1986 for the 1985 analysis, and be part of the Outpatient Utilization System (OPUS). The 1985 sample had substantially fewer observations than the 1980 sample, 842 versus 1,545 subscribers and 2,332 versus 4,446 individuals, respectively, because of the effect of the lower sampling ratio for the outpatient utilization data. The proportion of female subscribers was much higher in 1985, up from 33% in 1980 to 40%. This parallels overall demographic trends and labor force participation rates for women in the economy. It is not surprising that women are increasingly likely over time to have jobs and gain access to health care benefits through employment. Male subscribers in the 1985 sample were somewhat older than male subscribers in the 1980 sample (average age of 42.8 years versus 41 years), and female subscribers were similarly distributed across age groups for both samples (average age 39.6 years in 1985 versus 39.3 years in 1980). No subscribers were below the age of 18. The distribution of all individuals (subscribers plus dependents) reveals that the 1985 sample was slightly older than the 1980 sample, but the proportion of males to females was virtually identical.

RESULTS

We begin with the results of the estimations of ten different specifications for risk-assessment models using the 1980 and 1985 Membership Surveys. These models vary somewhat across the two data sources because the questionnaire items differed, and some variables were available on only one of the surveys. While this allowed us to explore a wider variety of predictors, it presented obstacles to validation when a strong predictor was not available on both surveys.

Estimation: 1980 Survey

Model 1 (Table 1) is a prior use model; it measures overall prior use by the number of self-reported outpatient visits in the past year. Each additional visit added about $35 in *future* expense. This simple model accounts for about 1.6% of the variance in per capita annual expense. The sample size for Model 1 is less than half the available cases because the survey item only asked about subscriber and spouse, not dependents.

Model 2 (Table 1) is a demographic model, using a series of 28 five-year age/gender dummy variables (plus newborns) with males age 20-24 as the omitted reference group; this model explains about 2.1% of the variation in expense. The pattern of the relative risk coefficients—U-shape for males and U-shape with an earlier rise associated with child-bearing for females—provides a test of the model's plausibility. While the sample size is nearly twice as large as for Model 1, it is still sufficiently small that some instability is introduced, as evidenced by the high number of insignificant coefficients. Males age 40-44 and above age 50, and females in child-bearing years and in their 50s, have statistically significant coefficients. The choice of this number of demographic cells (28) enables comparison with other research on portions of this population (Hornbrook, Goodman, and Bennett, 1991) to reveal that the demographic factors perform much more predictably for samples ten times as large as the one used here.

Model 3 (Table 1) is an expanded demographic model, adding variables for education, occupation, and marital status. These are variables that, for the subscriber, might be included in an employer's personnel files and, therefore, available for risk assessment. We are testing them, however, at the individual level. Adding these additional variables improves R^2 very slightly. Only marital status is statistically significant, with married persons having higher expenses the next year compared to unmarried persons. Very low and very high educational attainment also correlates with higher future expense. A number of missing observations reduces the sample size from that for Model 2.

Model 4 (Table 1) combines demographics and prior use for adult *subscribers* only (under-age dependents are omitted). This produces a slight improvement over Model 1 in explained variance and reduces the size of the coefficent for prior use. Demographic coefficients for males aged 40-44 years and females aged 55-59 years are statistically significant, and overall the coefficients roughly resemble the expected age/gender gradients.

Model 5 (Table 1) is a subjective health status model with a global perceived health status indicator: excellent, good, fair, poor, and mixed. Persons in excellent health are expected to be less expensive than those in good/fair/poor/mixed health. This hypothesis is supported—excellent is the least expensive—but the proportion of variance explained by this model is less than 1%. This variable was measured at the family level, so while the number of

Table 1. Estimation of Prediction Models: Total Expenses, 1981 (Estimation Data Set)

	Model									
Variable	*1*	*2*	*3*	*4*	*5*	*6*	*7*	*8*	*9*	*10*
Intercept	325.05*	83.87	−87.65	24.21	353.26	222.57	357.38	231.59*	85.49	223.74
Visits, Last 12 Months	35.07*			31.67*						27.44*
Male Newborn		433.87	461.87						446.64	
Male 1-4		203.71	204.79						195.88	
Male 5-9		176.76	209.69						192.59	
Male 10-14		66.23	85.83						63.94	
Male 15-19		27.35	167.66	−0.92					16.42	27.78
Male 20-24		Omitted	Omitted	Omitted					Omitted	Omitted
Male 25-29		123.79	6.38	106.88					136.44	118.59
Male 30-34		93.29	−10.11	74.13					93.12	70.25
Male 35-39		43.47	−54.55	28.09					45.03	2.54
Male 40-44		618.53*	605.72*	612.63*					617.83*	607.84
Male 45-49		314.76	188.66	315.30					329.07	254.52
Male 50-54		434.02*	205.42	434.29					432.08*	431.23
Male 55-59		526.62*	395.83	496.67					527.69*	446.74
Male 60-64		483.56*	108.78	447.57					483.02*	446.74
Female Newborn		332.83	241.51						350.82	
Female 1-4		69.63	69.21						80.76	
Female 5-9		9.15	22.20						6.96	
Female 10-14		93.40	100.36						93.89	
Female 15-19		169.83	311.64	606.82					182.96	586.75
Female 20-24		347.17	289.28	377.35					350.33	355.65
Female 25-29		566.14*	518.55*	473.73					569.56*	482.15

Female 30-34	353.59*	250.37	285.85					365.80*	175.90
Female 35-39	422.62*	336.40	334.13 n					424.33*	263.44
Female 40-44	179.96	49.99	138.09					171.30	93.64
Female 45-49	344.94	281.18	305.01					362.46	275.35
Female 50-54	643.79*	341.87	409.89					651.15*	323.28
Female 55-59	709.38*	666.81*	614.96*					712.07*	509.64
Female 60-64	462.77	162.56	429.73					458.98	292.83
Grade 0-8		77.01							
Grade 9-11		−119.28							
Some College		−43.85							
College Grad		−147.59							
Post-College		78.89							
Professional/Technical		143.45							
Manager		43.64							
Clerical/Sales		102.13							
Semi-Skilled		55.96							
Service		74.71							
Laborer		−91.75							
Not In Labor Force		101.26							
Married		284.63*							
Excellent Health				−76.78	−74.14			−51.45	
Fair Health				63.74	27.61			−46.91	
Poor Health				523.06	−726.91			399.28	
Mixed				97.51	−23.15			137.07	
Number of Conditions					29.55				
Number of Workdays Missed in Last 4 Weeks					93.89*				−0.15
Smoker					−34.04				
Alcohol Problem					−96.53				

(*continued*)

Table 1. (Continued)

	Model									
Variable	*1*	*2*	*3*	*4*	*5*	*6*	*7*	*8*	*9*	*10*
Little Exercise						−32.07				
Weight Class 1**						310.09				
Weight Class 2**						150.42				
Weight Class 3**						259.47				
Weight Class 4**						341.49				
Asthma							226.80			
Allergies							−116.04			
Arthritis/Rheumatism							396.03*			306.33
Cancer							−233.80			
Cataracts							543.59			
Bronchitis							−551.08			
Deafness/Hearing Loss							395.11			
Depression							155.84			
Diabetes							609.40*			57.54
Emphysema							−333.61			
Epilepsy							−365.66			
Heart Disease							291.17			
Hemorrhoids							13.04			
Hypertension							87.86			
Kidney/Bladder							286.14			
Liver Disease							−110.01			
Nervousness							−7.88			
Obesity							−37.69			
Skin Problems							140.51			

Sinus Trouble							−1.95			
Back/Neck/Spine							30.30			
Stress							−293.44			
Ulcer/Stomach							358.61			
Thyroid							−311.86			
Varicose Veins							219.50			
Other Problems							299.72*			79.23
Should Have Seen MD Last Year								115.59		
Have Regular MD								114.14*		−112.00
Very Satisfied with KP								23.55		
Neutral								116.83		
Dissatisfied with KP								−38.54		
Very Dissatisfied with KP								−250.91		
Adj. R^2	0.016	0.021	0.023	0.017	0.001	0.027	0.007	0.002	0.021	0.017
F-Ratio	20.261*	2.741*	2.109*	2.034*	1.755	3.123*	1.315	1.712	2.546*	1.731*
n	(1,175)	(2,222)	(1,883)	(1,175)	(2,192)	(1,004)	(1,260)	(1,951)	(2,192)	(1,073)

Notes: $^*p < 0.05$.

**These variables are combinations of two items. They are defined as follows:

Weight Class 1 = Self-reported normal or under weight and attempted to lose weight in the last year.

Weight Class 2 = Self-reported slightly or quite overweight and attempted to lose weight in the last year.

Weight Class 3 = Self-reported normal or under weight and no attempt to lose weight in the last year.

Weight Class 4 = Self-reported slightly or quite overweight and no attempt to lose weight in the last year.

Weight Class 5 = The omitted category—normal, under, or slightly overweight, and not necessary to attempt to lose weight in the last year.

observations indicates that most individuals are included in the analysis, the variable omits information on intra-family differences in health status.

Model 6 (Table 1) adds several variables to perceived health status: health-related habits (smoking and drinking), obesity, number of health conditions, and workdays missed. This model explains about 3% of the variation. Only workdays missed is significant, and it is responsible for nearly all the explained variance (as revealed by a step-wise regression not presented here). The reversal of signs on the coefficients for poor and mixed health indicates that workdays missed is picking up most of the prediction effect these variables carried in Model 5. Workdays missed was measured only for subscriber and spouse, so the number of observations is much smaller for this model.

The 1980 survey presented respondents with a checklist of health conditions. Model 7 (Table 1) uses dummy variables for 25 conditions. People who did not check any of the conditions are the omitted reference group. Of these conditions, only arthritis, diabetes, and the residual "other" category have statistically significant positive risk coefficients. Allergies, cancer, bronchitis, emphysema, epilepsy, liver disease, nervousness, obesity, stress, and thyroid problems all have seemingly implausible negative coefficients, but these are not statistically significant. Measuring at the subscriber level while estimating at the individual level may be the cause of this result. Model 7's explained variance is less than 1%.

Model 8 (Table 1) includes measures of health plan integration, access, and satisfaction. The only significant variable is having a regular physician, which has a positive coefficient, but only a negligible amount of variance is explained by these variables. Since the satisfaction variables were pertinent to the overall purpose of the Membership Survey, these items had a higher completion rate than some of the other items, thus increasing the number of observations.

Model 9 (Table 1) combines the age/sex cells (Model 2, Table 1) with perceived health status (Model 5, Table 1). The explained variance is the same as the pure demographic model (Model 2, Table 1). In addition, the coefficients on the demographic variables are similar for both specifications. Controlling for age and gender, persons in "fair" health become less expensive next year relative to persons in "good" health. This is not true for Model 5, which does not include the demographic variables.

Model 10 (Table 1) includes the strongest predictors from the previous models: prior use, demographics, workdays missed, three diseases/health problems, and regular physician. These account for about 2% of the variance in expense, which is almost no improvement over previous, simpler versions. The primary deficiency of this model is its low sample size—only subscribers and spouses who responded to these items are included. The instability of small samples is illustrated by the fact that only one variable—prior use—reaches statistical significance in this version, despite the strong showing of all included variables in other specifications. This lack of statistical significance could also reflect high correlations among the included variables.

No specification employing the 1980 Membership Survey data explained more than 3% of the variance in expense. The single strongest predictor for this data set was the number of workdays missed; age and gender were the next strongest predictors, followed by prior use of ambulatory services. These results must be conditioned on the fact that each model employed a slightly different set of observations because of missing data problems.

Estimation: 1985 Survey

In 1985, the simple prior use model (Model 1, Table 2), based on self-reported outpatient visits in the past year, explained 2.2% of the variance in expense, slightly higher than the 1.6% for 1980. Each visit added about $50.

The pure demographic model (five-year age/gender cells plus newborns, Model 2, Table 2) explained nearly 2% of the variance. The relatively small sample reduces the number of significant coefficients and the degree to which the model matches the shape of the expected distribution. Only males aged 50-55 and females aged 55-59 had statistically significant coefficients. A very high expense outlier explains the extremely large coefficient for 50-55 year-old males.

Model 3 (Table 2) includes demographics, education, occupation, and marital status. The explained variance falls below 1%, probably because of the instability introduced by the small sample size (missing values remove individuals from the estimation). Inconsistencies make interpreting coefficients from this model more difficult. High school graduates, the comparison group, are more expensive than persons with all other levels of educational attainment. None of these variables is statistically significant. Males, aged 50 to 55, is the single significant predictor.

Model 4 (Table 2) combines demographics and prior use for subscribers only. This produces an improvement over Model 1 in explained variance ($R^2 = .026$). The coefficent for prior use declines slightly, and statistical significance is lost for females aged 55 to 59.

Model 5 (Table 2) uses a global subjective health status indicator: excellent, good, fair, and poor. Excellent is the least expensive, but poor health is less expensive than fair health. Again the single outlier case explains the large coefficient on "fair" health. Health status was measured as an individual variable, and the R^2 is .047, showing good predictive potential.

Model 6 (Table 2) adds functional indicators, such as requirements for assistance in housework, to Model 5. This model explains 18% of the variance in next year's expense. Workdays missed, along with the functional measures "trouble getting around" and "bedridden," were statistically significant. Note that the bedridden variable has a coefficient of over $13,000. This represents

Table 2. Estimation of Prediction Models: Total Expenses, 1986 (Estimation Data Set)

	Model									
Variable	*1*	*2*	*3*	*4*	*5*	*6*	*7*	*8*	*9*	*10*
Intercept	299.10*	175.66	247.33	54.53	355.93*	342.98*	291.85*	20.31	334.27*	−124.55
Visits, Last 12 Months	50.12*			48.73*						21.52*
Male Newborn		281.94	270.15					473.75		
Male 1-4		24.34	48.40					199.54		
Male 5-9		52.36	19.55					211.40		
Male 10-14		−24.87	−9.78					162.62		
Male 15-19		24.85	24.96	490.57				175.65		751.99
Male 20-24		Omitted	Omitted	Omitted				Omitted		Omitted
Male 25-29		−54.29	−64.37	−46.70				103.53		197.05
Male 30-34		8.67	4.10	11.96				163.13		227.40
Male 35-39		109.70	167.44	151.01				183.53		311.90
Male 40-44		235.26	274.69	309.59				391.81		516.11
Male 45-49		188.93	217.02	147.18				262.01		334.67
Male 50-54		1346.65*	1588.97*	1486.40*				1545.35*		475.95
Male 55-59		107.71	193.22	23.41				120.05		287.13
Male 60-64		478.22	470.48	422.57				622.81		692.22
Female Newborn		268.42	304.65					448.25		
Female 1-4		−33.12	−8.74					184.13		
Female 5-9		−83.37	−86.61					112.92		
Female 10-14		10.79	−0.86					167.05		

Female 15-19	109.03	117.86	−164.77				195.34		32.76
Female 20-24	173.47	226.11	162.62				344.00		416.83
Female 25-29	340.23	289.53	275.19				470.49		535.10
Female 30-34	500.77	564.85	187.92				674.33*		475.75
Female 35-39	297.09	207.24	233.87				389.48		461.63
Female 40-44	380.97	421.63	378.60				466.95		601.96
Female 45-49	167.88	186.79	112.59				130.76		264.47
Female 50-54	256.45	192.45	294.72				380.19		427.99
Female 55-59	636.14*	725.45	580.48				533.38		696.67*
Female 60-64	576.28	511.76	358.17				317.89		309.33
Grade 0-8		−47.17							
Grade 9-11		−64.07							
Some College		−65.28							
College Graduate		−30.42							
Post-College		−169.41							
Professional/Technical		−33.57							
Manager		−86.00							
Clerical/Sales		15.76							
Semi-Skilled		6.17							
Service		−146.42							
Laborer		25.84							
Not In Labor Force		−50.65							
Married		1.73							
Excellent Health				−114.11	−46.07		−65.64	−40.47	−1.24
Fair Health				1100.54*	1308.44*		1097.54*	717.51*	783.71*
Poor Health				954.46*	1298.92*		1025.77*	1207.34*	1451.14*
Mixed				104.40					

(continued)

Table 2. (Continued)

	Model									
Variable	*1*	*2*	*3*	*4*	*5*	*6*	*7*	*8*	*9*	*10*
Bedridden						13067.00*			12794.00*	
House-bound						−444.999			−582.75	
Need Help from Other Person						−360.57			−361.92	
Need Help from DME						−88.98			−175.88	
Trouble Getting Around						−1091.07*			−780.65*	−876.57*
Number of Workdays Missed in Last Four Weeks						60.04*			70.10*	
Should Have Seen MD Last Year							−45.60			
Have Regular MD							184.96*			
Very Satisfied with KP							−35.28			
Neutral							−136.59			
Dissatisfied with KP							−49.10			
Very Dissatisfied with KP							−51.02			
Adj. R^2	0.022	0.019	0.009	0.026	0.047	0.182	0.002	0.062	0.349	0.087
F-Ratio	15.578*	1.845*	1.215	1.826*	14.674*	16.993*	1.323	3.404*	39.658*	3.371*
n	(657)	(1,165)	(995)	(623)	(1,104)	(649)	(1,132)	(1,085)	(648)	(600)

Note: $*p < 0.05$.

a single case that had $15,091 in expenses in 1986. This illustrates the critical importance of including risk measures for outlier cases if at all possible.

Model 7 (Table 2) examines measures of health plan integration, access, and satisfaction. As was the case in 1980, the only significant variable is having a regular physician, with only negligible variance explained overall.

Model 8 (Table 2) combines the age/sex cells (Model 2) with perceived health status (Model 5). The explained variance increases to 6.2%.

Model 9 (Table 2) is Model 6 with one extreme outlier case removed. Note that the R^2 for this model increases to 0.35. The coefficient on "fair" health drops by 45%, and the coefficient on use of mobility aids increases in absolute value 100%. Outliers have been routinely dropped from other risk-assessment analyses on the argument that they carry too much influence on the coefficients and produce instability in the estimates (Anderson et al., 1990; Feldman et al., 1989). We estimated this model to show that single extreme cases can have substantial effects on risk-assessment models, especially when sample sizes are small. The problem with this approach is that outliers are a part of the phenomenon under investigation and removing them ignores reality. The most appropriate way of handling outliers is to increase sample size so that, as the distribution is "filled in," its true shape becomes more apparent and stable. The highly skewed nature of medical care consumption is not corrected by truncating it above some level, either by analytic fiat or by a policy initiative to create a separate reimbursement for outliers—a skewed distribution still remains. We need to develop better ways of handling the underlying nature of this distribution.

Model 10 (Table 2) combines the best predictors from previous models—prior use, demographics, perceived health status, and trouble getting around. The proportion of variance explained is 8.7%, even with only 600 observations.

In summary, functional health status is the strongest predictor, followed by perceived health status, prior use, and demographics. The 1985 data offers strong hope for self-report data. The lack of consistent performance between the surveys is, however, troubling.

Prediction Performance: 1980 Survey

Table 3 summarizes the prediction performance of the various models on the validation data set for the 1980 Membership Survey. One criterion for prediction performance is overall accuracy. The models estimated from the 1980 survey range in prediction error from an average of $101.36 over-payment to $5.82 under-payment. This represents an error as great as nearly 27% of the mean per capita annual expense. Clearly, such bias or instability is not tolerable to any payer (or health plan). Model 5 (Table 1)—simple perceived health status—yields the least overall prediction error, less than one-half of 1%. This model, however, explains very little of the expense variation, so the

Table 3. Prediction Results: Total Expenses, 1981 (Validation Data Set)

	Model									
Variable	*1*	*2*	*3*	*4*	*5*	*6*	*7*	*8*	*9*	*10*
Under- / Over-Payment	27.67	4.33	8.23	31.01	1.47	101.36	28.93	−5.82	6.07	20.50
Under- / Over-Payment as Percent of Mean	6.54%	1.26%	2.48%	7.32%	0.43%	27.02%	6.99%	1.66%	1.77%	4.68%
Intercept	−156.23	103.41*	194.52*	34.61	−70.43	215.49*	241.75*	113.94	98.98*	51.11
Predicted Expenses	1.29*	0.69*	0.40*	0.86*	1.20*	0.33*	0.39*	0.69*	0.70*	0.84*
Adj. R^2	0.039	0.023	0.012	0.043	0.006	0.018	0.009	0.003	0.026	0.047
F-Ratio	50.853*	53.884*	22.773*	55.361*	14.999*	20.271*	13.116*	7.457*	60.457*	54.797*
n	(1,226)	(2,222)	(1,872)	(1,225)	(2,191)	(1,045)	1,331)	1,905)	(2,191)	(1,104)
Age Prediction Error	−6.29	1.34	0.85	−0.81	−6.09	0.68	−0.07	−7.05	1.29	0.24
Gender Prediction Error										
Males	125.02	4.15	−9.63	68.66	61.69	202.11	154.74	51.31	4.25	83.34
Females	−57.33	4.51	25.36	−1.80	−57.76	10.11	−82.62	−60.84	7.85	−33.37

Note: $*p < 0.05$.

prediction accuracy is obtained from extrapolation of the mean. Models 2 and 9 have average prediction errors around 1% of the mean, demonstrating the utility of demographic predictors. Model 8 is another example of the mean being a good prediction—overall prediction error is low but so is the estimation R^2.

The predicted values from Models 3, 5, 7, and 8 (Table 1) explain 1% or less of the variance in actual expense for 1981. The models with the best fit of predicted to actual expenses, as measured by the R^2, are those containing prior doctor office visits, Models 1, 4, and 10. Models containing demographic predictors (Models 2, 3, and 9) and functional health status (Model 6) produce the next level of goodness-of-fit on this criterion.

Another measure of goodness-of-fit is the regression of actual on predicted expenses for 1981. An intercept of zero with a slope of unity indicates that the model is unbiased on average across the full range of prediction, that is, that it does not disproportionately under-predict or over-predict at either end of the range of annual per capita expense. The results presented in Table 3 reveal that the self-report models for 1980 are unstable on this criterion. Eight of the models (2 through 4 and 6 through 10) have slope coefficients less than 1 and large positive intercept terms. This indicates that at low levels of predicted expense the actual expense is on average much higher, and that at high levels of actual expense, predicted expense is on average lower than actual. This is to be expected as a manifestation of the regression technique—outliers cannot be predicted with accuracy, so to achieve the mean prediction, low values are over-predicted to compensate for under-prediction of the high values. Models 1 and 5 have negative intercept terms and slopes greater than 1. This indicates that the model over-predicts for some higher range of values sufficiently to overcome the expected level of under-prediction for low values of expense. Note that these two models still over-predict for low values and under-predict for high values, but the mid-range is biased.

A good risk-assessment model should not leave unacceptable patterns of cross-subsidy among the residuals. Specifically, after adjusting for health risk, we would expect that any remaining differences between men and women or between younger and older persons were purely random. We should not observe strong associations between the residuals (prediction error is computed as actual minus predicted) and age or gender. The sensitivity of the models to age-related selection bias can be explored with scatter plots of predicted values, as in Hornbrook, Goodman, and Bennett (1991). Models that do not include age will have a negative slope, which indicates a subsidy from young to old. Linear regression provides a descriptive measure of these scatter plots. The slope of the regression of average prediction error on age is shown in Table 3. Ideally, the prediction error should be random, so that the slope in this plot would be 0. Thus, the smaller the absolute value of the slope, the less biased the model with respect to age-related cross-subsidy. By this criterion, Models 3, 4, 6, 7, and 10 have the least age bias. All but one of these models include age as a predictor. Finally, the age bias inherent in the simple prior use model is shown by Models 1 and 8. Over-predicting for infants and children and under-predicting for older adults creates substantial intergenerational transfer.

The second finding is the heteroscedasticity of the models; the variance of prediction error generally increases as age increases.

The gender bias test is simpler. If there is a large difference between the residual for each gender and if the differences have different signs, then the models have a subsidy by gender. The worst, by this criterion, are Models 1, 3, 4, 5, 7, and 10 (Table 3). The best are Models 2 and 9 where both genders are over-predicted by less than 2% of the mean.

While none of the models dominates on all performance criteria, of those with the highest R^2 in the estimation data set (Models 2, 3, 6, 9), Model 2 (pure demographics) has the lowest overall error and acceptable age- and gender-related prediction errors.

Prediction Performance: 1985 Survey

The smaller sample size for the 1985 survey produces poorer prediction results, as shown in Table 4. The overall prediction errors are very high, ranging from about 9% to over 18% of the mean. All models over-predict. The effect of removing the one outlier observation in the estimation data set is shown by the improved prediction accuracy of Model 9, an overall error of less than 1%. However, when the validation data set does not contain the outlier, but the prediction model is set up to predict the influence of such a value, the model performs rather poorly.

The prediction distributions from all the models have very bad fits with the actual distribution of expenses in the validation data set. The prediction R^2 values never exceed 2% (Table 4). For Model 6, which had an R^2 of .18 in the estimation data set, the prediction R^2 drops to .004 with a 17% over-prediction. This apparent drop in performance is caused by a difference in the shapes of the expense distributions between the two split-half samples. The estimation data set happened by chance to have the extreme outlier; since this case was not present in the validation data set, the models over-predict in an attempt to capture the contribution of this case to the overall mean. Note that all of the intercept terms are strongly positive and the slope values are less than 1 in the prediction validation regressions showing that, on average, the prediction errors are negative (under-payment) for lower expenses and positive (over-payment) for higher expenses.

Models 1, 5, and 7 require young persons to subsidize older persons, while Models 2, 3, 4, 6, 8, 9, and 10 reverse the subsidy pattern. None of the slope coefficients is near 0.

Table 4. Prediction Results: Total Expenses, 1986 (Validation Data Set)

	Model									
Variable	*1*	*2*	*3*	*4*	*5*	*6*	*7*	*8*	*9*	*10*
Under- / Over-Payment	55.16	38.87	49.10	43.13	56.29	72.47	31.65	61.37	4.03	21.60
Under- / Over-Payment as Percent of Mean	13.30%	11.64%	14.38%	11.00%	16.59%	17.00%	9.34%	18.14%	0.92%	4.98%
Intercept	251.32*	165.29*	210.33*	307.93*	274.85*	359.31*	124.49	259.58	309.63*	303.88*
Predicted Expenses	0.35*	0.45*	0.34*	0.26*	0.16*	0.15	0.58*	0.20*	0.19*	0.28*
Adj. R^2	0.006	0.018	0.011	0.006	0.003	0.004	0.004	0.009	0.010	0.006
F-Ratio	4.713*	22.230*	12.376*	4.929*	4.281*	3.515	6.000*	10.568*	7.208	4.552*
n	(646)	(1,165)	(983)	(607)	(1,091)	(650)	(1,130)	(1,078)	(650)	(580)
Age Prediction Error	−7.06	1.60	1.22	2.03	−2.45	3.44	−8.13	3.29	4.65	1.46
Gender Prediction Error										
Males	102.44	66.06	102.45	89.24	125.94	183.88	99.15	109.20	107.64	58.96
Females	12.99	12.50	−2.16	1.63	−11.61	−27.58	−33.39	15.20	−89.01	−11.97

Note: $*p < 0.05$.

Gender-related prediction error is a problem for Models 3, 5, 6, 7, 9, and 10: males cross-subsidize females. Models 1, 2, 4, and 8 require both males and females to subsidize some other subgroup, although males contribute disproportionately more.

Overall, these models perform much worse than the 1980 models. We suspect this is largely a sample size problem. Prediction analysis with less than 1,000 observations is a recipe for instability.

Tree Analysis

Even with the small number of variables available to this study from the Membership Surveys, the number of alternative specifications for the prediction models is exceedingly large. Rather than attempting to specify all these functional forms and inspecting them for relative performance, we undertook a regression tree analysis of the data with the University of Michigan's Automatic Interaction Detector (AID) (Sonquist and Morgan, 1964). Separate models were developed for each estimation data set.

For the 1980 data set, the first split is the number of workdays missed, which is not surprising given its strong performance in the a priori regressions (see Figure 1). This split produces the first terminal group, 27 cases, or about 1% of the sample, who missed seven or more days of work in 1980. The next split is number of office visits in the past year—256 cases, or 12% of the sample, had five or more visits in the past year. This group is split into two terminal groups—those who reported having arthritis (terminal group 2) and those who did not (terminal group 3). Persons with four or fewer visits to the doctor last year were split into two terminal groups on the basis of age: 40 years and above is terminal group 4, while 39 years and below is terminal group 5. Two-thirds of the entire sample is classified in group 5.

Newer regression-tree programs have more sophisticated pruning algorithms than are available in AID. These techniques determine splits based on the variance explained by the entire tree; AID determines each split independently. To replicate these techniques, the trees are reconstructed eliminating the variable used in the first split—workdays missed (Figure 2). The first split is now on visits (prior use), followed by marital status among the low users, which produces two terminal groups, and by weight status among the high users, which produces one terminal group for a small set of overweight persons. Persons with normal to below-normal weight, or those who attempted to lose weight if they were overweight, are split into two terminal groups on the basis of prior use, 5 to 14 visits versus 15 or more visits. Clearly, the last three terminal groups are persons with an above average use of services. Nearly half of the sample are classified in terminal group 1, unmarried persons with four or fewer doctor visits last year.

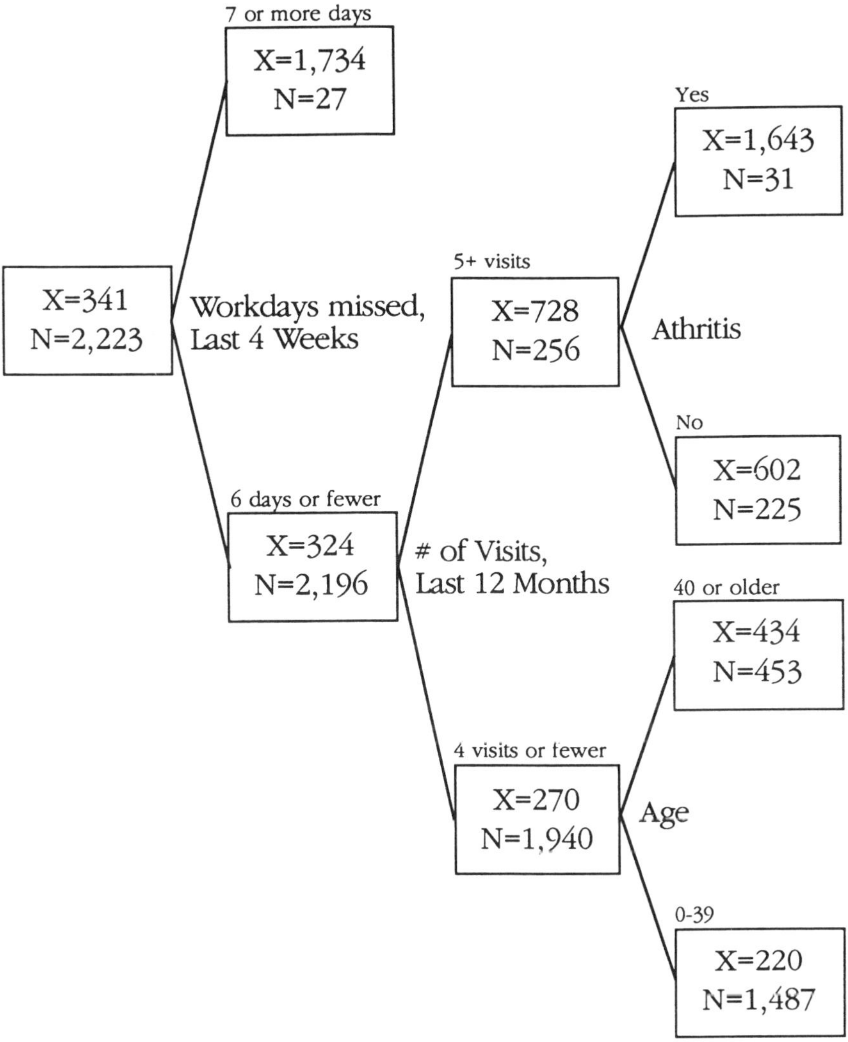

Figure 1. Regression tree, 1980-1981.

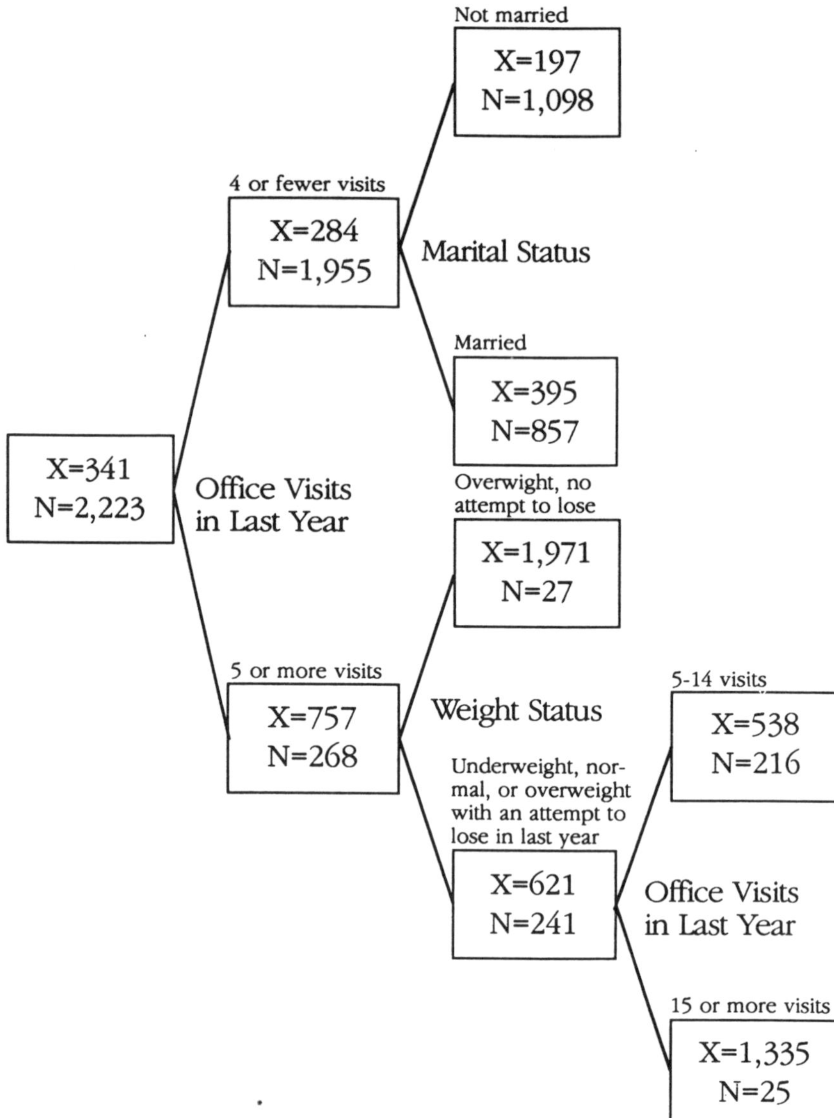

Figure 2. Regression tree, 1980-1981, excluding workdays missed.

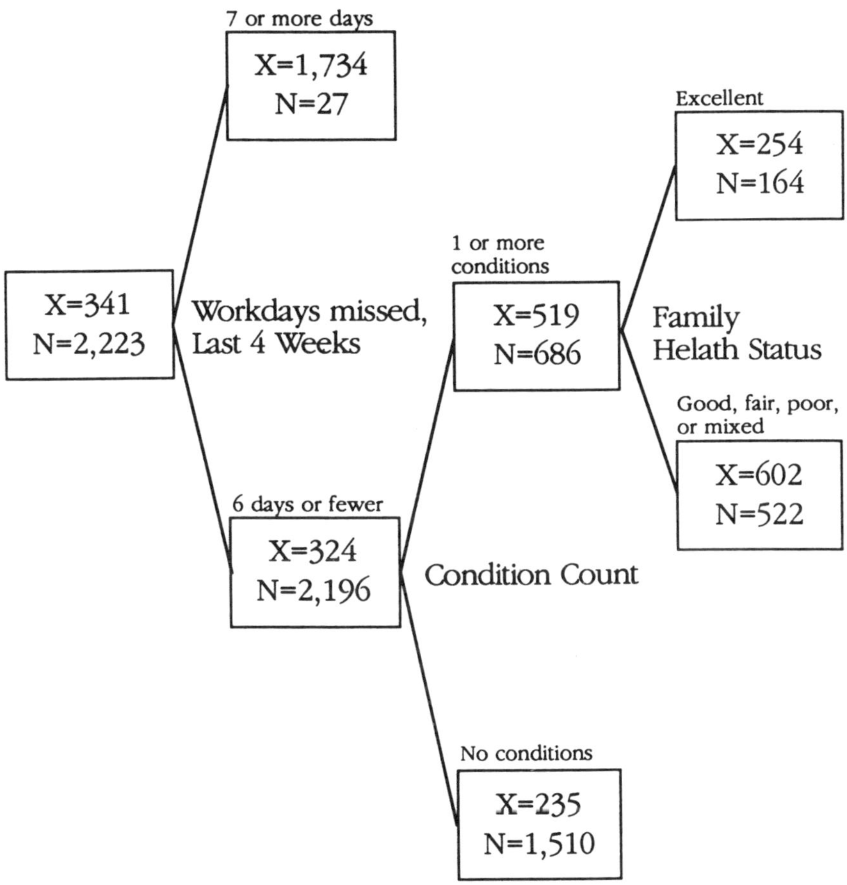

Figure 3. Regression tree, 1980-1981, excluding prior use.

The 1980 data set was also run without the prior use information available to the AID algorithm but with workdays missed included (Figure 3). This tree first splits on workdays missed, the same as in Figure 1. Then persons with no reported health conditions are split into a terminal group (68% of the sample). Persons with one or more conditions are split on perceived health status, with 7% of the cases classified into group 3, excellent health. The net effect of the 1980 tree analysis is to show that the strong predictors in the linear regressions are also strong in the AID splits. The data set will not support complex interactive models, except for a small hint of one in Figure 2 when prior use creates two different splits.

For the 1985 data set, prior use, measured as office visits, is the first split, with persons with six or more visits last year split into two terminal groups on the basis of perceived health status (excellent/good versus fair/poor, as shown in Figure 4). Workdays missed represent the second split for the majority of the sample (those who had five or fewer visits in the prior year). Terminal group 3 is persons who had five or fewer visits last year and four or more days of work lost. For persons with three or fewer days of work loss, the next split is on health status—excellent/good (82% of the cases) versus fair/poor. For those in fair or poor health, a final split on occupation produces two terminal groups—managers, service, crafts, and semiskilled workers versus professional, technical, clerical/sales, laborer, not in labor force, and missing data. This classification scheme is highly concentrated since a single group accounts for over four-fifths of the sample.

When prior use is omitted as a classification variable, the first split is on health status (Figure 5). Those in excellent or good health split on workdays missed (three days or fewer versus four or more), while those in fair or poor health split on age (above or below age 50), with the younger group then splitting on occupation as in Figure 4. In this tree, nearly 90% of the cases are classified in the first terminal group.

In each of the trees, a large portion of the sample ends up in a single cell. This is known in the literature as an end-splitting problem. In predictors with a large number of classes, the splitting algorithm has a tendency to split at either end of the distribution. Among the range of potential splits, of course, it is not clear that it is always better to split in the middle (Kass, 1980). Nevertheless, some variance-reduction algorithms, including AID, are more likely to split a category with a large number of classes at the end, while other techniques may arrive at more balanced splits. This complicates interpretation. For example, in the remaining large cell, the expense distribution may not be truly homogeneous.

The second step of the analysis is to test the predictive performance of a subset of the trees. The results of this analysis are shown in Table 5. The first step is to convert the trees into dummy variable regression models so they can be compared to the first set of models. In each data set, the first tree has the

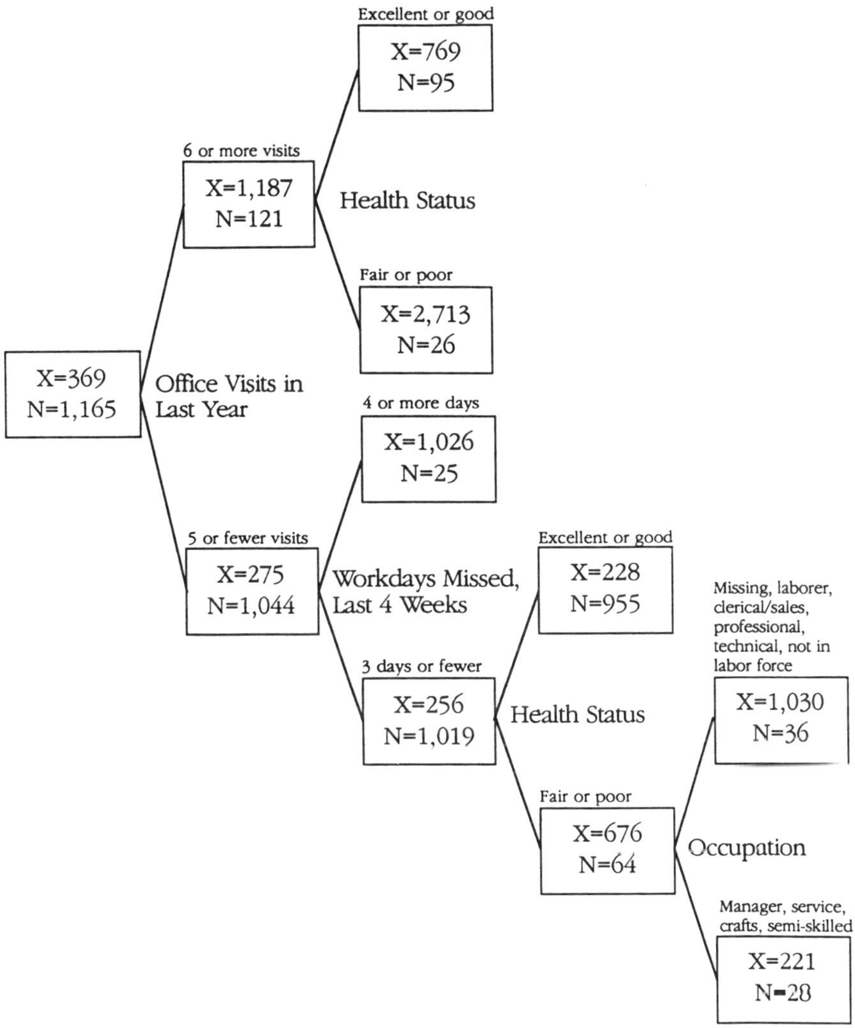

Figure 4. Regression tree, 1985-1986.

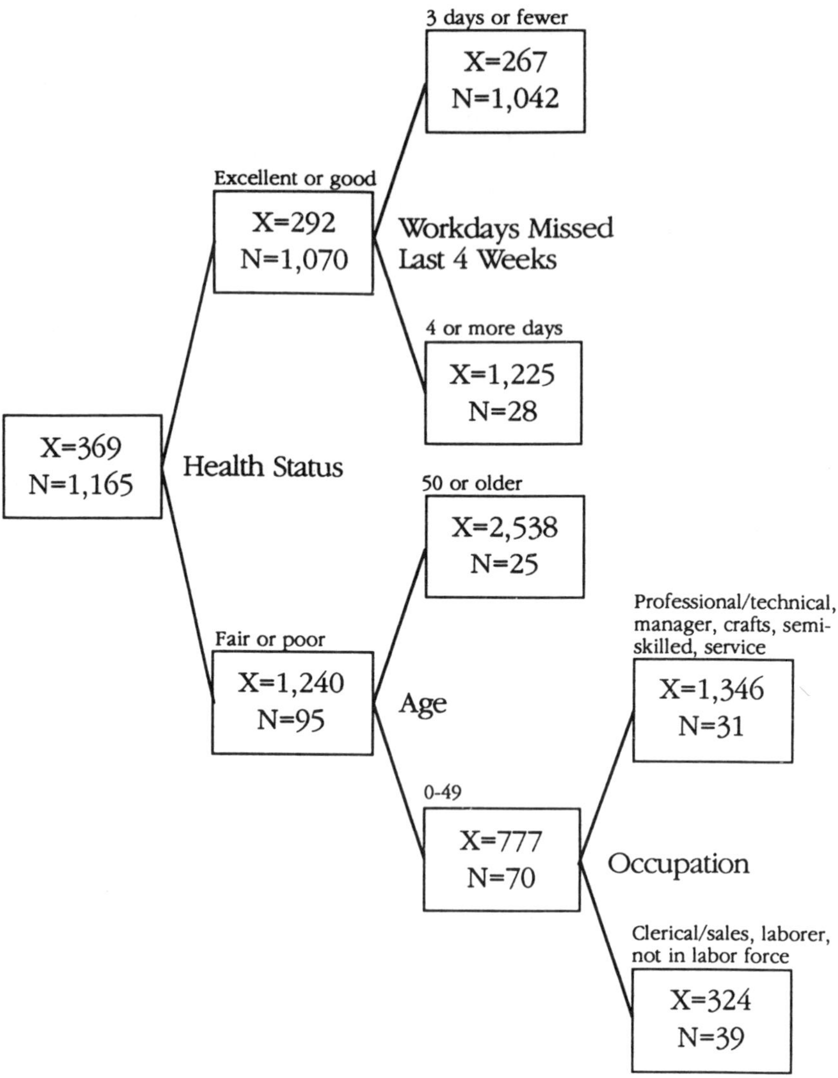

Figure 5. Regression tree, 1985-1986, excluding prior use.

highest proportion of variance explained, which is expected by construction. The 1980 estimation R^2 values are about twice as high as obtained with the best a priori specifications—5% for Tree Model 1, and 4.4% for Tree Model 2. For the 1985 data set, the estimation R^2 values are .104 and .091 for Tree Models 1 and 2, respectively. These demonstrate the effect of capitalizing on the sample variance structure in defining the models.

The overall average prediction error for the 1980 tree models is around 1%: Tree Model 1 over-predicts by about $3.50 per person per year, while Tree Model 2 under-predicts by $3.90 per person per year. Both tree models derived from the 1985 data set over-predict, from 8.4% for Tree Model 1 to 19.5% for Tree Model 2. Again, the different shapes of the estimation and validation distributions for 1985 defeat the tree models as well. None of the tree models generates predicted values that fit the observed expenses well; the prediction R^2 values are less than 3% for the 1980 data set and less than 1% for the 1985 data set. Finally, the tree models exhibit substantial age and gender bias because these variables are not forced into the specifications.

In sum, the 1980 tree models reveal more stable performance across the criteria than the 1985 tree models. Sample size may be the most pertinent distinction between the two data sets. The 1985 models appear promising in their estimation, but fail in validation.

CONCLUSIONS

Using data collected for other purposes, we set out to examine the efficacy of using self-reported perceived and functional health status to predict future expenses. The major conclusions and caveats emerging from our analysis reveal highly mixed results—some highly tantalizing findings that must be qualified by very poor showings in other areas.

First, measurement of perceived health status and other self-reported health attributes at the subscriber level and application to the individual level do not accurately predict health care expense in the next year. These models fail to confirm or deny whether perceived health status provides a realistic proxy for other, objective, but more difficult to implement, predictors of health care expense. Future researchers should use and, if necessary, design surveys that can obtain information for each individual in a household. Moreover, assessing risk via any ecological unit—family, subscriber unit, workplace, occupational group—loses too much information to be useful for most risk-assessment applications.

Second, until we can develop validated models that exhibit no age or gender bias, demographic factors must be included in our risk-assessment models. We also recommend that lost workdays be incorporated into any risk-assessment model for employed persons. This data should be available from most employer personnel files.

Table 5. Estimation and Prediction Results from Tree Analysis

	Model			
Estimation	*1980*		*1985*	
Results	*Tree No. 1*	*Tree No. 2*	*Tree No. 1*	*Tree No. 2*
Intercept	220.18*	196.54*	227.74*	266.65*
Node 1[a]	1,423.08*	1,138.37*	541.09*	
Node 2	382.14*	341.36*	2,485.12*	958.18*
Node 3	214.28*	1,774.60*	798.09*	2,271.74*
Node 4	1,513.41*	198.90*		57.21
Node 5			803.25*	1,079.81*
Node 6			−6.92	
R^2	0.50	.044	.104	.091
F-Ratio	30.088*	26.699*	28.115*	30.220*
n	(2,222)	(2,222)	(1,165)	(1,165)
Under- / Over-Payment	3.51	−3.90	28.133	65.23
Under- / Over-Payment as Percent of Mean	1.02%	−1.14%	8.42%	19.54%
Intercept	141.98*	164.49*	262.33*	294.11*
Predicted Expenses	0.58*	0.53*	.20*	.10*
Adj. R^2	.027	.0164	.008	.002
F-Ratio	61.809*	38.155*	10.36*	3.743
n	(2,222)	(2,222)	(1,165)	(1,165)
Age Prediction Error	0.77	−1.29	−3.57	2.16
Gender Prediction Error				
Males	48.31	45.61	70.62	144.67
Females	−40.62	−52.65	−13.08	−11.79

Note: Nodes do not correspond between models.

Third, the fact that perceived and functional health status performed significantly in both data sets confirms our hypotheses that these are pertinent variables to be included in risk-assessment models. We have conducted very rudimentary tests of these prediction factors. The assessment of functional health status, even via mail questionnaires, has progressed in the years since the KP Membership Surveys were constructed. We strongly recommend further research to develop a health status/habits instrument specifically for the purpose of predicting health care use over the next 12 to 24 months. In the nonaged population, such an instrument should be sensitive to chronic disease and conditions creating lost workdays.

Fourth, self-reported prior use of ambulatory services is a relatively strong predictor of next year's use. This suggests that social surveys can be used to obtain these data should they be unavailable from other sources (as for members of other HMOs that do not have automated claims or utilization reporting systems). More research is needed to examine the potential biases introduced by mixing claims data with self-report data on prior use. Under-reporting of prior use because of inaccurate recall may create bias if persons without claims data are disproportionately enrolled in managed care systems.

Fifth, behavioral risk factors—tobacco and alcohol consumption, overweight—do not perform very well in our models. The epidemiologic literature, from which these factors emerge, uses a much longer time frame than the 12- to 24-month horizon employed in this study. Thus, smokers are likely to be more expensive to treat in the future, but the probability of this increased expense does not necessarily manifest itself within a one-year window. Much more work is needed to develop short-term disease risk models for common and serious chronic conditions.

Several methodological limitations to this study merit emphasis. First, the survey was designed for purposes other than risk assessment and was administered over a period of months. Thus, for some individuals the survey took place during the last portion of the estimation year; for others, the survey was a year old at the start of the risk period. This variation in the interval between the administration of the survey and the beginning of the risk period added more variance to the models. Second, these were subscriber-level surveys applied to individuals. A survey designed specifically for individuals would be more valid and reliable. Third, the size of the samples, while large in survey terms, was relatively small for estimating future health care expense, a variable that is highly heterogeneous. Future research on self-report risk-assessment models should have very large samples—25,000 or more—to explore the structure of risk with a comprehensive health status and behavioral risk factors instrument. Moreover, personal interview techniques and clinical assessments should be explored and special efforts in design and administration should be made to obtain consistent and complete data on all persons in the sample.

A major attraction of self-report risk measures is that they may avoid, or at least reduce, the problem of selection bias associated with prior use. Jobe et al. (1990) found that recall accuracy for visits to medical providers varies by gender, self-reported health status, and number of visits. While these differences were not substantial, especially with respect to number of visits, future research on self-report methods must maintain vigilance for bias. The research by Jobe et al. (1990) also indicates that in-depth probing and opportunity for free recall can "uncover" visits lost to immediate recall.

The failure of our efforts to derive simple, valid, unbiased, and feasible risk-assessment models from a few self-administered questionnaire items is no reason to close off this avenue of inquiry. This field is still relatively undeveloped and the solutions to the risk prediction challenge may require much more creativity than has been engaged to date.

ACKNOWLEDGMENTS

This research was supported by a grant from the Kaiser Foundation Health Plan, Inc. The views expressed in this paper are those of the authors and no official endorsement by Kaiser Foundation Hospitals or Kaiser Foundation Health Plan is intended or should be inferred. An earlier version of this paper was presented at the Workshop on Risk Adjustment of Employer Contributions, sponsored by the Kaiser Permanente Center for Health Research, Otter Rock, Oregon, July 16, 1990. We would like to acknowledge the helpful insights of Arlene Ash, Nelda McCall, Richard Scheffler, Bill Thomas, Pete Welch, and the members of the Technical Subcommittee of the Kaiser Permanente Risk Adjustment Task Force at various stages of this work. We are grateful for the assistance of the following persons: Barbara J. Mendius, who provided all the programming required to create the data files for this study; Gregory N. Nichols, who conducted and documented the statistical analyses; and Margaret R. Sucec and David Porter, who provided assistance with technical editing.

REFERENCES

Anderson, G.F., E.P. Steinberg, N.R. Powe, S. Antebi, J. Whittle, S. Horn, and R. Herbert (1990). "Setting Payment Rates for Capitated Systems: A Comparison of Various Alternatives." *Inquiry* 27:225-233.

Brown, J.B. (1991). Personal Communication.

Ellis, R.P. and A. Ash (1988). *Refining the Diagnostic Cost Group Model: A Proposed Modification to the AAPCC for HMO Reimbursement.* Final Report, Grant No. 18-C-98526/1-03. Baltimore, MD: Health Care Financing Administration.

Ellis, R.P. and A. Ash (1989). *The Continuous-Update Diagnostic Cost Group Model.* Final Report, Grant No. 18-C-98526/1-03. Baltimore, MD: Health Care Financing Administration.

Feldman, R., B. Dowd, M. Finch, and S. Cassou (1989). *Employer-Based Health Insurance.* Rockville, MD: Department of Health and Human Services, National Center for Health Services Research and Health Care Technology Assessment

Garfinkel, S.A., G.F. Riley, and V.G. Iannacchione (1988). "High-Cost Users of Medical Care." *Health Care Financing Review* 9:41-52.

Greenlick, M.R., D.K. Freeborn, and C.R. Pope (Eds.) (1988). *Health Care Research in an HMO: Two Decades of Discovery.* Baltimore, MD: Johns Hopkins University Press.

Harlow, S.D. and M.S. Linet (1989). "Agreement between Questionnaire Data and Medical Records." *American Journal of Epidemiology* 129:233-248.

Heckman, J.J. (1979). "Sample Selection Bias as a Specification Error." *Econometrica* 45: 153-161.

Hornbrook, M.C., M.D. Bennett, and M.R. Greenlick (1989). "Adjusting the AAPCC for Selectivity and Selection Bias Under Medicare Risk Contracts." In R. M. Scheffler and L. F. Rossiter (Eds.), *Advances in Health Economics and Health Services Research* (Vol. 10, pp. 111-149). Greenwich, CT: JAI Press.

Hornbrook, M.C., M.D. Burnett, and M. R. Greenlick (1991). "Prior Use Risk-Adjustors for the AAPCC Based on an HMO's Experience." Final Report, Cooperative Agreement No. 18-C-98804-1/04. Submitted to Office of Research. Baltimore, MD: Health Care Financing Administration.

Hornbrook, M.C. and M.J. Goodman (1991a). "Adjusting Health Benefits Contributions to Reflect Risk." In M. Hornbrook (Ed.), *Advances in Health Economics and Health Services Research: Vol. 12. Risk-Based Contributions to Private Health Insurance* (pp. 41-76). Greenwich, CT: JAI Press.

Hornbrook, M.C. and M.J. Goodman (1991b). "Health Plan Case Mix: Definition, Measurement, and Use." In M. Hornbrook (Ed.), *Advances in Health Economics and Health Services Research: Vol. 12. Risk-Based Contributions to Private Health Insurance* (pp. 111-148). Greenwich, CT: JAI Press.

Hornbrook, M.C., M.J. Goodman, and M.D. Bennett (1991). "Assessing Health Plan Case Mix in Employed Populations: Ambulatory Morbidity and Prescribed Drug Models." In M. Hornbrook (Ed.), *Advances in Health Economics and Health Services Research: Vol. 12. Risk-Based Contributions to Private Health Insurance* (pp. 197-232). Greenwich, CT: JAI Press.

Idler, E.L. and R.J. Angel (1990). "Self-rated Health and Mortality in the NHANES-I Epidemiologic Follow-up Study." *American Journal of Public Health* 80:446-452.

Idler, E.L., S.V. Kasl, and J.H. Lemke (1990). "Self-Evaluated Health and Mortality among the Elderly in New Haven, Connecticut, and Iowa and Washington Counties, Iowa, 1982-1986." *American Journal of Epidemiology* 131:91-103.

Jobe, J.B., A.A. White, C.L. Kelley, D.J. Mingay, M.J. Sanchez, and E.F. Loftus (1990). "Recall Strategies and Memory for Health-Care Visits." *The Milbank Quarterly* 68:171-189.

Kass, G.V. (1980). "An Exploratory Technique for Investigating Large Quantities of Categorical Data." *Applied Statistics* 29:119-127.

Lee, L. (1983). "Generalized Econometric Models with Selectivity." *Econometrica* 51:507-512.

Lichtenstein, R.L. and J.W. Thomas (1987a). "A Comparison of Self-Reported Measures of Perceived Health and Functional Health in an Elderly Population." *Journal of Community Health* 12:213-230.

Lichtenstein, R.L. and J.W. Thomas (1987b). "Including a Measure of Health Status in Medicare's Health Maintenance Organization Capitation Formula: Reliability Issues." *Medical Care* 25:100-110.

Lubitz, J. (1987). "Health Status Adjustments for Medicare Capitation." *Inquiry* 24:362-375.

Mullooly, J.P., T.M. Vogt, and C.R. Pope (1989). "Objective and Self-rated Health: Predictors of Mortality." Paper presented at the 1989 American Public Health Association annual meeting, Chicago, October 24, 1989.

National Center for Health Statistics, Bonham, G.S. (1983). *Procedures and Questionnaires of National Medical Care Expenditure and Utilization Survey.* National Medical Care Expenditure and Utilization Survey, Series A, Methodological Report No. 1, DHHS Pub. No. 83-20001, U.S. Public Health Service, March.

Newhouse, J.P., W. E. Manning, E.B. Keeler, and E.B. Sloss (1989). "Adjusting Capitation Rates Using Objective Health Measures and Prior Utilization." *Health Care Financing Review* 10:41-54.

Olsen, R.J. (1980). "A Least Squares Correction for Selectivity." *Econometrica* 48:1815-1820.

Olsen, R.J. (1982). "Distributional Tests for Selectivity Bias and a More Robust Likelihood Estimator." *International Economic Review* 23:223-240.

Paganini-Hill, A. and R.K. Ross (1982). "Reliability of Recall of Drug Usage and Other Health-related Information." *American Journal of Epidemiology* 116:114-122.

Sonquist, J.A. and J.N. Morgan (1964). *The Detection of Interaction Effects: A Report on a Computer Program for the Selection of Optional Combinations of Explanatory Variables.* Survey Research Center Monograph No. 35. Ann Arbor, MI: The University of Michigan Institute for Social Research, Survey Research Center.

Whitmore, R.W., J.E. Paul, D.A. Gibbs, and J.C. Beebe (1989). "Using Health Indicators in Calculating the AAPCC." In R. M. Scheffler and L. F. Rossiter (Eds.), *Advances in Health Economics and Health Services Research,* (Vol. 10, pp. 75-109). Greenwich, CT: JAI Press.

Wilensky, G.R. and L.F. Rossiter (1986). "Patient Self-Selection in HMOs." *Health Affairs* 5:66-80.

Advances in Health Economics and Health Services Research

Edited by **Richard M. Scheffler,** *School of Public Health, University of California, Berkeley* and **Louis F. Rossiter,** *Department of Health Administration, Medical College of Virginia, Virginia Commonwealth University*

Volume 7, Mergers in Health Care: The Performance of Multi-Institutional Organizations
1986, 300 pp. $63.50
ISBN 0-89232-573-9

CONTENTS: Conference Program Committee. Preface. PART I. ORGANIZATION AND FINANCING. Diversification of Health Care Services: The Effects of Ownership, Environment, and Strategy, *S.M. Shortell, E.M. Morrison, S.L. Hughes, B.S. Friedman, and J.L. Vitek, Northwestern University.* **A Descriptive and Financial Ratio Analysis of Merged and Consolidated Hospitals: United States, 1980-1985,** *R. Mullner, American Hospital Association, and R.M. Anderson, Johns Hopkins University.* **Hospital Participation in Multihospital Systems,** *M.A. Morrisey and J.A. AleXander, University of Alabama, Birmingham.* **Capital Markets and the Growth of Miltihospital Systems,** *F. Sloan, Vanderbilt University, M.A. Morrisey, University of Alamaba, Birmingham, and J. Valvona, Vanderbilt University.* **Comments on Diversificaiton of Health Care Services,** *J.B. Christianson, University of Arizona.* **Comments on Ratio Analysis of Merged Hospital,** *A. Woodward, Coopers and Lybrand.* **PART II. BEHAVIOR AND PERFORMANCE. Multihospital Systems and Access to Health Care,** *M. Schlesinger and J. Bentkover, Harvard University, D. Blumenthal, W. Custer, R. Musacchio, and J. Willer, American Medical Association.* **Hospital Reorganization: Examining the Effects on Medical Education,** *C.M. Russe and G.F. Anderson, Johns Hopkins University.* **Walking Softly: The Role of Management in Altering Physician Practice Patterns in the Hospital Corporation of America,** *D. Barrett and P.H. Campbell, Harvard University.* **Horizontal and Vertical Concentrations in the Evolution of Hospital Competition,** *D.B. Starkweather and J.M. Carman, University of California, Berkeley.* **Strategic Behavior Patterns of Small Multi-institutional Health Organizations,** *J.W. Begun, R. Luke, T.A. Jensen, and L.H. Warner, Medical College of Virginia.* **Comments on Behavior and Performance,** *D. Ermann, National Center for Health Services.* **PART III. ANTITRUST ISSUES. Antitrust Treatment of Nonprofit and For-Profit Hospital Mergers,** *R.D. Blair, University of Florida and J.M.*

JAI PRESS

J A I

P R E S S

Fesmire, University of Tampa. **Antitrust Considerations for Hospital Mergers: Market Definition and Market Concentration,** *R.P. Wilder and P. Jacobs, University of South Carolina.* **Comments on Antitrust Issues,** *H.E. Frech III, University of California, Santa Barbara.* **Summary and Reflections. Mergers in Health Care: Implications for the Future,** *A. Dobson, Health Care Financing Administration.*

Volume 8, The Economics of Mental Health Services
1987, 305 pp. $63.50
ISBN 0-89232-735-9

Edited by **Thomas G. McGuire,** *Department of Economics, Boston University* and **Richard M. Scheffler,** *Graduate School of Public Health and Public Policy, University of California, Berkeley.*

Reduction of Health Care Costs: A Four-Year Study of U.S. Federal Employees Enrollment with the Aetna Life Insurance Co., *H.D. Holder, Prevention Research Center, Berkeley and J.O. Blose, The Human Ecology Institue, Chapel Hill.* **A Comparison of Psychiatric Service Utilization in A Single Group Practice Under Multiple Insurance Systems,** *K. Jennison, Massachusetts General Hospital and R.P. Ellis, Boston University.* **Discrimination and Insurance Coverage of the Mentally Ill,** *J. Rubin, Rutgers University.* **The Demand for Outpatient Mental Health Care from Nonspecialty Providers,** *C. Horgan, Brandeis and D. Salkever, Johns Hopkins University.* **Monopolistic Competition and Consumer Information: Pricing in the Market for Psychologists' Services,** *A.K. Klevorick, Yale University and T.G. McGuire, Boston University.* **Demand for Psychiatric Services: A Clinical Episode Model for Specifying "The Product",** *H.H. Goldman, University of Maryland, R.M. Scheffler, and Allen, Cheadle, University of California, Berkeley.* **Comments on Demand for Psychiatric Services,** *J.M. Mitchell, Health Economics Research, Inc.* **Markov and Other Models of Episodes of Mental Health,** *E.B. Keeler,The Rand Corporation, K.B. Wells, University of California, Los Angeles and W.G. Manning, The Rand Corporation.* **Comments on Markov and Other Models of Mental Health Treatment,** *D. Haas-Wilson, Smith College.* **Concluding Remarks,** *B. Weisbrod, University of Wisconsin, Madison.*

Volume 9. Private Sector Involvement In Health Care: Implications For Access, Cost, and Quality
1988, 265 pp. $63.50
ISBN 0-89232-937-8

CONTENTS. Conference Program Committee. Preface, *L.F. Rossiter and R.M. Scheffler.* **I. PRIVATE INITIATIVES FOR PUBLIC PROGRAMS. Employer Financing of Long-Term Care,** *D.J. Chollet and R.B. Friedland, Employee Benefit Research Institute, Washington, DC.* **A Broker Model for Joint Public-Private Supplemental Insurance for the Medicare Population: A Transition to Long-Term Care Insurance,** *J. Sangl, U.S. Health Care Financing Administration, Baltimore, Maryland and A. Dobson, Consolidated Health Care, Inc., Washington, DC.* **Innovative Concepts in Public-Private Coordination of Benefits for Retirees,** *B.M. Edington and R.W. Deacon, U.S. Health Care Financing, Administration, Baltimore, Maryland.* **Enrollment Patterns in Medicare HMOs: Implications For Access To Care,** *R.S. Brown, and K. Langwell, Mathematica Policy Research, Inc., Washington, DC.* **II. PRIVATE INNOVATIONS TO DEAL WITH SPECIAL POPULATIONS. Health Insurance for the Uninsured: An Evaluation**

JAI PRESS

JAI PRESS

of Plan Design Preferences, *R. Crittenden and C.W. Madden, University of Washington.* **Uncompensated Hospital Care In California: Private and Public Hospital Responses To Competitive Market Forces,** *T.G. Rundall, University of California, Berkeley, S. Sofaer, University of California, Los Angeles, and W. Lambert, University of Michigan.* **Private Long-Term Care Insurance: Alleviating Market Failures with Public-Private Partnerships,** *J. Knickman, New York University.* **Use of Nursing Care in Continuing Care Retirement Communities,** *C.E. Bishop, Brandeis University.* **III. MANAGEMENT STRATEGIES IN HEALTH CARE SYSTEMS. Health Care Coalitions: Continuity and Change,** *R.M. Mullner, University of Illinois at Chicago, G.W. Young, American Hospital Association, and R.M. Andersen, University of Chicago.* **"May the Third Force Be With You": Community Programs for Affordable Health Care,** *L.D. Brown and C.G. McLaughlin, University of Michigan.* **Private Sector Medical Care Management for High Cost Illness,** *M. Henderson, A. Bergman, A. Collard, B. Souder, and S. Wallack, Brandeis University.* **The CHAMPUS Reform Initiative: Tailoring Private Sector Innovations to Public Sector Needs,** *S.B. Clauser and B.S. Cooper, Office of Health Affairs, U.S. Department of Defense.*

Volume 10, Risk-Based Payments Under Public Programs
1989, 376 pp. $63.50
ISBN 0-89232-976-9

CONTENTS. Preface, *L.F. Rossiter, The Williamson Institute Medical College of Virginia and R.M. Scheffler, University of California, Berkeley.* **Foreword,** *C. Ross Anthony, U.S. Department of Health and Human Services.* **A NEW PAYMENT FOR RISK-BASED PROGRAMS UNDER MEDICARE. Medicare's Expanded Choices Program: Issues and Evidence From The HMO Experience,** *L.F. Rossiter, The Williamson Institute Medical College of Virginia, K.M. Langwell, Mathematica Policy Research, Inc., Washington, D.C., R. Brown, Mathematica Policy Research, Inc., Princeton, New Jersey, K.W. Adamache, Health Economics Research, Inc., Needham, Massachusetts and L. Nelson, Mathematica Policy Reserach, Inc., Washington, D.C.* **The Health Status [illegible]ation Patterns of the Elderly: Implications for Setting Medicare Risk-Based Payments,** *L. Gruenberg, C. Tompkins and F.W. Porell, Brandeis University.* **Using Health Status Indicators in Calculating the AAPCC,** *R.W. Whitmore, J.E. Paul, D.A. Gibbs, Research Triangle Institute, and J.C. Beebe, U.S. Department of Health and Human Services.* **Adjusting the AAPCC for Selectivity and Selection Bias Under Medicare Risk Contracts,** *M.C. Hornbrook, M.D. Bennett and M.R. Greenlick,*

Kaiser Permanente. **WHAT WE KNOW ABOUT RISK-BASED PROGRAMS UNDER MEDICAID. Interim Findings From the Medicaid Competition Demonstrations,** *D.A. Freund, Indiana University, R.E. Hurley, Pennsylvania State University, J.E. Paul, Research Triangle Institute, C. Grubb, Consultant, Durham, North Carolina, L.F. Rossiter, THe Williamson Institute Medical College of Virginia and K.W. Adamache, Health Economics Research, Inc.* **Selection of Prepaid or Fee-For-Service Care by Medicaid Families: Examining the Health Risk Hypothesis,** *A.R. Davies, New England Medical Center.* **NEW RESULTS FROM INDIVIDUAL STATE EXPERIENCES. Wisconsin: The Impact of an HMO-Based Health Plan for Indigent Adults,** *N.C. Dunham, New York University, M.H. Dunham, New York City Health and Hospitals Corporation, D.A. Kindig, S. Lastiri, University of Wisconsin-Madison, and J. Vanderburg, Robert Wood Johnson Foundation.* **Arizona: The Arizona Health Care Cost Containment System and Plan Structure,** *N. McCall, SRI International.* **New York: Design and Implementation of a Voluntary Medicaid Case-Management Demonstration,** *L.M. Manheim, Northwestern University, S.M. Davidson, Boston University, S.M. Werner, M. Hohlen and B.K. Shapiro, American Academy of Pediatrics.* **Minnesota: Plan Choice by the Mentally Ill in Medicaid Prepaid Health Plans,** *I.S. Moscovice, M. Finch and N. Lurie, University of Minnesota.* **NEW DIRECTIONS FOR PUBLIC PROGRAMS AND RISK-BASED PAYMENTS. Capitation of Mental Health Care in Public Programs,** *J.B. Christianson, University of Minnesota.* **Competitive Bidding for Medicare Outpatient Laboratory Services,** *S.T. Mennemeyer, Abt Associates, Inc.* **Should Risk-Based Payments Be Used for Long-Term Care?,** *T. Grannemann, Mathematica Policy Research, Inc.* **The Provision of Long-Term Care in Risk-Based HMOs,** *C.L. Polich and L.H. Iversen, Interstudy, Excelsiior, Minnesota.*

Supplement 1, Comparative Health Systems: The Future of National Health Care Systems and Economic Analysis
1990, 256 pp. $63.50
ISBN 1-55938-006-3

Edited by **Jean-Jacques Rosa,** *Institut d'Etudes Politique de Paris*

CONTENTS: Preface. The United Kingdom, *Alan Maynard, University of York.* **The Netherlands,** *Jacques van der Gaag, The Work Bank, Frans F. H. Rutten, Limburg University, and Wynand P.M.M. van de Ven, Erasmus University.* **The United States,** *H.E. Frech III, University of California, Santa Barbara.* **Switzerland,** *Peter Zweifel, University of Zuruch.* **Canada,** *Peter C. Coyte, University of Toronto.* **The Federal Republic of**

JAI PRESS

J A I P R E S S

Germany, *Klaus-Dirk Henke, University of Hanover.* **Health Systems and Policies for Japan,** *Shigeru Tanaka, Keio University.* **France,** *Jean-Jacques Rosa and Robert Launois, Universite de Rennes.* **Health Care in Sweden An Economist's Perspective,** *Ingemar Stahl, University of Lund.* **Italy,** *Domenicantonio Fausto, University of Naples.* **Health Care Systems in Ten Industrial Countries,** *Jean-Jacques Rosa, Universite de Rennes.*

Volume 11, Health Economics and Health Policy in the 1990s: Surprises from the Past, Forecasts for the Future
1990, 250 pp. $63.50
ISBN I-55938-137-X

CONTENTS: Conference Program Committee. Preface, *L.F. Rossiter, Virginia Commonwealth University.* **Hospital Supply Response to Prospective Payment as Measured by Length of Stay,** *J.R. Lave, University of Pittsburgh and R.G. Frank, Johns Hopkins University.* **Macro Forecasting of National Health Expenditures,** *T.E. Getzen, Temple University.* **The Relationship Between Physician Fees and the Use of Medical Services in Ontario,** *J. Hurley, R. Labelle, McMaster University and T. Rice, University of North Carolina, Chapel Hill.* **Policy and Research on Health Manpower Regulation: Never Too Late to Deregulate?,** *J.W. Begun, Virginia Commonwealth University and R. Feldman, University of Minnesota.* **The Economics of Group Practice: A Reassessment,** *R.H. Lee, University of North Carolina, Chapel Hill.* **Tax Exemption and Community Benefits of Not-For-Profit Hospitals,** *B.S. Friedman, P.A. Hattis, and R.J. Bogue, American Hospital Association, Chicago.* **Medical Malpractice, Technological Change, and Learning-by-Doing,** *M. Shroder and B.A. Weisbrod, University of Wisconsin, Madison.* **The Cost-Effectiveness of Community Care for Former Long-Stay Psychiatric Hospital Patients,** *M. Knapp and J. Beecham, University of Kent at Canterbury.* **The Future of Nursing Home Policy: Should Policy Be Based on an Excess Demand Paradigm?,** *J.A. Nyman, University of Minnesota.*

Also Available:
Volumes 1-6 (1979-1985) $63.50 each

JAI PRESS INC.
55 Old Post Road - No. 2
P.O. Box 1678
Greenwich, Connecticut 06836-1678
Tel: 203-661-7602